Discriminating Risk

Discriminating Risk

*The U.S. Mortgage Lending Industry
in the Twentieth Century*

Guy Stuart

CORNELL UNIVERSITY PRESS

Ithaca and London

First published 2003 by Cornell University Press

Printed in the United States of America

Library of Congress Cataloging-in-Publication Data

Stuart, Guy, 1966–
    Discriminating risk : the U.S. mortgage lending industry in the twentieth century / Guy Stuart.
        p. cm.
Includes bibliographical references and index.
    ISBN 0-8014-4066-1 (cloth : alk. paper)
    1. Mortgage loans—Unites States. 2. Discrimination in housing—United States. 3. Discrimination in housing—Illinois—Chicago. 4. Race discrimination—United States. 5. United States—Race relations. I. Title.
    HG2040.5.U5S747 2003
    332.7'22'0973—dc21   2002154180

Cornell University Press strives to use environmentally responsible suppliers and materials to the fullest extent possible in the publishing of its books. Such materials include vegetable-based, low-VOC inks and acid-free papers that are recycled, totally chlorine-free, or partly composed of nonwood fibers. For further information, visit our website at www.cornellpress.cornell.edu.

Cloth printing   10   9   8   7   6   5   4   3   2   1

To Jenny

Contents

Figures and Tables

Acknowledgments

This book would not have been possible without the cooperation of many professionals in the mortgage lending and real estate industries. I am grateful to the people whom I interviewed for their willingness to tell me how they go about their business. I am also grateful to the executives without whose cooperation I could not have conducted such in-depth interviews.

Many people have read drafts of various chapters and provided me with sound advice. I thank them all.

I received financial assistance from the Mellon Foundation and the Alfred Taubman Center for State and Local Government at the Kennedy School of Government at Harvard University. This support was of great assistance in giving me large blocks of time in which to concentrate on research and writing.

G. S.

Cambridge, Massachusetts

Discriminating Risk

Introduction

In 2000 the U.S. mortgage lending industry made 9.56 million loans with a total value of $1.16 trillion for the purchase or refinance of 1- to 4-unit homes. The total volume of outstanding loans at the end of that year was $5.2 trillion.[1] It is a massive industry, and it rests on millions of individual decisions made each year, which in turn rest on a plethora of minute details about every aspect of every home loan applicant's life. In 1992 the *Chicago Tribune* reported on the efforts of lenders to become more flexible in how they assess mortgage loan applications. The story provided an example of how a particular lender had extended a loan to a couple who might have been rejected under existing loan evaluation criteria; it read in part:

> [The applicants] qualified with respect to employment stability. . . . And their debt-to-income ratios were well within the guidelines. . . . Commonly used ratios are a maximum of 28 percent of total income going to housing expenses and 36 percent to all expenses. . . . The applicants had excellent ratios of 15 and 25 percent.
>
> So far the loan looked good. But there were two problems. First, a credit report showed that the couple had been 30 days late with payments 10 times within the previous six months, 60 days once and 90 days once. . . . In addition, a student loan had been reported 90 days late 10 times before it was ultimately repaid in full in 1991. . . .
>
> Still, because the ratios were so good, the questionable credit history wouldn't have been enough to warrant a denial of the loan. . . . [Also] the couple was paying $435 in rent, had been in good standing with rent payments and would be paying only $483 on the new mortgage. (Linn 1992, 6)

The *Chicago Tribune* account captures both the variety of information mortgage lenders in the United States consider when looking at a loan application and some of the reasoning they use to evaluate it. They look at an applicant's employment record, income, credit record, past housing payments, and myriad other factors. They evaluate each piece of information against a set of rules, using such calculations as debt-to-income ratios and

2 loan-to-value ratios, but also consider all the information together. They not only run the numbers, but also look at the story the numbers tell.

This book examines how home mortgage lenders make decisions. More accurately, it examines how lenders construct risk, and shows that this process can be understood only when one examines the cultural, institutional, and spatial context in which lenders operate. In brief, the argument is the following. The language of financial risk is an economic language, imbued with the legitimacy of "formal rationality," but the risk criteria used to decide who gets a mortgage and who does not lose their "formal" patina when one investigates their origins and the way they are implemented. Their origins show that the contemporary decision-making rules are a mix of rules of thumb, accepted norms, and theoretical assumptions imposed on reality. Their implementation shows that the loan application is a process in which the right risk profile has to be constructed, and that the decisions are often self-fulfilling. This does not mean that these rules and practices are irrational or ad hoc, but it does mean that they constitute a version of rationality that is not the only possible one. In other words, when lenders explain what they are doing when they make loan decisions, it mostly makes sense — they provide good reasons for how they make their decisions. But those reasons are grounded in a certain set of values or established ways of doing things, and they often make sense only because other lenders adhere to them as well.

This argument is of both theoretical and practical import. In terms of theory it provides a general framework for analyzing how people construct economic concepts and institutions. It does so by describing the interaction among three theoretical concepts — rules, networks, and the production of space — using the U.S. mortgage lending industry as an example. In terms of practical import, the book reframes the debate about racial and ethnic discrimination in the mortgage lending industry. It moves the focus from an often fruitless theoretical and methodological debate about whether or not illegal discrimination takes place to a practical debate about how to embed social justice in the process of delivering financial capital to all people and neighborhoods that need it. The theoretical and practical purposes of this book are closely tied together. The data in support of the theoretical contention show that the risk decisions that financial institutions make every day are, in essence, political decisions, and therefore rightly belong in a public debate that includes all people with an interest in who gets what loans. This is what antidiscrimination activists have been asserting for over thirty years. The data support their position and also show that the issue of "who gets what" is relevant even in the absence of racial and ethnic discrimination.

Constructing Risk

A risk decision is a decision that has consequences, gains or losses, in the future. The mortgage loan decision is a decision about the future. A lender makes a loan in anticipation of being repaid the full amount of the principal with interest, at some time in the future. Within the current legal framework in the United States, lenders expose themselves to two broad types of losses: losses resulting from changes in expected cash flow from the investment that the loan represents—in other words, losses resulting from both voluntary and involuntary prepayment; and losses incurred when the loan amount is not repaid in full—losses due to default only. Voluntary prepayment occurs when the borrower chooses to prepay; involuntary prepayment occurs in cases of default or the sale of the home to avoid default. In chapter 2 I outline more fully what type of losses prepayment produces, but, in brief, they have to do with the fact that lenders incur a large number of costs when they first make a loan that they can recoup only through the receipt of interest payments, which are not paid if the loan is paid off early. Prepayment also results in losses if the interest rate at the time the loan is paid off is lower than the interest rate at the time it was made—especially if the loan was bought by an investor who was anticipating a particular yield over a particular period of time.[2] Default can result in losses because the proceeds of the lender's sale of the home are not sufficient to cover the outstanding loan balance and the administrative expenses the lender incurs in taking over the home (whether by deed-in-lieu of foreclosure or foreclosure).

Generally, there are three ways in which people construct risk: through the process of risk assessment; by managing what Heimer (1981) calls "behavioral risk" after a risk decision is made; and through the effect their past and present decisions have on the future. I explain each in turn.

Risk Assessment: Translating Uncertainty into Risk

Following the lead of Frank Knight and John Maynard Keynes, we can usefully distinguish between a risk decision and one made under conditions of uncertainty (Knight 1921; Keynes [1921] 1979; Douglas 1985). A decision is a risk decision if the person making the decision knows the probability of all the relevant events that may happen in the future and the losses and gains that will accrue to her in the case of each event. A decision is an uncertain one if the person making it does not know the probability of relevant future events and/or the losses and gains stemming from them.[3] People making decisions use their reasoning powers applied to relevant in-

4   formation about the future to try to translate uncertainty into risk. It is in this way that people *construct* risk.

Mortgage lenders attempt to translate uncertainty into risk by defining the concepts they deem relevant to their decisions, by setting the rules for gathering information about them and the rules for assessing that information, and by implementing those rules of information-gathering and assessment. In particular, lenders try to assess the probability that they will be exposed to losses from default. Such losses are, first and foremost, contingent on the willingness and ability of the borrower to make the monthly mortgage payments. The size of the lender's loss is contingent on the extent to which the outstanding balance on the loan, including any costs incurred in trying to help the borrower get back on track, can be recouped by the sale of the property standing as collateral. The lender, at the time a loan application is made, attempts to assess the willingness and ability of the applicant to make the payments and the ability of the property to stand as collateral for the loan. The assessment of the borrower and the assessment of the value of the property both inform the risk decision. They both contribute to the translation of future uncertainty into present-day calculations about the probability of loss that a particular loan entails.

But lenders and people in general face a problem when constructing risk. They have to decide what information to gather, how to gather it in a cost-effective manner, what criteria to use to evaluate the information, and how to make a decision when the information does not quite conform to the established criteria. There are, of course, ways to decide on relevant information and gather it systematically to make an informed decision. Inference from statistics describing the frequency of past events occurring among a group of people, say the frequency of default among a group of borrowers, is possible so long as the people about whose future we are concerned share the same characteristics and they will be in an analogous environment (Keynes [1921] 1979, 368–69). Such inference will result in a probability proposition about the frequency of future events occurring among a group of similar people. But, as Keynes is at pains to point out, such inference is very difficult because it is difficult to capture information on all the relevant characteristics of the people in question for several reasons: the information is so varied; it is uncertain that they will be operating in the same environment in the future as in the past; and it is uncertain that people's actions are independent of each other.[4] Knight also acknowledges the information problem, and at one point notes: "It probably occasions surprise to most persons the first time they consider seriously what a small portion of our conduct makes any pretense to a foundation in accurate and exhaustive knowledge of the things we are dealing with" (1921,

210). Herbert Simon makes a similar point about economic decision-making in general when he argues that people are "boundedly rational"— even if a person wants to, he cannot process all the information necessary to make a fully informed decision (1983, 18–20).

Yet just because the process of constructing risk is fraught with difficulty does not mean that people making decisions do not try to do it. As I have described, lenders have a plethora of information when they make a loan decision and a plethora of rules for interpreting that information. But why do lenders pay attention to a particular set of information, and how do they evaluate and interpret it? Douglas argues:

> The wrong way to think of the social factors that influence risk perception is to treat them as smudges which blur a telescope lens and distort the true image. This metaphor justifies a negative approach. But the social point of view thus dismissed includes moral judgments about the kind of society in which we want to live. . . . A better kind of analysis might treat such transformations of the image not as distortions but as improvements: the result of a sharper focus that assesses the society along with its assessments of risks. (1985, 18)

Douglas's insight is important because it points us toward an analysis that asks not just whether people's construction of risk is "right," but, rather, what the ways people construct risk tell us about their values. The values that lenders reveal in their perceptions of risk are a critical focus of this book. But there are more prosaic reasons why people perceive risk as they do. It is not just their values that are reflected in their risk perceptions but also the type of information they are privy to and the reasoning that they have learned to use to process that information. Granovetter (1985) argues that people are embedded in a social context and it is that context which structures the information that they receive and the way they process it, even when they are making economic decisions. Lawson argues that Keynes's concept of "direct acquaintance" of objects, which results in direct, and therefore reliable, knowledge of them, implies the same thing. He notes: "Behaviour therefore, and unsurprisingly, is highly dependent upon the context in which (context related) knowledge is obtained" (1985, 917). On this reasoning what we need is a way to understand the context in which lending rules are developed and implemented. Later in this chapter I elaborate a theoretical framework for organizing an analysis of this context, based on the concepts of rules, networks, and the production of space.

It is important to emphasize that people who construct risk are pro-

6   ducing information as well as receiving it and processing it. The information they produce does not just disappear into the ether—it is received and processed by others. As a result, the product of decision-makers makes them answerable to a wider audience and the conception of risk arrived at is underpinned by a logic that is accepted by this audience. Thus an analysis that seeks to show how risk is constructed must both reveal the logic employed by those involved in the construction process and define the audience to which they were and are answerable, thus revealing the support-base for the particular construction of risk used. Of course, the best place to look for the audience is in the same social context in which the process took and takes place.

Managing Behavioral Risk

Decisions based on the future actions of other people run into danger from what Heimer (1981) calls "behavioral risk." She argues, in the context of the insurance industry, that this is the risk that insurers face once they enter into a contract with the insured, as a result of the incentives that the very contract creates for the insured. In the economics literature this is called moral hazard. In essence, behavioral risk is contingent on the relationship between the various parties to the insurance contract *once the contract has been signed*. There are three ways in which insurers deal with such risks. First, they make the signing of a contract contingent on the proper behavior of a prospective client—the adoption of loss prevention practices is an example of proper behavior. Second, they make the insured share in the gains and losses resulting from the latter's behavior—deductibles do this. And finally, they get third parties to police the contract.

     Mortgage lenders are exposed to behavioral risk once they have disbursed the loan to the borrower. Lenders manage the post-disbursement behavior of the borrower by requiring the borrower to make a downpayment toward the purchase price of the mortgaged home. The downpayment gives the borrower the incentive not to default on the loan, for the simple reason that she will lose the money she invested in the home if she does.[5] In the same way, the amortization of the loan's principal over the life of the loan creates an increasing community of interest between borrower and lender. Lenders can also manage the risk of prepayment through stipulating prepayment penalties in the loan contract. And, finally, the servicing of the loan—the monthly receipt of installment payments by the lender from the borrower—creates an ongoing relationship between the two parties to the loan contract.[6] How this servicing relationship is managed can affect the borrower's willingness and ability to stay current on the loan. This is especially the case when the borrower shows the first signs of becoming delinquent. I pay most attention to the first and second ways in which lenders manage risk, but the third is also extremely important.

Though it is analytically useful to distinguish between risk assessment and managing behavioral risk, they are not completely distinct activities. For example, the downpayment a lender requires of a borrower features in the discussion of both risk assessment and managing behavioral risk. And there is no reason why lenders should not try to assess the risk that someone will prepay and deal with it accordingly. This commonality rests on the fact that risk assessment and management both involve decisions about the future. As a result, how someone manages behavioral risk is as context-dependent as how someone assesses risk. So the arguments I made above about how context matters are equally relevant to the ways in which people manage behavioral risk. In fact context is likely to be even more relevant because the process of managing risk is an ongoing one in which borrower and lender, in our case, may construct a context for their interactions out of past interactions. In other words, the process of managing risk may result in a relationship between borrower and lender, which becomes part of the context in which the lender manages risk.

Self-Fulfilling Prophecies and Consensus

Risk assessment assumes that the risk someone incurs is something external to the decision that that person makes. Managing behavioral risk is grounded in the idea that a risk-taker can manage some of the risks to which he is exposed through some deliberate set of actions. Risk decisions that are self-fulfilling prophecies actually change the risks to which a lender exposes itself, simply through the act of making the decision. A pure example of a self-fulfilling prophecy that I examine in this book is one in which the concentration of mortgage loans in a given geographic area lowers the inherent risk of lending in that area. The self-fulfilling prophecy works in the following manner. So long as financing is available, people will be able to buy homes in a particular geographic area. So long as people are able to buy homes, people will be able to sell them. So long as people can sell their homes, the likelihood of losses due to foreclosure is diminished, because either a delinquent borrower will sell the property and pay off the mortgage or a lender who takes possession of the property will be able to sell it easily. And, finally, so long as this foreclosure risk is diminished, loan money will continue to flow into the area.[7]

The logic of this cycle indicates that lenders have the capacity to construct the risks they face. This argument comes with two caveats. First, even the ready availability of mortgage money may not be enough to sustain demand in a particular geographic area if it is not desirable for other reasons. Second, the cycle still requires the active decisions of countless people for its sustenance—it is contingent and susceptible to disruption and reversal. This is particularly obvious in the example I have given because of the way in which lenders and real estate appraisers define and relate to particular geographic areas. For the cycle of concentrated geographic lending to play out, the people involved first have to define, and then sustain, the boundaries of the favored geographic area.

The self-fulfilling cycle results in a consensus about the risk of lending in a particular neighborhood. As a result, we do not have a situation in which lenders are spreading themselves across different neighborhoods looking for different opportunities to take risks and generate profits. Rather they are seeking the protection that the activity of other lenders affords them.[8] It may be the case that this consensus emerges out of a set of uncoordinated decisions of independent lenders—maybe because one lender takes the lead and others follow. But there are other ways in which consensus may be achieved, in terms not only of geographically concentrated lending but also of the general way that lenders assess and manage risk.

One way in which consensus may be generated is through the use of third-party information providers—to the extent that they use the same definitions and methodology regardless of which client they are supplying, third-party providers are going to supply the same information to different lending institutions, resulting in consensus decisions. A further possibility in this regard is that, owing to network externalities, the consensus spreads across the whole industry, not just across localized networks of lenders served by the same third party. Network externalities exist where a consumer or supplier of a good or service (including information) finds that he derives benefits from simply belonging to the network, even at the expense of supplying or consuming a good or service that is not the best from his point of view. For example, local credit bureaus are likely to encounter network externalities from membership in a network of credit bureaus, if the network has sufficiently wide coverage, because the network allows them to supply credit-grantors more complete loan applicant credit histories.[9] Another possibility is that financial institutions, faced with a future full of uncertainties, simply copy each other (Keynes 1937, 214). A fourth possibility is the desire for legitimacy. Financial institutions do not want to be seen as making irresponsible decisions, and working within the consensus provides them with the cover of legitimacy. Concomitant with that is the role that government regulation might play in promoting consensus—lenders make decisions in compliance with government regulations and, as a result, enact the government's version of how risk should be constructed. And finally, it is possible that lenders reach consensus because of the liquidity it generates (Carruthers and Stinchcombe 1999). Consensus results in the production of loans that are standardized and that can be bought and sold like commodities. This means that once people or institutions have taken a risk, they are not committed to continued exposure to the risk over its full term, but, rather, they can sell it at their convenience. This allows them to manage their risk exposure in a way that serves them best.

There are then a number of reasons why lenders may not compete in the way they construct risk, but seek consensus instead. This means that lenders may not, as many assume, be looking for the most accurate risk assessment and management process, but, rather, they may be making do with whatever everyone else is doing. In some cases this consensus actually creates the conditions for its own success, through the process of a self-fulfilling prophecy or by creating a liquid market for loans. And in other cases, the consensus may be institutionally "locked in"—by network externalities or a collective agreement that one way of constructing risk is the right way. Whether consensus exists and, if it does, in what form are integral to an empirical investigation of the way lenders construct risk. Furthermore, as in the cases of the risk assessment and management processes, it is in the analysis of the social context of decision-makers that we will find the building blocks out of which consensus and self-fulfilling prophecies are built.

"Economic Rationality" and Racial Discrimination

The argument thus far, that lenders construct risk in a manner informed by their social context, has immediate implications for our understanding of economic rationality and for the debate regarding racial and ethnic discrimination in mortgage lending. There are two ways we can understand the construction process in a social context. One is that economic decisions involve noneconomic considerations; another is that economic decisions are social and political decisions. These are two different ideas; the first is about how social context structures economic decisions, while the second is about how the building blocks of economic decisions, the very concepts used, are reflections of the values of those who use them.[10] Or, to put it differently, the first is designed to show that often people act in ways that are not economically rational when making economic decisions, while the second is designed to show how economic rationality is itself constructed. For example, Carruthers (1996) shows how financiers on the

10   London Stock Exchange at the beginning of the eighteenth century
       traded stocks for political ends, though he also spends a lot of time show-
       ing how the state helped to construct that exchange. This raises the ques-
       tion as to whether the actions of the financiers were economically "irra-
       tional" when they traded for political ends, or whether they had
       constructed a version of rationality that made their actions rational. This
       distinction is important from both a theoretical and a substantive point of
       view. From a theoretical point of view the distinction highlights the fact
       that the first version of the story requires an assumption—that we can de-
       fine what is economically rational and then identify departures from that
       rationality—while the second requires no such assumption and simply re-
       quires us to examine the reasoning used in a particular circumstance and
       its origins. From a substantive point of view, allowing the assumption that
       there is an economic rationality constrains public policy debates within
       the parameters set by those who define what is economically rational.[11]

       This is what has happened to the debate about racial discrimination in
       mortgage lending decisions. The explicit racist and sexist theories and
       practices of the mortgage lending industry have been extensively docu-
       mented, especially for the period up until the 1970s (see for example,
       Jackson 1985, Abrams 1955, and Bradford, 1979). Both the federal gov-
       ernment and the private sector were complicit in these practices. The
       1960s and 1970s were decades of great activism directed against this
       racism and sexism. The first major change occurred in November 1965
       when the commissioner of the Federal Housing Administration (FHA) an-
       nounced a change in its policies, which up until then had redlined black
       and other minority neighborhoods and excluded many other central city
       neighborhoods from its insurance coverage.[12] In 1968 Congress passed
       the Fair Housing Act, which prohibited discrimination in housing, includ-
       ing the financing of home purchases. In the 1970s there was a change in
       the explicitly racist policies of the appraisal profession through a consent
       decree between the Department of Justice, on the one hand, and the Soci-
       ety of Real Estate Appraisers and the American Institute of Real Estate
       Appraisers, on the other. Other achievements in the 1970s were the pas-
       sage of the Home Mortgage Disclosure Act (HMDA) in 1975, the Equal
       Credit Opportunity Act (ECOA) in 1974 and amendments in 1976, and
       the Community Reinvestment Act (CRA) in 1977. HMDA required
       lenders to report where they made their loans each year. This was
       amended in 1989 to require that lenders report from whom they received
       loan applications, by race, gender, and income and location of the prop-
       erty, and what action they took with regard to the applications. In 1974
       ECOA added Title VII, which prohibited discrimination on the basis of

sex and marital status, to the Consumer Credit Protection Act of 1968, and the 1976 amendments amended Title VII to include race, color, religion, national origin, age, and source of income from public programs. Finally, the CRA required "each appropriate Federal financial supervisory agency to use its authority when examining financial institutions, to encourage such institutions to help meet the credit needs of the communities in which they are chartered" (PL 95-128 Sec. 802(b)). This last provision addressed the fact that many deposit-taking financial institutions were taking deposits in minority and low-income city neighborhoods and lending elsewhere.[13]

Largely as a result of the data made available by HMDA, there exists a large literature on the extent to which the U.S. mortgage lending industry in the past 20 years has practiced discrimination against minority populations, in particular blacks and Hispanics, notwithstanding the advances made in the 1960s and 1970s. Prima facie, this literature is consistent with the thesis of this book. But the literature has its limitations because it is couched in a paradigm in which it is assumed that risk can be objectively measured and that discrimination can be detected when decision-makers use measures that are not objective. And the ultimate test of the objectivity of the decisions made is whether they are profitable. The following quotes are typical statements of those on one side of the debate:

> Personally, I find it difficult to reconcile the notion that there is widespread racial discrimination in mortgage lending with the fact that bankers want to make loans; not only to strengthen their financial prospects for the short-term, but to ensure that the community in which they operate thrives. (John LaWare, of the Federal Reserve System, before the Subcommittee on Consumer and Regulatory Affairs; U.S. Congress, Senate, Committee on Banking and Urban Affairs 1989, 6)

> Illegal discrimination simply does not make good business sense in this context. (Robert J. Herrmann, of the Office of the Comptroller of Currency, before the Subcommittee on Consumer and Regulatory Affairs; ibid., 46)

Three years after these statements were made, the Federal Reserve Bank of Boston published a landmark study of racial discrimination. Using traditional econometric methods, the authors modeled the decision of lenders using "objective" economic information about each applicant for a loan, and looked for any additional effect of race or ethnicity of the applicant on the lenders' decision. They found a wide disparity in the rates at which white, Hispanic, and black applicants, with the same *eco-*

12   *nomic* characteristics, were being turned down for loans—the first having the lowest rates and the last having the highest. Since the publication of this study there has been an extensive debate about the validity of the results, and subsequent debates about the presence or absence of discrimination have been conducted in roughly the same mold: can you identify race as a significant variable after controlling for all other objective economic factors?[14]

But the authors of the Boston Fed study prefaced their reporting of the results with a statement worthy of note. Though they stated that "to determine whether race plays a role in the lending decision, it is necessary first to account for all the economic factors that might bear on the financial institution's decision" (Munnell et al. 1992, 9), they acknowledged that "because little is known about the relationship between applicant characteristics and actual loan performance, any model must by necessity explain what lenders actually consider when making their decisions rather than what they ought to consider" (13).[15]

This statement suggests that the supposedly "objective" economic characteristics that lenders use in their assessment of a loan application are loosely tied to the actual performance of a loan. It also suggests that an important set of data has been omitted from the debate about racial discrimination in the U.S. mortgage lending industry: data about the origins and nature of the loan assessment criteria used by lenders. This book presents these data and argues that an understanding of the logic and nature of the loan assessment criteria, and of the institutional support that they receive, results in a complete reframing of the debate about racial discrimination and about the definitiveness of economic reasoning in general. In particular, the argument reframes how we should think about illegal discrimination. The current regulatory position on discrimination, as articulated by the Interagency Task Force on Fair Lending, is that not only are overt discrimination and disparate treatment illegal, but so is the uniform application of a practice that has a disparate impact on minorities but cannot be justified as a "business necessity" (Interagency Task Force on Fair Lending 1994, 4). Implicit in the idea that lenders might uniformly engage in practices that have no "business necessity" is the idea that their risk assessment criteria are not necessarily very good at translating uncertainty into risk. This is wholly consistent with my argument. But I also argue that we should question the distinction between disparate impact stemming from discrimination, on one hand, and "business necessity," on the other. The data I present show how hard it is to identify a true "business necessity," especially in a context where decisions can be self-fulfilling prophecies.

The policy implications of this additional step are fairly straightforward. At the level of the loan application process itself, we should stop looking for the "smoking gun" of discrimination and start looking at disparate impact as a bureaucratic problem in the context of a given set of bureaucratic rules. In other words, at one level this is a management problem. But at another level it is a political problem, because of the political nature of the economic concepts underpinning the decision-making rules—what constitutes a "business necessity" is a political issue. As a result, the debate should be about the appropriate institutional framework in which the rules themselves are critically assessed and revised as needed.

Rules, Networks, and the Production of Space

I have made much reference already to the context in which lenders develop rules and make loan decisions. To explain how people construct risk out of uncertainty, I will be using the concepts of rules, networks, and the production of space to create a theoretical framework for understanding how the context of decisions affects them. The first two concepts are commonly found in the economic sociology literature; the third is less common. In contrast, the literature on the money–space nexus, mostly the product of British social geographers, has a focus on space but has tried, with varying amounts of success and clarity, to incorporate rules (norms of behavior) and networks into accounts of the way that financial markets structure and are structured by space.[16] In this section I briefly describe how these concepts are relevant to the process of constructing risk out of uncertainty in mortgage lending, and then highlight the kinds of insights they provide to the empirical analysis in the following chapters.

The most obvious construction process is through rules of assessment, which define the concepts that decision-makers use, the information they gather, and the criteria with which they evaluate that information. Rules can also be used to prescribe future behavior through contracts. And finally, rules can lock in a particular construction of risk if people generally accept them, or find it too costly to break with convention.

As I show in chapter 3, the risk assessment process takes place within the context of a network relationship between a loan officer and a real estate broker who often refers clients to that loan officer. Lenders also access a wide variety of information through existing informational networks, which are themselves built on further networks. Furthermore, lenders can use networks of relations to monitor and control the behavior of borrowers.[17] Finally, networks may also lock in a particular construction of risk if network externalities take effect, thus resulting in a consensus.

The very process of risk assessment in the mortgage lending industry

14   requires the construction of spatial boundaries demarcating neighbor-hoods. Such demarcation is necessary for the identification of "compara-ble" properties that have recently sold in the same or a "competing" neigh-borhood, on the basis of which the appraiser estimates the value of the home securing the mortgage loan. There are also ways in which lenders can use spatial categories to monitor their loan portfolio, and so manage the behavioral risk they face. For example, the Federal Housing Adminis-tration monitors the concentration of foreclosures by particular lenders in particular geographic areas, and the Federal National Mortgage Associa-tion (Fannie Mae) and the Federal Home Loan Mortgage Corporation (Freddie Mac) regularly put in place emergency servicing measures in areas which have been hit by a natural disaster or some other crisis. Fi-nally, the production of space through the lending process can create a self-supporting construction of risk.

This brief sketch indicates the general use I will make of the concepts of rules, networks, and the production of space. But the sketch obviously fails to convey the full theoretical power of the concepts. Each of these concepts has three dimensions: the informational, the structural, and the social. What distinguishes the last from the first two is the involvement of people and the uncertainty they perceive and create. The exact nature of these dimensions can most easily be understood if we look at each concept separately.

Rules contain information—they are directives about what to do, how to behave. They do not exist in a vacuum; they are the product of, and re-produce, institutions—the structural dimension. Embodied in rules are a set of institutional priorities, some established recently, others established a long time ago, that reflect the values and concerns of those in a position within the institution to write the rules and change them. But rules were meant to be broken, and there is strong evidence that they routinely are, whether it is because the rules get in the way (DiMaggio 1990, 121) or be-cause the rules do not cover all eventualities and require the use of discre-tion or judgment. In other words, the exercise of discretion or evasion is as likely to ensure the persistence of an institution as it is to undermine it. Many rules do not require implementation by people and so are not sub-ject to evasion or the exercise of discretion, except insofar as people exer-cise discretion in setting up the automatic implementation of a rule. But, as soon as one introduces people into the mix, evasion and discretion soon follow.

People exchange information through networks—information flows through them. Networks are also relationships of trust that go beyond the service they provide in the delivery of information. Some networks are purely mechanical lines of communication—information of a prescribed sort flows through them, such as television transmissions picked up by televisions in individual homes across the country—but they still involve people because someone has to produce the information. As a result, even these networks invoke questions of trust: do I trust the information sent to me? Though it is people, in the last instance, who build up and break down social networks, it is a feature of networks that these processes of building up and breaking down are not easy to do. Thus networks of relations persist; they have a structural dimension. Networks matter in the analysis of the construction of risk because of their persistence, which results in a particular structure of relations, and means that information flows to some people and not to others. This matters because people with access to more or better information are able to make better decisions for themselves. And people who have access to the same information are more likely to agree with each other.

Lefebvre (1991) argues that the production of space entails the production of abstract and social space. Abstract space has both an informational dimension and a structural one. Its informational dimension is the space that cartographers, planners, architects, and others depict on paper or on computer screens. But these depictions do not take place in a vacuum. They articulate the vision of a particular institution that has the power to impose the depiction on others—the structural dimension. They can also depict a particular social order. For example, zoning laws demarcate spaces according to the uses to which they can be put. A map showing the boundaries of zones with symbols identifying the category of zone within each boundary, and a "dictionary" explaining the types of building allowed in each category of zone, provide sufficient information to allow someone to know what they are allowed to build in any particular location. But the zoning map also represents the authority of the government to regulate the use of land in the area over which it has jurisdiction. And the boundaries between zones articulate a social order that the government, either as an autonomous agent or as a representative of its electorate (or a mix of both), has chosen to impose on those living and working within its spatial jurisdiction.

The production of space also involves people who live in the space, who enjoy and endure it. In doing so, they produce social space. Walking down a street alters the meaning of the street for others, either fleetingly or, if it is a regular route one takes, more permanently. Buying a house in a particular neighborhood alters the experience of that neighborhood for others living there, or even alters the way others think about what constitutes their neighborhood. In these ways, and many others, people produce social space. The processes by which people produce abstract and social space interact. People use spaces that have been defined for them, through abstraction, and those spaces are nothing, neither successes nor failures (for both the planner and people in general), until we see how people use them. Furthermore, abstract spaces do not come out of nowhere. They build on or react to what is already physically in place and in use.[18]

The informational/structural/social trichotomy is also useful for understanding how rules, networks, and the production of space interact. Rules and networks interact in a complex manner. People use rules to define what information flows through what networks. Thus, for example, an organization's reporting requirements determine who gets what reports. Of course the efficacy of the rules defining information flows is contingent on there being a preexisting distribution network. Furthermore, networks determine the flow of information to those involved in making or adapting rules. In this light we can see how people can use rules and networks to try to exert control over the flow of information and the content of rules. But such control is elusive, because networks are not simply information flows, but are grounded in trust, and rules require the exercise of discretion. A person may know with some certainty what information she is likely to receive on a regular basis because of her position within a network. But she cannot be certain as to what information from what source to trust. People have to build and maintain trust, so that when they act they do so on trustworthy information only. Kollock (1994) shows that uncertainty helps build trust, because the only way people can test whether someone is trustworthy is to see how the person acts when someone depending on him has no control over what he is going to do. The corollary to this is that a well-negotiated relationship in which the rules for future behavior are stipulated in advance does not require trust, because behavior that benefits the relationship is stipulated to in the rules. In other words, rules destroy the need for trust. But that is the case only if rules are absolute and cover all future contingencies. They are not and do not; they require discretion or even evasion if their intentions are to be carried out properly. People exercise discretion in implementing rules that cannot predict all possible situations in which the rules will be applied. As a result, discretion reinstates the need for trust in even a rule-based relationship.

The relationship between rules and networks is further complicated if we look at their structural dimensions. The network structure of an institution does not map directly onto the authority relations established in its institutional rules. Informal networks of relations develop that are not in the organization chart, either because they are embedded within networks of relations that exist outside the institution or because they have developed out of the everyday interaction of people who regularly cross each other's paths (the "water cooler" phenomenon—a spatial phenomenon). Such informal relationships maybe functional for the institution because they may enable the exchange of important information in an efficient manner that either allows for better compliance with the rules of the institution or is another form of discretion.

Rules are involved in the production of space. The rules of planners and others define abstract spaces. But, as I noted, those planners and others are not working on a tabula rasa—there are people and structures that they can choose to incorporate or ignore through their production of abstract spaces. Those people themselves have ideas as to the proper way to demarcate the space in which they live. Thus the extent to which the process of abstraction takes into account the social meaning that people in particular spaces attach to those spaces depends on the extent to which people know about and can challenge the abstraction process. In this regard, it also depends on the network of relations in which the rule-makers are embedded. Furthermore, the abstraction process may be informed by clear-cut rules, but it still falls foul of the problem of discretion, because the rules cannot cover all contingencies that emerge on the ground. This, as I will show, is most prominent when appraisers have to value a home in a neighborhood whose boundaries are being redefined.

Networks contribute to the production of space in two ways. They can cut across existing spatial boundaries to create new spatial agglomerations, or they can bring together people living or working near each other in ways that confirm existing spatial boundaries. As Martin (1994) notes with regard to the impact of the extension and greater efficiency of global financial networks, it is not clear which force is dominant. He argues that the greater capital mobility facilitated by these global financial networks creates two contradictory forces: (a) the ability of footloose capital to go where it pleases, thus nullifying spatial differences and creating indistinguishable social spaces; and (b) the advantage it gives to those places where capital is concentrated to gain further by being best able to exploit the new opportunities that greater mobility creates. Dow gives a succinct explanation of what advantages financial centers enjoy that reinforce themselves over time: "localized concentration of expertise, specialized institutions, networks of information and trust, and market confidence that these advantages help to promote" (1999, 41). Furthermore, in an analysis of the London financial district, Thrift shows that world financial centers still rely on face-to-face interactions that are part of an effort to create relationships built on trust (1994, 348). At the level of the residential neighborhood, where the mortgage lending industry constructs risks out of loan applications, the same issues are at play. Do lenders' marketing networks reach across all neighborhood boundaries, or are they parochial in whom they serve? How do people construct their neighborhoods through their everyday interactions and movements? And how do these efforts at boundary-drawing coincide with, or jar with, those practiced by real estate brokers and appraisers?

One thing to keep in mind is that what I have described is a *process*. The term "production of space" makes this clear in the case of the spatial concept, and it is implied in my discussion of rules and networks. The idea that people are continuously engaged in a process of creating and, more often, maintaining networks and rules is an important one for understanding the theoretical thrust of the argument that follows. We can use rules, networks, and the production of space to analyze the way people construct risk in the mortgage lending industry, but we always have to keep in mind that it is people doing the constructing of both rules, networks, and space, and, through them, of risk. The process orientation is also an important point from a public policy perspective, because the focus on how people are doing the constructing enables policy-makers to understand how those constructing risk might go about the process differently—the concepts are there to help policy-makers understand the context in which people are operating. Furthermore, the idea that it is a process results in a focus on the fact that people produce as well as receive information, and future decisions are contingent on what information has been produced in the past. This most clearly matters when risk is constructed through the locking-in of certain practices or through self-fulfilling prophecies. And, again, from a public policy perspective this is important, because policy-makers should look at how certain practices have become locked in or have become self-supporting if they want to work out a way to change them.

The U.S. Mortgage Lending Industry

As the figures that I cited at the start of this introduction testify, the mortgage lending industry is a massive one. It is also highly centralized, especially with regard to rule-making power, which is of prime interest in this book. Figures I.1 and I.2 give a sketch of the structure of the industry from a regulatory and a financial perspective respectively. The diagram of the regulatory structure includes only federal regulators and omits state regulators. In Figure I.1 the lines between entities are lines of authority, whereby the entity higher up on the page has the authority to regulate the practices and decisions of those below it. In Figure I.2 the lines without

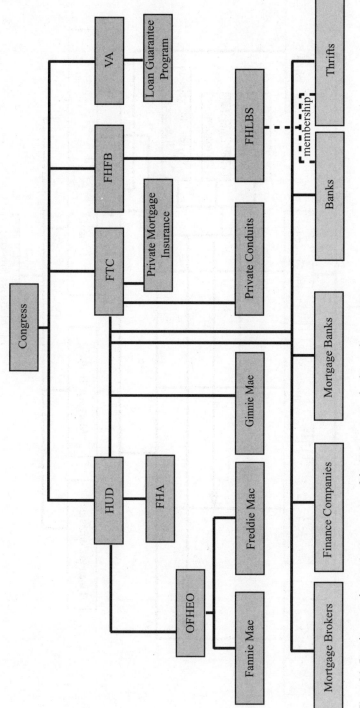

Figure 1.1. Regulatory and supervisory structure of the U.S. mortgage lending industry, 2000.

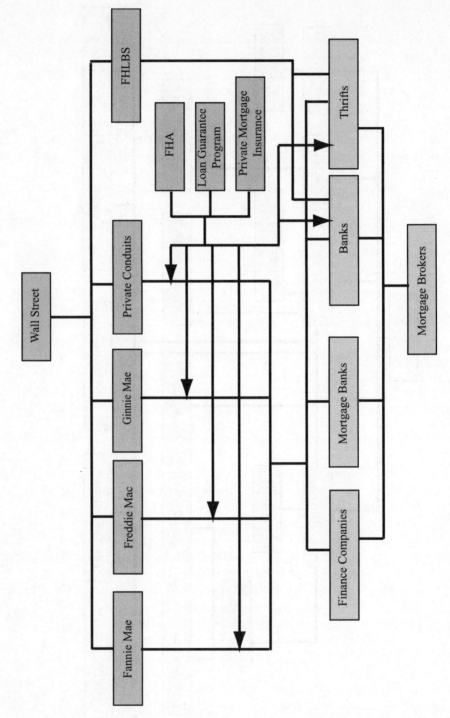

Figure 1.2. Financial structure of the U.S. mortgage lending industry, 2000.

arrows between the entities are flows of capital, information, and contract rights: capital flows down the hierarchy, while information and contract rights flow up, in exchange. The lines with arrows indicate the provision of loan insurance.

At the top of the regulatory structure of the industry is the U.S. Congress. Below Congress are the government regulatory bodies. These regulators are of two sorts. There are the bank regulators: the Federal Deposit Insurance Corporation, the Federal Reserve Bank, the Office of Thrift Supervision, and the Office of the Comptroller of the Currency. These supervise the practices of depository institutions—banks and thrifts—with regard to such issues as safety and soundness, the Community Reinvestment Act, the Home Mortgage Disclosure Act, and fair lending laws.[19] The other regulators, the Department of Housing and Urban Development (HUD) and the Federal Trade Commission, are charged with enforcing federal consumer protection laws that apply to real estate transactions: the Real Estate Settlement Practices Act (RESPA) and the Truth-in-Lending Act (TILA) respectively. These laws apply to banks, thrifts, mortgage banks, and finance companies. HUD is also the regulator of mortgage banks with respect to HMDA, and it has supervisory authority over much of the secondary mortgage market. The secondary market is composed of the Government National Mortgage Association (Ginnie Mae), the Federal National Mortgage Association (Fannie Mae), the Federal Home Loan Mortgage Corporation (Freddie Mac), and private "conduits." Ginnie Mae is under the direct supervision of HUD because it is a part of that government department. Fannie Mae and Freddie Mac are privately owned, government sponsored enterprises (GSEs). Despite their private ownership they receive an implicit government guarantee of the risks they bear. The 1992 Federal Housing Enterprises Financial Safety and Soundness Act (FHEFSS Act) established the Office of Federal Housing Enterprise Oversight under HUD, which monitors the safety and soundness of the GSEs and establishes targets they have to meet with regard to lending in low-income and minority neighborhoods and to low-income borrowers. These secondary market institutions buy or pool mortgages originated by financial institutions, as reflected in the lines linking the financial institutions and the secondary market in Figure I.2. The government insurers, the Federal Housing Administration (FHA) and the Veterans Administration (VA), are subordinate to their respective government departments as shown in Figure I.1. Along with private sector insurers (PMIs) they insure many of the mortgages that are sold to the secondary market and also mortgages kept in portfolio by the financial institutions, as shown in Figure I.2.

The centralization in terms of rule-making power is the result of the fact that for either Fannie Mae or Freddie Mac to purchase or pool conventional "conforming" mortgage loans originated by a financial institution, the loans must meet their underwriting guidelines.[20] For either of these institutions to purchase or pool government-insured loans originated by financial institutions, the loans must meet the underwriting criteria of the two government departments that insure mortgage loans: the FHA and the VA. Ginnie Mae buys or pools only government-insured mortgages, which again must conform to the rules of the FHA and the VA. As a result, apart from mortgage loans that remain in the portfolio of a financial institution without government insurance, any loan originated in the United States must directly comply with either Fannie Mae, Freddie Mac, FHA, or VA underwriting rules. I say directly because these institutions' influence extends beyond their direct activities. Even if a lender keeps its loans in portfolio it may want to be able to sell them at some time in the future. For it to do so the loans would have to be in compliance with the rules of Fannie Mae or Freddie Mac.

Of all loans on 1- to 4-family buildings made in the United States in 2000, 49.3 percent were sold into the secondary market (this excludes sales of seasoned loans). Fannie Mae, Freddie Mac, and Ginnie Mae controlled 86 percent of the secondary market in that year (in terms of $ volume of loans made). As a result, 42.6 percent of all loans went through one of these three institutions in 2000 (Fannie Mae 2001). This does not completely capture the dominance of these institutions and the FHA and VA, because financial institutions hold loans in portfolio that they may later wish to sell into the secondary market (seasoned loans), and they also hold FHA- and VA-insured mortgages in their own portfolios, in addition to selling them (Fannie Mae 2001).

Fannie Mae, Freddie Mac, the FHA, and the VA do not deal directly with the borrowing public. All loans are made through financial institutions—mortgage banks, commercial banks, and thrifts. Mortgage banks do not have deposits and so are unlikely to hold the mortgages that they originate. They may sell them to a parent company that is a bank, to a private investor, or to Fannie Mae, Freddie Mac, or Ginnie Mae. Commercial banks and thrifts do have deposits and so have the capacity to hold mortgages that they originate. Even at this tier there is a great deal of concentration of activity. In 1998 the top 25 lenders in the country accounted for over 55 percent of the mortgage loan originations (Office of Federal Housing Enterprise Oversight 1999, 37).

Parallel to and overlapping with the secondary market and individual financial institutions is the Federal Home Loan Bank System (FHLBS).

This is a network of 12 cooperatively owned banks whose members are deposit-taking institutions (no longer restricted to thrifts) that hold at least 10 percent of their assets in mortgage loans.[21] The 12 banks issue advances to their member institutions against the security of the mortgage loans the latter hold. The funds for the advances come from securities that the FHLBS issues on the capital markets (Figure I.2). Like Fannie Mae and Freddie Mac, the FHLBS is a GSE, but has its own supervisor, the Federal Home Finance Board (FHFB), which monitors the system's safety and soundness as shown in Figure I.1. Unlike Fannie Mae and Freddie Mac, the FHLBS does not specify the rules according to which member institutions should underwrite the loans they sell to the system. This means that there is some decentralization of decision-making authority within the system, but it is circumscribed by two constraints. First, FHLBS does evaluate the loans submitted to it by its members using its own underwriting model, and its evaluation affects the pricing of the loans. Second, members of the system are still subject to regulation by their supervisory agencies, as shown in Figure I.1.

The GSEs, government insurers, and an increasingly consolidated banking system make up the mainstream of the mortgage lending industry. There is a group of lenders that operates outside of this mainstream. These are the finance companies, which have traditionally provided home equity loans and first-lien refinance loans to borrowers wanting to consolidate their consumer debt. Much of this type of lending is "subprime" lending because the finance companies extend credit to people who cannot get a "prime" loan that meets the guidelines of the secondary market or what is common among the mainstream financial institutions. In return for this "leniency" the finance companies are able to charge a higher interest rate. Many of the finance companies are unregulated, except for federal consumer protection regulations enforced by the Federal Trade Commission (FTC) and HUD. But there are also lenders within the mainstream that operate in the subprime market. These are finance companies that are owned by regulated financial institutions, or, even, the institutions themselves that offer subprime loans as one of their loan products. Also, the GSEs, as I will describe in chapter 3, are flirting with subprime lending.

The subprime market is a rapidly growing market, but it is still small—in 1998 it made up 12 percent of the refinance market, but only 4.6 percent of the home purchase market. From the perspective of this book the subprime market is important not because of its size, but for two other reasons. First, it defines itself against a prime market—its very existence as a clearly identifiable market segment is indicative of the extent to which the rest of the market operates, more or less, under a consensus about

24   what constitutes a good risk and what does not. Second, subprime lending
is a precursor of "risk-based pricing" in the prime mortgage market—the
practice of charging borrowers a different interest rate depending on the
level of risk they represent. This again highlights a feature of the mainstream mortgage lending industry. It largely operates on a "one size fits
all" basis. On this basis a loan applicant either fits the criteria and gets a
loan at the going rate, or does not fit the criteria and does not get a loan at
all.[22] In this regard, risk-based pricing is a radical break from the current
dominant practice and, to the extent that it may become more widely
adopted, merits some attention, which it gets in the last chapter.

Finally, at the bottom of the industry structure are the mortgage brokers. Whether they are prime lenders or subprime lenders, many financial
institutions use mortgage brokers. Mortgage brokers take applications,
process the paperwork, and "pre-underwrite" the application to ensure
that it conforms to the requirements of one of its correspondent financial
institutions. Mortgage brokers do not fund the loan and do not make the
final credit decision. Most of the time they have correspondent relationships with a number of different financial institutions, which allows them
to offer borrowers a wide variety of loan products and rates. Some banks
or thrifts operate almost like mortgage brokers in that they will take the
application and process it at their branch, but the loan will actually be underwritten and financed by another entity.[23] A loan applicant enters the
loan application process either through a mortgage broker or through a
loan officer.

The industry was not always this way. The contemporary mortgage
lending industry has its roots in the changes made by the federal government in the 1930s. In 1932, Congress established the Federal Home Loan
Bank Board (FHLBB) in response to the liquidity crisis that thrifts were
suffering during the Great Depression. In 1933, under the Roosevelt administration, Congress established the Home Owners Loan Corporation
(HOLC), which was the first direct intervention of the federal government into the mortgage market. The HOLC, which was under the control
of the FHLBB, issued government-insured bonds which it exchanged for
delinquent mortgages held by thrifts and commercial banks. The HOLC
then refinanced the delinquent mortgages at a 4 percent interest rate,
amortized over 15 years. Though the HOLC stopped issuing loans in
1939, it was an important first step in the creation of the contemporary
mortgage loan industry. In 1934 Congress passed the National Housing
Act, which created the FHA. For the purposes of this book the most important aspect of the act was Title II, which authorized the FHA to insure
mortgage loans issued by approved financial institutions, very much as it

does today. The great financial innovation of the FHA was to establish high loan-to-value, fully amortizing, long-term loans.[24] The act also created the Federal Savings and Loan Insurance Corporation, now part of FDIC, which provided insurance for deposit accounts in thrifts. The 1934 act also allowed for the creation of private national mortgage associations that could buy mortgage loans. No private sector investors stepped forward to set up such an association, but in 1938 Congress itself chartered the Federal National Mortgage Association (Fannie Mae) to buy FHA-insured loans. In 1944 the Servicemen's Readjustment Act (section 501) established a home loan guaranty program for veterans which provided for an even higher loan-to-value ratio. Fannie Mae was authorized to buy loans insured by the VA.

The industry did not change again until the 1960s. In 1965 the FHA and Fannie Mae were brought into the newly established Department of Housing and Urban Development. In 1968 Fannie Mae was divided into Ginnie Mae and a new Fannie Mae that was privately owned. The former was established to purchase the new loans that the FHA would be insuring as a result of policies established by the 1968 National Housing Act. These loans were considered more risky than the traditional FHA loans and so were channeled into a separate entity (Hays 1985). The new Fannie Mae continued to buy the traditional FHA mortgages. In 1970 Congress authorized Fannie Mae to purchase conventional mortgage loans, and chartered a new institution under the control of the FHLBB, whose three board members were the sole members of the Freddie Mac board (Stanton 1991, 22).[25]

The structure of the industry remained roughly the same until the late 1980s when, in response to the savings and loan industry crisis, Congress altered and reinforced the regulatory structure. In 1989 Congress, under the Financial Institutions Reform, Recovery and Enforcement Act (FIRREA), dissolved the FHLBB and transferred its functions to three different organizations: the oversight function went to the newly created OTS; the insurance function went to the FDIC; and the bank system function went to the FHLBS, supervised by the FHFB. Under the same act Freddie Mac's board became shareholder controlled (ibid.). In 1992 Congress created the OFHEO to monitor the safety and soundness of Fannie Mae and Freddie Mac.

There are two important phenomena to note here. One is the prominent role the federal government has played in the industry since 1932. The second is the long-term tendency toward centralization of the industry, mostly as a product of the growth of Fannie Mae and Freddie Mac, though the consolidation of the banking industry through mergers and ac-

26   quisitions in the 1990s has also contributed to this centralization. Both the role of the federal government and the increasing centralization of the industry play an important part in the process I describe in the next two chapters.

Plan of the Book

This book presents data showing how the various actors in the mortgage lending industry have constructed risk, both historically and in today's everyday practices. Chapters 1 and 2 focus on the origins of the underwriting rules that are generally in use in the industry today. Much of the analysis focuses on the origins of the rules that Fannie Mae, Freddie Mac, and the FHA use, because these are the industry's dominant institutions. But the analysis also includes the rules and practices of the thrifts under the regulatory structure of the FHLBB and the Federal Savings and Loan Insurance Corporation, prior to 1989, and of the VA. In addition, I discuss significant regulatory issues that affect the practices of the industry today.

    Chapter 1 traces the current appraisal process to its roots in the debate about the definition of value in the 1920s. The analysis runs along two tracks. One is an institutional track that examines the professionalization of the practice of appraising. It shows how networks of relations between key actors in this process enabled a particular solution to the appraisal problem to gain primacy in the implementation of government interventions in the home loan market during the Great Depression. But the institutional analysis also shows how relatively slowly this solution was disseminated to savings and loans across the country, the most important providers of home mortgages in the 30 years after World War II.

    The second track focuses on the way in which the particular solution to the appraisal problem the profession adopted produced a particular kind of urban space. It is clear from the evidence that even before professionalization, and even before they agreed on one definition of value, appraisers agreed that the presence of minorities in a neighborhood was detrimental to home values. They also agreed that people of different incomes should live in separate neighborhoods. But it is clear that the very definition of value, and the methodology used to measure value, endorsed and institutionalized this consensus. Furthermore, despite the fact that the explicit endorsement of segregating people by race has been expunged from appraisal handbooks, the explicit endorsement of segregating people by income remains and, as a result, there remains an implicit endorsement of racial segregation. Chapter 2 traces the origins of the rules by which the industry currently evaluates the risk presented by the borrower—a borrower's willingness and ability to pay the mortgage—and the way the industry manages behavioral risk through loan-to-value ratio rules and prepayment penalties. The chapter shows the variety of ways in which these rules were formulated in different institutional settings, and how debates about their validity have been constrained by those settings.

Chapters 3 and 4 detail the application of the rules of risk assessment in practice. Both these chapters rely heavily on data gathered in Chicago during the 1990s. Chapter 3 discusses how employees of lending institutions solicit and process loan applications. Using interview data I focus on the marketing and loan preparation practices of loan officers and the decision-making heuristics of underwriters. I show the importance of networks of relations between real estate brokers and loan officers to the marketing efforts of lenders, and the importance of loan officers in helping an applicant get a loan. The interviews with underwriters reveal how they use their judgment in making loan decisions, and the extent to which that judgment is itself grounded in the rules of decision-making established by the secondary market and the FHA. This chapter also presents data on the use of credit scoring and automated underwriting systems that began in the mid-1990s. I focus on the extent to which these two developments have changed the loan application and underwriting process, especially with regard to the exercise of discretion. Chapter 4 examines how appraisers value properties. The analysis focuses on the process of neighborhood definition that they must employ to complete their valuation. By defining neighborhoods in a way consistent with both the appraisal rules and their own understanding of the Chicago housing market, appraisers are forced to draw lines that have racial and class significance. I look at the significance of the way appraisers, real estate brokers, and home owners draw boundaries for the processes of racial and ethnic succession and gentrification.

In chapter 5, I continue to use data from Chicago to analyze the determinants of racial disparities in the distribution and approval of home purchase loan applications, within the theoretical framework of rules, networks, and the production of space. I show how a network analysis can explain why lenders serve particular neighborhoods, and how a mix of neighborhood boundaries and the race of a loan applicant affects the results of a loan application.

Chapter 6 provides a summary of the evidence presented in the previous five chapters, with a focus on the extent to which the mortgage lending industry operates on the basis of consensus around a core set of rules. I use this summary account to flesh out the bones of the theoretical framework that I have outlined in this chapter. Finally, in chapter 7 I address

28   the broad policy implications of the way risk is constructed in the mortgage lending industry, within the context of radical changes in the industry brought about by automated underwriting and risk-based pricing. Specifically, I outline strategies designed to change the current process of construction by changing the way in which rules, networks, and the production of space currently operate. I recommend a regulatory strategy that takes a constructivist view of the loan application process, which requires that regulators conducting fair lending exams not only look for racial and ethnic discrimination as it is traditionally defined, but also require lenders to aggressively address situations in which their loan application process is failing minority applicants. At an institutional level I recommend a strategy that does not take for granted the validity of the current rules, but sets in motion a political dialogue about how the financial risk inherent in lending money to buy a home should be shared. I recommend a network strategy that is designed to put useful information in the hands of the prospective home buyer and loan applicant. And I recommend a spatial strategy designed to disrupt the construction of boundaries between people of different races and classes.

1

The Meaning of Value

A mortgage lender uses an appraisal to determine the value of the collateral securing a home mortgage loan. The determination of the value of the home is a crucial part of the risk assessment process. The lender reduces its risk exposure by placing a mortgage on the property the borrower is buying that allows it to take possession of that property (foreclose on it) if the borrower defaults on the loan. The lender then sells the property to try to recoup the amount it lent out. The lender also knows that the borrower may want to sell the property to pay off the loan. In either case the lender wants to make sure that the home is of sufficient value to cover the amount of the loan. So part of the process of constructing risk is constructing the value of the property.

Nowadays the lender hires an appraiser to conduct the appraisal of the property. If the home is a 1- to 4-family building, the appraiser uses the Uniform Residential Appraisal Report (URAR) form to capture the relevant information used in the valuation and to make the appropriate calculations to come up with a final monetary value (the form is reproduced in the appendix to this book). On the back of this form is some-

30   thing curious: there is space for three different approaches to valuation. At the top is the "Cost Approach," which is assigned about two inches of space. Below it is the "Sales Comparison Analysis," which takes up about ten inches of the page. And finally, there is one line for the "Indicated Value by Income Approach (If Applicable)." At the bottom of the form is a "Reconciliation" section in which the appraiser "reconciles" the potentially divergent values reached by the different approaches. The structure of this form is not an accident. It reflects historical debates about the definition of value and the best method for determining that value. Yet, despite the seemingly eclectic nature of the valuation process, the URAR also reflects a convergence within the real estate industry on a particular definition of value and a particular methodology for measuring it.

This chapter unfolds in two ways: on the one hand, as a discussion of the theory of value in real estate appraisal and its implications and, on the other hand, as an institutional history of the debate about and practice of real estate appraisal. The discussion of the theory of value looks at the various ways different people defined value and the implications of this for the shape our cities have taken since the 1920s. It goes beyond the existing body of literature that has examined the racism of the appraisal industry to look at the underlying logic implicit in past and present theories of value. In doing so it exposes a logic of class segregation that is still in place today. The institutional history shows how lending institutions, professional associations, and the government constructed definitions of real estate value for their own purposes, sometimes at odds with one another and at other times in coordination. Localized lending institutions were, for the most part, happy to retain their own individual definitions and approaches to value. The government also suffered from parochialism at different points in time, with different agencies employing different definitions of value for different political ends. But professional associations and national lending institutions, most prominently the secondary market after 1970, sought standardization. The parallel analysis of both the theoretical underpinnings of appraisal practices, past and present, and the history of those institutions engaged in the practice of appraising is important because together they explain how theories and practices that we now take for granted came to be so. In this way the analysis shows that the concept of real estate value has been constructed over the years to reflect a certain set of values that tend to advantage one group of people over another.

The Meaning of Value in Dispute

Defining and Measuring Value

Appraisers are confronted with a classic problem of economics, that of determining the value of something. The problem is twofold: defining what is meant by value; and developing a sound methodology for measuring it. In the 1920s considerable disagreement existed among appraisers about how to define and measure real estate value. There were three camps. First, there were those who used the cost approach to valuation, often referred to as the summation method, which was the most common at that time.[1] The cost approach estimated the value of a property by calculating the reproduction cost of the building (minus physical depreciation) plus the value of the land. Those using the cost approach did not show much interest in defining value; rather their interest was in measuring it in a sound manner. For example, Knox, whose book is an articulation of the cost approach, noted that "mortgage loans are always based on a fair selling price" (1924, 8), but failed to define what he meant by that.

There were also those who defined value in terms of "market value," drawing on marginal utility economics and the courts for support. For example, McMichael and Bingham argued:

> Economists suggest a rule for the determination of market price, stating that purchasers with the highest subjective exchange values are paired off against sellers with the lowest subjective exchange values until the process results in a pair exchanging at a price which is then considered the market price. This price is reached by a process of bargaining, a practice as old as the ages. (1923, 223–24)

And they went on:

> Market value is the expression, in money, of the meeting of the minds of a buyer willing but not compelled to buy, and a seller willing but not compelled to sell. This rule is recognized by the law as applicable to real estate transactions although the units dealt in are not alike. (Ibid., 224)[2]

As a result, they advocated the sales comparison approach to valuation. It stipulates that the value of the property is best estimated through an analysis of the sales prices of comparable properties in the area.

Finally, there were those who defined value as the "the present worth of all the rights to future benefits arising from ownership," though it was not uncommon for advocates of this definition to acknowledge that value was "established in exchange." What distinguished them from the market

32   value advocates was their desire to identify the "warranted" or "justified" value of real estate. They advocated the income approach to valuation, which estimated value by capitalizing the future income stream of the property. They argued that this approach to valuation was designed to capture its "warranted" value by getting at the heart of the usefulness of a property. In the case of single-family, owner-occupied homes these theorists saw their value in the "amenity income" stream accruing to the owner of the property, though they recognized that the sales comparison method was more appropriate to their valuation. For example:

> *The theoretical method of valuation commences by studying the future utility of the property.* . . . Thus, in the valuation of a home, the returns which are forecast are amenities—sunshine, shelter, comfort, warmth, beauty of surroundings, and congeniality of neighbors. Such returns are, in theory, discounted to an equivalent present money value in the form of a price for the home. This is precisely what the market does. It compares the various sets of anticipated amenities offered by the available homes and assigns present values to them. . . . Thus appraisal by comparison with market prices (which is the method applied to houses) follows the valuation theory outlined but can make little use of its implied precision. (Babcock 1932, 165–66; see also Ely and Morehouse 1924 for the origins of this idea.)

Some appraisers advocated the use of all three approaches, either using each approach to check the others in any appraisal, or favoring one approach over the other depending on the task and the type of property. For example, Zangerle wrote: "Any attempt to transmute exchange value into utility value, intrinsic value, real value or speculative value involves the study of philosophy and metaphysics in the realms of idealism and materialism. Especially in the subject of real estate will there be violent resentment by dealers and owners against theorizing the market into abstractions" (1924, 23–24). Nevertheless, he defined value in terms of "a price at which an owner is willing to sell who does not have to sell to a buyer who is willing to buy but who does not have to buy" (23), and went on to discuss all three approaches to appraising.

Urban Structure and Dynamics

The warranted value theorists were particularly critical of the traditional approach to valuation, because it largely ignored the structure and dynamics of the city in which the subject property was located. For example, Frederick Babcock drew this contrast:

Habitually an appraiser, when asked to make a valuation, seizes his note-
book and several pencils, jumps into his car, and drives rapidly to the property. Arrived he immediately rivets his gaze upon the property. Into the hall
he goes, and then to the basement, the attic, and every part of the building. . . . If he looks at a window in some room, his attention is on the
weather stripping.

All of this is distinctly proper except that that very window frames a
view of something of vast importance in arriving at his valuation—the
neighborhood and district.

A clever appraiser commences his field work before he reaches the
property. He drives rather slowly and observes the transition from one district to another as he proceeds. He circles around in the neighborhood of the
property. He sees stores, schools, churches, paving, traffic movements, the
condition of yards and buildings, and, if he would do the very best job, people. (1931, 94–95)

The warranted value theorists abhorred the fact that the "summation"
method ignored the relationship between the building and the lot. It is
clear from reading Knox 1924 that this critique had a large element of
truth to it. Knox did discuss the importance of the neighborhood in the
valuation process, in the valuation of the lot, but the emphasis of his book
is on calculating the costs of the building and adding that to the price of
the lot. His scant description of depreciation encompassed only the wear
and tear on the building and did not take into account "functional" and
"economic" obsolescence on which the income theorists placed so much
emphasis, and which they used to capture the effects of changes in the surrounding neighborhood on the value of the subject property.[3]

Yet despite the disagreements about the definition and measurement
of value, there was a general consensus among appraisers of all stripes that
a certain urban structure was desirable. That structure was a separation of
city districts by uses and the separation of residential areas by social class,
country of origin, and race. Fisher explained quite clearly why people of
different incomes and social class should remain separate:

Thus if a professional man is looking for a house site, he prefers to go where
the homes are of the general type which he expects to build. Likewise the laborer prefers a section where the homes are of the sort he expects to build
because a standard of living in such a neighborhood is more nearly the same
as his. In the exclusive neighborhood the laborer would frequently feel ill at
ease. He would also find that his income would not enable him to build or
keep up the kind of home prevalent in the neighborhood. (1923, 116)

Knox explained the importance of keeping people of different countries of origin separate: "In communities composed largely of native Americans the presence of people of foreign birth is sometimes regarded as objectionable, but where foreigners are present in such numbers that they constitute a considerable element in the community, their presence makes it easier to sell to others of the same nationality" (1924, 9).

And, of course, there was the well-documented consensus that people should be separated by race (Abrams 1955; Bradford 1979; Jackson 1985; Massey and Denton 1993). In the eyes of appraisers and the real estate industry in general, any breaches of this desired structure resulted in a decline in real estate values. Abrams reviewed the *Appraisal Journal* of the American Institute of Real Estate Appraisers and the *Residential Appraisers Review* of the Society of Residential Appraisers from 1933 to 1945 and found 15 articles on race and real estate, of which 14 took the view that nonwhite and foreign-born people were detrimental to real estate values (1955, 166).[4] Babcock (1924) includes both race and occupations as the "real factors" that affect real estate values. And McMichael and Bingham argued:

> There are certain elements which have a detrimental influence on the desirability and value of residential areas. Among these may be noted:. . . .
> 2. Tenements and apartment houses, creeping into fine residential streets, where expensive detached homes have been built, soon cause a diminution in value. (1928, 230–31)[5]

Despite general disagreement about how to define and measure real estate value, there was a general consensus that the violation of neighborhood lines (supposedly) separating people by social class, country of origin, and race would result in a decline in values.

Unlike the cost and market definitions of value, the warranted value definition was a systematic attempt to make sense of the structure and dynamics of the city grounded in a particular theory of value. As I noted, the traditional cost definition focused mainly on the property itself. The market definition required that the appraiser define the neighborhood in which the property was located, because that defined the area from which the appraiser drew his comparables. But, though such advocates of the market value definition such as Bingham and McMichael were clearly concerned with the impact of city dynamics on real estate values, they did not use this definition as the starting point for a general theory of urban structure and dynamics. In contrast, the advocates of the warranted value theory clearly grounded their understanding of urban structure and dynamics in their value concept, because an appraiser had to assess the income that a particular building on a particular lot would yield and had to assess the future size of that income stream. In other words, the warranted value theory required the appraiser to pay attention to the relationship between the building and its lot and to the future. At the heart of the theory of urban structure and dynamics derived from the warranted value theory was what Babcock (1924) called the "principle of uniformity," which had been first articulated by Hurd (1903). Hurd argued that the competitive mechanism yielded uniformity in the types of building in an area of the city through the workings of time:

> The time element in this definition [of the most suitable building for a location] eliminates such buildings as a factory in a residence district, or a saloon in a business location, which while yielding a large rent injures the surrounding property. . . . The main principle seems to be that the best neighbors any building can have are buildings similar to itself, business buildings and residences being most keenly responsive to environment, and public buildings, factories, churches, hospitals, transportation terminals, etc., being more independent. (1903, 116–17)

In other words, the future benefits that a particular building derived from a given location were contingent on that building's effect on other buildings around it, and vice versa. Hurd also argued that there was a tendency for like uses to cluster together in order to save customers the "time, trouble and uncertainty of seeking through scattered shops," and because a successful shop will attract others to its area in order to take advantage of the increased street traffic it promotes (ibid., 82–83). Thus uniformity of both land values and uses was the result of the workings of two mechanisms: clustering of like uses and expulsion or exclusion of unlike uses.

Babcock was not a great believer in the reality of the principle of uniformity, even though he accepted it in theory. He offered a pared down version of the principle, which ignored the type of use to which the land was put, and posited that uniformity of land values would hold because the rent yielded by uses in the same area would be the same due to competition. But this applied only in a static city. In a dynamic city uniformity was undermined by the fact that as the city grows the areas become home to new uses while still being home to older, different uses established in a previous stage of growth. There was a tendency toward uniformity but this was never fully realized, because the different uses to which land in a particular area was put resulted in different values (1924, 54–57). As a result, Babcock rejected the practicality of using the principle of uniformity

36   in appraising (whereby the value of the land could be established with data from the sale of other parcels of land in the district).

This ambivalence about uniformity was also reflected in a study that emerged out of the huge *Regional Survey of New York and Its Environs,* which compiled an inventory of land uses in the area. Using data from this survey Robert M. Haig of Columbia University argued:

> The forces of competition do tend to approximate the ideal layout, and the trends actually in operation are the surest indication as to what is economically sound. However, the trends are the result of the individual decisions of persons in search of a dollar profit.
>
> It also happens that unless social control is exercised, unless zoning is fully and skillfully applied, it is entirely possible for an individual to make for himself a dollar profit but at the same time cause a loss of many dollars to his neighbors and to the community as a whole, so that the social result is a net loss. (1926, 433)

In other words the "forces of competition" seemed to work, but not well enough, so zoning was needed.

Much of the focus of theoreticians of the city was on commercial and industrial land uses. The theory of residential districts' structure and dynamics was less well developed. Nevertheless this did not stop the theorists from making assertions about residential neighborhoods, in line with the consensus described above. For Hurd the mechanisms of clustering and exclusion worked in residential neighborhoods in the same way they did in commercial areas:

> The basis of residence values is social and not economic—even though the land goes to the highest bidder—the rich selecting the locations which please them, those of moderate means living as near by as possible, and so on down the scale of wealth, the poorest workmen taking the final leavings, either adjacent to such nuisances as factories, railroads, docks, &c., or far out of the city. . . . The main consideration in the individual selection of a residence location is the desire to live among one's friends or among those whom one desires to have for friends; for which reason there will be as many residence neighborhoods in a city as there are social strata. (1903, 78)[6]

Babcock (1924) said little about residential areas in his discussion of different districts in the city, but again agreed with the consensus regarding neighborhood uniformity. He offered no evidence in support of the idea of uniformity and did not explain how he could agree given his ambivalence regarding the likelihood of uniformity in districts in general. His

1932 *Valuation of Real Estate* included a discussion of the valuation of homes and of the gradual decline of residential neighborhoods due to the infiltration of people of lower social classes. Similar to Hurd in this regard, Babcock noted the drawing and driving processes that underlay the movement of people of different social classes in and out of neighborhoods: "a class of persons is *drawn* to newer districts where newer buildings are available for occupancy, but it is equally true that they are *driven* to the newer districts by the growing class distinctions mentioned" (1932, 89). He emphasized the gradual nature of this process because the movement was of individuals whose marks of class distinction, though real, were imperceptibly different from those above and below them. Only racial change was likely to be rapid and have a commensurate impact on values. Overall, he believed that all residential neighborhoods experienced a decline in value over time, even with zoning in place (ibid., 88–91).

Babcock's pessimistic view of the plight of values in residential neighborhoods reflected a general public concern regarding the effect of urban dynamics on the mix of land uses and people within districts and neighborhoods. The spread of zoning across the nation's cities in the years after the First World War was a response to what were seen as the incompatible uses of neighboring lots. Though found to be unconstitutional, the first such zoning ordinances were passed by cities in border states to ensure the segregation of black and white residential areas. In 1916 New York City instituted the first comprehensive city zoning ordinance, which heralded the beginning of the zoning boom that sought to separate areas of the city by use. One of the consequences of this boom was a debate over the constitutionality of ordinances that zoned areas of the city for single-family homes only (see Williams 1922, 284–85, for a list of court cases). The concern here was that, *contra* Hurd, wealthy residents of a neighborhood could not exclude poorer residents through the simple mechanism of high land values, because the latter could always afford to move into such districts by renting apartments built there. So long as those apartments generated sufficient rent, high land values did not act as a barrier. Wealthy residents sought protection in zoning ordinances creating areas in which only single-family homes could be built. The Supreme Court's decision in favor of such zoning came in the case of *Euclid v. Ambler* (1926).

A parallel concern with the planning and "preservation" of residential neighborhoods was also apparent in the publications of the Institute of Public Utilities and Land Economics. For example, Gries (1925) and Bartholomew (1925) in the *Journal of Land and Public Utility Economics* complained about the haphazard nature of city growth and the unplanned development of new subdivisions. J. C. Nichols (1929) in the same journal

38 gave a "Developer's View of Deed Restrictions," in which he outlined the challenge of creating a development controlled by deed restrictions but sufficiently flexible to accommodate city growth and changes in taste. The emphasis was on the coordination of individual actions for the greater good of all.

The concerted efforts to regulate the distribution of land uses through zoning and deed restrictions were part of an attempt to make practical sense of the city. The warranted value theory was a parallel attempt to make theoretical sense of the city. The important connections between the two sets of sense-making activities were their concern with the future and their concern with the relationship between the building and its lot. The contradiction between the two was that the theory of value implied an orderly city, while the evidence that the practitioners encountered was of cities with a "dispersion and . . . complexity of districts" that belied the theory. Babcock recognized this contradiction in the case of commercial and industrial areas. In the case of residential neighborhoods, all he was willing to see were uniform neighborhoods facing inevitable decline. It was only later when he became chief of underwriting at the FHA that he fully developed a way to address this problem. To understand how he came to be in that position requires an understanding of the institutional context of the debate about value.

The Institutional Context of the Debate

The debates about value played out in the 1920s within the National Association of Real Estate Brokers (NAREB), whose political power was to grow exponentially in the following decade (Abrams 1955, 151–52). Table 1.1 lists the major works on real estate appraising published in the 1920s in the United States and shows NAREB's interest in promoting the education of appraisers.[7] It also shows the diversity of views that NAREB was willing to endorse, reflecting the variety of opinion among those who were seriously thinking about valuation. But within this diversity NAREB forged a strong link with the Institute for Research in Land Economics and Public Utilities (IRLEPU)[8] at Northwestern University. Those affiliated with the Institute were heavily influenced by Richard Ely, who was its director and a prominent economist. They were advocates of the warranted value definition, using the capitalization of income method to arrive at a value, though they recognized the importance of the workings of supply and demand in determining the price of a property. Frederick Babcock and Ernest Fisher were the two most important links between the Institute and NAREB. They were members of both organizations, and Fisher at the time of his 1923 book was serving as assistant executive secretary of

NAREB, while Babcock was a member of NAREB's Appraisal Division and a founding board member of the American Institute of Real Estate Appraisers. Henry Babcock, Frederick's brother, was also a prominent member of NAREB and the AIREA.

During the late 1920s the warranted value theory gained prominence within NAREB (see NAREB 1925–29). In 1927 a brief course in real estate appraising published by NAREB (*Real Estate Appraisal,* by Arthur Mertzke) endorsed the income approach for income properties, and described a cost approach for the valuation of homes that incorporated many of the criticisms of that approach being made at the time. Wendt (1974, 27–28) notes that Mertzke's influence on appraisal theory lay in his reconciliation of the three approaches to value—though a careful reading of his chapter on appraising a residential home shows a consideration of only the cost and market approaches. Mertzke's work for NAREB was also representative of an effort to accommodate new *definitions* of value without throwing out old *approaches* to value. This was readily apparent in NAREB's 1929 statement of the "Standards of Appraisal Practice for Realtor Appraisers and Appraisal Committees of Member Boards," in which the warranted value theory held sway.[9] In article 3 under the title "Value," the following definition of market value was given: "The market value of a property at a designated date is that competitively established price which at that date represents the present worth of all the rights to future benefits arising from ownership" (NAREB 1929, 886).

But article 3 also acknowledged the impracticality of this definition in many circumstances. The article distinguished between three different types of property: investment, noninvestment, and service properties. The first type could be appraised by the "direct" method—the capitalization of net income. The second type, which were largely owner-occupied residential properties, could be appraised by the comparison sales approach, which the article termed the "indirect" method, thus making clear that it was a deviation from the most accurate method:

> This *indirect* method of appraisal, in conformity with this definition of value, determines that competitively established price which represents the present worth of all the rights to future benefits arising from ownership by comparison with the competitively established prices of comparable properties. (Ibid.; emphasis added)

Finally, the third type of property, which included such things as parks and churches, which neither yielded income nor could be compared to like properties, could be "estimated" by the cost approach, though the article

Table 1.1. Books on real estate appraisal published in the 1920s in the United States

Title	Author	Year	Publisher	Institutional endorser	Author's institutional affiliation	Definition of value and methodology
Real Estate Principles and Practices	Philip A. Benson and Nelson L. North	1922	Prentice-Hall	NAREB	Both lecturers at New York University	Value of land=capitalized income. Appraise improved lot using modified cost approach; have to take into account suitability of improvement to lot.
City Growth and Values	Stanley L. McMichael and Robert F. Bingham	1923	Stanley McMichael Corporation	NAREB	Real estate broker and attorney in Cleveland, respectively	Willing buyer, willing seller. Sales comparison method in strong market; cost and income method in a slow market.
Principles of Real Estate Practice	Ernest M. Fisher	1923	Macmillan	NAREB	Assistant executive secretary of NAREB and research assistant at the Institute for Research in Land Economics and Public Utilities (IRLEPU)	"value arises from . . . scarcity and . . . desirability." Focus on income method of valuation.
	Robert Bingham and Elmore Andrews	1924	Stanley McMichael Corporation	NAREB	Both attorneys in Cleveland	Modified cost approach; have to take into account suitability of improvement to lot.

Title	Author	Year	Publisher	Organization	Position	Approach
Elements of Land Economics	Richard T. Ely and Edward W. Morehouse	1924	Macmillan	NAREB	Director of and research assistant at IRLEPU, respectively	Mostly interested in land value. Capital value = selling price in a competitive market. Capitalization of income method.
Real Estate: A Comprehensive Manual on All Branches of the Real Estate Business	George Kirkman	1924	Southland Publishing House, Inc., Los Angeles	None	Real estate practitioner	Cost approach for residential properties, though taking into account future trends.
The Appraisal of Real Estate	Frederick M. Babcock	1924	Macmillan	NAREB	IRLEPU	Present value of future income/amenity stream. Sales comparison approach for owner-occupied homes.
Principles of Real Estate Appraising	John Zangerle	1924	Stanley McMichael Corporation	None	Inheritance tax appraiser for Cuyahoga County, Ohio	Willing buyer, willing seller. Cost, sales, and income approaches.
Principles of Real Estate Appraising	Charles C. Knox	1924	R. C. Knox	None	Vice-president and appraiser of The Home Savings and Loan Company in Youngstown, Ohio	"Fair selling price." Cost approach.
"The Appraisal of City Property," in *The Real Estate Handbook*, ed. Blake Snyder	James A. Webb	1925	McGraw-Hill Book Company	None	Cleveland real estate firm. Chair of Appraisal Committee of NAREB	All approaches, but emphasis on cost approach minus depreciation and obsolescence.

Table 1.1 Books on real estate appraisal published in the 1920s in the United States (*continued*)

Title	Author	Year	Publisher	Institutional endorser	Author's institutional affiliation	Definition of value and methodology
The Basis of Real Estate Values	John P. Kennedy	1925	Bank Business Builders, Associates	None	Chief appraiser, Security Trust & Savings Bank	Income definition. No guidance on application to appraising residences.
"Real Estate Appraisal," in *Pointers on Real Estate*, ed. James R. Murphy	Robert Simon	1926	James R. Murphy, New York	James R. Murphy Real Estate School	Real estate developer and speculator	People make value; improvement must suit lot.
Practical Real Estate	W. Carlton Harris	1926	International Textbook Company	None	Lawyer	Willing buyer, willing seller; but cost approach based on sum of land value and building reproduction cost, minus depreciation and obsolescence.
The Science and Practice of Urban Land Valuation	Walter Pollock and K. Scholz	1926	The Manufacturer's Appraisal Co.	None	Tax assessors	"Comparative usefulness . . . to the life of the community." Community survey approach for tax assessment.
Fundamentals in Real Estate	Blake Snyder and Ralph Roby	1927	Harper and Bros.	NAREB and IRLEPU are acknowledged as the stimulus for writing the book	Snyder member of NAREB Education Committee; Roby lecturer at Columbia University	Value based on "the service which the property is capable."

Title	Author	Year	Publisher			
Real Estate Appraisal	Arthur Mertzke	1927	NAREB	NAREB	NAREB (received Ph.D. from University of Wisconsin, Madison—previous home of IRLEPU)	Long-run cost=normal value. Three approaches to value.
Practical Suggestions for the Appraisal of Residential Properties for Real Estate Loans	Philip Kniskern	1927	National Reserve Corporation	Presented at NAREB convention	National Reserve Corporation, NAREB	"Value is what the average individual is justified in paying for a piece of property." Cost approach to measure value.
Urban Land Economics	Herbert Dorau and Albert Hinman	1928	Macmillan	None	Both at IRLEPU	"the price it would bring if sold." Income and comparative methods (where no income data are available). Use one as a check on the other.

repeatedly noted that this was not the property's value (see ibid., 889 and 893). NAREB's standards were an institutional compromise both between practice and theory and between the old guard and the new.

In 1932 NAREB established the American Institute of Real Estate Appraisers, which published the highly influential *Appraisal Journal*. Its first issue reflected the still fluid nature of the debate over the definition and measurement of the value of real estate. This was clearly articulated by Philip W. Kniskern, the first president of the AIREA, in a discussion printed there, in which he noted: "a feeling on the part of some of the Committee that possibly one of the reasons we get so much variation in the values found in appraisal work is because we are not all working with the same definition, implying that if we do not travel to the same point we naturally do not come out together. And it was believed that one of the big jobs for this Institute to undertake was to develop by discussion or otherwise a definition of value" (AIREA 1932, 23–24).

Not everyone agreed, however, that it was necessary to come up with a definition of "true" value. For example, an essay by Harry S. Cutmore[10] argued, "I would get away from all attempts at rigid definitions of value," and concluded that an appraisal simply be "provable to all reasonable individuals" which would "do away with any necessity of presenting a scholastic definition of value" (AIREA 1932, 18–19). Another item in this stew of differing opinions, the first edition of *McMichael's Appraising Manual*, did not offer much direction. In his chapter "Measuring Value" McMichael cited numerous authors and their definitions of value, without comment except to conclude: "Property may be appraised on the assumption that it possesses one or more of the above indicated types of value" (1931, 8).

Meanwhile the warranted value theorists continued to push their line. Fisher in the revision of his 1923 textbook, published in 1930 as *Advanced Principles of Real Estate Practice*, had already shown the tendency of this school of thought toward increased dogmatism. He committed himself wholeheartedly to the definition of value as being the present worth of future benefits (1930, 148–49). In Frederick Babcock's 1932 publication, *The Valuation of Real Estate*, the same was true, though he made an exception for the valuation of owner-occupied homes. In the *Appraisal Journal*, Peter Hanson (1933) attacked the courts' definitions of value as being too oriented toward the notion of market value as opposed to warranted value, and Ivan A. Thorson (1933) promoted the same theory of value. But they came under fire because of the impractical nature of the method their theory of value required, though, of course, their critics were also committed to putting appraising on a sound scientific footing.

The attempt to professionalize real estate appraising went hand in hand with the debates about value. The very impetus to professionalize stemmed from the realization that appraisers' current practices were inadequate. It was those who were critical of those practices that gained prominence in the AIREA, because it was they who needed to organize to change current practices. As a result, when the federal government turned to the private sector to staff its newly created positions to implement policies intervening in the mortgage market, those most prominent in the only professional association of real estate appraisers were called to service. They came to government service fresh from the ongoing debates about the meaning of value and with their own perspectives on how to best define and measure real estate values. Philip Kniskern was appointed chief of the Appraisal Division of the Home Owners Loan Corporation, while Arthur Mertzke headed up its Economics and Statistics Division. Ernest Fisher was already working for the Department of Commerce on its real property inventory before he became head of the Economics and Statistics Division of the Federal Housing Administration. He in turn brought into the organization his long-time colleague Frederick Babcock who became chief underwriter (FHA 1959, 11).[11] What these men did in these new positions of power is the subject of the next section.

The New Deal and the Meaning of Value

The Federal Home Loan Bank Board and the Home Owners Loan Corporation
The stock market crash of 1929 and the subsequent Great Depression had a profound effect on the real estate market in the United States. In 1933, with foreclosures running at over 20,000 a month across the nation and half of all mortgages in the United States "technically in default" (Jackson 1985, 193), President Roosevelt asked the newly created Federal Home Loan Bank Board (FHLBB) to develop a solution.

The FHLBB recommended the formation of the Home Owners Loan Corporation (HOLC) which would exchange the first mortgages on properties held by financial institutions for bonds it issued, the interest payments on which were guaranteed. The HOLC would then refinance the mortgage it held to a longer-term mortgage at a lower interest rate. The HOLC was created by the passage of the Home Owners Loan Act in 1933. The act restricted the value of the bonds issued by the HOLC to 80 percent of the value of the home securing the original mortgage. This immediately created a valuation problem, because the dramatic decline in real estate values in the 1930s put many lenders in the situation where they were owed more than the home was worth. The solution, according to Horace Russell, general counsel of the FHLBB at the time, was the adoption of "some kind of *intrinsic worth* formula for appraisal which would arrive at a valuation about 25% in excess of current market values. . . . The board finally adopted an appraisal formula providing for a value equivalent to one-third of the current market value plus the current reproduction cost, plus a capitalization of rental value the past 10 years" (1956, 55; emphasis added).

The success of the HOLC in completing its mission hinged on how it defined value. Russell attempted to justify the valuation formula adopted by the HOLC by labeling it an "intrinsic worth formula," but it is clear that the definition was an expedient one. Such expediency was possible because the definition of value at the time was in sufficient dispute to allow for the kind of flexibility that the HOLC needed. It was also consistent with the multifaceted approach to value developed by Mertzke in 1927 and the position of the AIREA under the leadership of Kniskern when it was founded in 1932.

As Jackson (1985, 197–202) notes, the HOLC was also responsible for developing a neighborhood rating system that institutionalized the racial and class attitudes of the real estate industry. The fact that, as Jackson also shows, the HOLC did not exclude lower-rated neighborhoods is not a complete endorsement of its commitment to its mission — many of the neighborhood rating maps do not seem to have been ready for use until 1936 or 1937 after the bulk of the HOLC's lending activities were over.[12] But it did show what could be achieved in the mortgage market by a sheer commitment of resources.[13] Despite the fact that the HOLC bought a large number of loans that were either delinquent or in default in neighborhoods that it later rated as either "definitely declining" or worse, it ended its life as a solvent institution that had achieved its mission of shoring up the private housing market through massive intervention.

The Federal Housing Administration

The Federal Housing Administration (FHA) was the brainchild of the Roosevelt administration. Its original purpose was to stimulate the building industry to create employment for the approximately 2 million building tradesmen unemployed at the time of its passage.[14] The National Housing Act that set up the FHA was passed in June 1934 and contained four sections: Title I established a loan insurance program to stimulate rehabilitation loans on existing properties, under the administration of the FHA; Title II established the Mutual Mortgage Insurance Fund to insure mortgages on homes, to be administered by the FHA; Title III provided

federal charters for privately financed secondary market "national mortgage associations" that would buy FHA-insured mortgage loans; and Title
IV established the Federal Savings and Loan Insurance Corporation to insure the deposits of qualified savings and loan associations.

The focus of this section is on the development of the appraisal rules
for the administration of the Mutual Mortgage Insurance Fund, which,
since its inception, has insured about 10 percent or more of the mortgages
originated in any given year in the United States. Unlike the HOLC's, the
Federal Housing Administration's definition of value had all the appear-
ance of a "scientific" formula. Its 1936 *Underwriting Manual* (henceforth the
Manual), written by Frederick Babcock, laid the ground work for today's
appraisal theory and practices. As such it deserves close scrutiny.

AXIOMS OF VALUATION. The Manual established the following "Axioms of Valuation:"

(1) Valuation presupposes the existence of a buyer.

(2) Valuation presupposes the existence of a seller.

(3) Valuation presupposes a sale in which the buyer is well-
informed, and acts intelligently, voluntarily, and without necessity.

(4) Valuation presupposes a sale in which the seller is well-informed,
and acts intelligently, voluntarily, and without necessity.

(5) *Valuation endeavors to estimate prices which are fair and warranted, that
is, prices which represent the worth at the time of appraisal of the future benefits
which will arise from ownership, rather than prices which can be obtained in the
market.*

(6) Valuation recognizes the importance and usefulness of sales
prices provided it is determined whether or not such sales prices were
fair and warranted; and provided the motives, intelligence, and wis-
dom of the parties to the sales, as well as other conditions surrounding
them and influencing the determination of the sales prices, are ascer-
tained and weighed.

(7) Valuation presupposes and recognizes that intelligent buyers and
sellers consider the utility of real property.

(8) Valuation recognizes that replacement cost at the time of appraisal sets one approximate upper limit of possible value.

(9) Valuation recognizes that value may be less than replacement
cost.

(10) Valuation recognizes that the prices at which competing properties are available for purchase set or tend to set the approximate upper
limit of possible value.

(11) Valuation presupposes and recognizes that well-informed buyers and sellers are commonly aware of the existence of competing properties and compare their respective asking prices, desirability, advantages, and disadvantages, and future prospects.

(12) Valuation presupposes and recognizes that well-informed buyers and sellers compare and contrast the advantages and disadvantages of renting with those involved in ownership. (FHA 1936, para. 303 (1); emphasis added).

These axioms established the preeminence of the warranted value theory, provided in item (5), but made reference to all three approaches to valuation. In doing so, they defined the logic of the relationship among the three methods, and their relationship to the true value of the property. Most simply, the replacement cost of the property (building cost minus depreciation plus land) provided an approximate upper limit to the value of the property. Less simply, the market price of the home paid by a willing buyer to a willing seller was a good guide to the value of the home and could be established through the process of gathering comparative sales data on properties. But this market price had to be checked to see whether it was "fair and warranted," because it was not a true reflection of the value of the property and was subject to the vagaries of market speculation and individual taste.[15]

These axioms show that Babcock and his colleagues' ultimate concern was to establish the valuation process on the foundations of a solid theory of value.[16] That theory was the warranted value theory. On that the Manual built a methodological structure that sought to demarcate and then shape the residential settlement patterns of metropolitan areas throughout the country. The demarcation and shaping of settlement patterns made it possible, methodologically, for appraisers to rely on comparative sales data to determine the value of a home. The methodological structure was built on the two fundamental principles of the warranted value theory of value: the realization of the value of a property took place in the future; and the principle that the building and the land on which it rested had to be compatible with each other. It was on this basis that the Manual promoted the "principle of uniformity" as the ideal for residential neighborhoods. And it was in the context of such uniformity that the FHA could safely rely on comparative sales data to measure the value of a home.

PRINCIPLE OF UNIFORMITY. Despite the ambivalence he expressed with respect to the "principle of uniformity" in his writings about the com-

mercial and industrial districts of cities, Babcock clearly stated his belief in
the uniformity of residential neighborhoods in the Manual:

> It is common to find residential communities of considerable area in which
> the characteristics of the individual properties are substantially alike, and in
> which influences originating in neighboring districts, or in the city as a
> whole, or in larger regions, operate substantially alike upon each of the
> properties in the districts under consideration. From this fact arises the
> principle of uniformity upon which the comparative method of land valua-
> tion is based. (Pt. 1, para. 337(2))

> The best type of residential district is one in which the values of the in-
> dividual properties vary within comparatively narrow limits. In such a dis-
> trict one is likely to find people whose living standards likewise are substan-
> tially the same, although their individual tastes in some respects may be
> widely different. Such a district is characterized by uniformity and is much
> more likely to enjoy relatively great stability and permanence of desirability,
> utility, and value than a district in which the residential values are found to
> vary within wider limits. In both cases one of the first steps the Valuator
> must take is to determine the characteristics of that which he would con-
> sider the typical (not the average) residential property in the district. In so
> far as properties in an area depart from that which is typical, it will be found
> that fair values will be less than replacement costs. (Pt. 1, para. 316)

The principle of uniformity recited in the Manual served a number of
purposes. It was an empirical statement—"it is common to find." But it
was an empirical statement unsupported by any data, and, in fact, contra-
dicted by the Residential Security Maps developed by the HOLC. For example, the HOLC map of the Chicago metropolitan area, an area with
which Babcock was very familiar, included 396 neighborhoods within the
city. To the extent that the HOLC maps were an attempt to delineate
neighborhoods by social class and race, this map belies Babcock's assertion in the Manual: Chicago covered 133.8 square miles in the 1930s,
which means that each neighborhood delineated by the HOLC covered,
on average, one-third of a square mile, hardly the "considerable area" that
the Manual asserted was "common to find."[17] More important, the statement was a methodological one establishing the validity of the comparison
sales method. And it was a value statement of two kinds: (a) a general
statement of class prejudice; and (b) an economic articulation of that prejudice—"much more likely to enjoy relatively great stability and perma-
nence of desirability, utility, and value." In addition, uniformity was a pro-

tection, of sorts, against what Babcock had previously described as inevitable neighborhood decline. How this protection could be provided was spelled out in the Manual's risk rating procedures.

RISK RATING OF PROPERTY AND LOCATION. Section 205(a) of the National Housing Act specifically required that the loans insured by the FHA be classified in terms of the risk they represented.[18] The Manual stated that the risk rating system was established: "(1) to determine whether or not a mortgage is eligible for insurance, and (2) to rate the risk represented by the mortgage so that it may be grouped correctly for mutual insurance purposes. The risk-rating process accomplishes both objectives simultaneously" (pt. I, para. 213). There were four distinct categories in which the mortgage was rated: property, location, borrower, and the mortgage as a whole. This section is concerned with the property and location ratings both in and of themselves and as extensions of the valuation process.

Value and risk (as I defined them in the introduction) are related in two ways. First, value statements are not 100 percent accurate. This uncertainty about the value of the property can be expressed in risk terms by assigning a certain probability to the fact that the value statement made by the appraiser is in fact correct.[19] Second, value and risk are related because value can change in the future. The uncertainty of the size and direction of a change in value can be translated into a risk statement by attaching probabilities to the future value of a home. If value is defined in terms of the home's ability to provide services in the future, then this second aspect of the relationship between value and risk can be collapsed into the first. That is, if an assessment of the future is part of the valuation process, then any risk presented by future changes in value becomes part of the measurement problem.

As noted previously, the definition of value in the Manual required an assessment of the future as part of the valuation process:

> A dwelling property is valuable solely because of its ability to produce a stream of returns in the future for the benefit of its owner. The size of the stream of returns, the future increase or decrease in its size, and the constancy and permanency of the stream will determine the value of the property. In the case of rental property, the returns are in the form of streams of dollar incomes. In the case of new single-family residential properties, the returns are usually in the form of amenity income-streams, that is, in the form of direct satisfactions. Residential properties are of both types. Both

types of streams produce income, the one measurable in dollars, and the other not concretely measurable but, nevertheless, ratable comparatively in terms of assumed standards with regard to quantity, quality, and duration. The Valuator must make forecasts of the sizes of these incomes, their probable future sizes, and their probable future duration. He cannot avoid such forecasting in his work for he is dealing constantly with future contingencies, which being unknowable, can only be estimated, and which very largely determine present value. (Pt. I, para. 334(1))

But contrary to the logic that any estimate of value should by definition already take into account any future risk, the Manual also established a risk rating system, which:

involves forecasting and prediction. It deals with probabilities. Mortgage risk lies in the future. It exists throughout the life of a loan. It relates to the possibility of default and loss. . . . Risk-rating, therefore, is equivalent to predicting chances or likelihoods as seen at the time of analysis. (Pt. I, para. 215)

Though the National Housing Act required the FHA to adopt a risk rating system, Babcock also gave a methodological justification for using such a system. In the July 1935 issue of the *Appraisal Journal* he cited the problems involved in valuation as a reason for adopting a risk rating approach:

1. They [valuations] are relatively inaccurate. . . . Advances in appraisal technique are not evident among the great majority of the men and institutions who do such work and the very nature of the valuation problem is such that some considerable degree of disparity between appraisals will probably always be present. At the present time the wide disagreement as to proper methods is sufficient to show the inevitability of divergence of estimates.
2. Appraisals are made at and as of the time the loans are made. They represent estimates of values at that time. . . . It [the appraisal] measures the value on foreclosure only indirectly. . . .
3. Valuations are not descriptive of mortgage risk except in an indirect manner. Mortgages do not become delinquent because the value of the security declines; they go into default because the borrower is unable or unwilling to meet his payments. Borrowers are unable to meet payments because their incomes, usually, from the earnings of the property itself, decline. In other words, the amount, certainty, and duration of the income of the property constitute a much greater factor in mortgage risk than does the capital value of the property.

4. Reliance on valuations as the basis of mortgage credit extension is fraught with danger because it tends to divert attention from the zone of mortgage risk and to introduce an element of confidence, which is sometimes not justified by investigations which follow the risk rating line of thought. (Babcock 1935, 319)

Here Babcock argued that both the uncertainty surrounding the valuation process and the future prospects of the value of the property required the use of the risk rating system.

Even though the authors of the Manual adopted a definition of value that was theoretically sound (according to the authors) and required an assessment of future value trends, institutional and methodological imperatives led to the development of the FHA's risk rating system. Despite Babcock et al.'s insistence on a risk rating process distinct from valuation, the former process provided data that were incorporated into the comparative sales method of value estimation (FHA 1936, pt. I, para. 339(2)). The Manual recommended the use of risk ratings as a way of gauging the desirability of the subject property in comparison with "representative type houses," whose values the chief valuators in the regional offices had already established (pt. I, para. 339(1)). In this way the risk rating system provided methodological support for the comparative sales method.

What resulted was a sophisticated model of the city in which residential neighborhoods were delineated according to the principle of uniformity. This provided a basis for the rating of neighborhoods and the properties within them, in terms of both their place in the static order of the city and their vulnerability to its dynamics.[20]

THE STATIC ORDER OF THE CITY—BOUNDARIES, BENCHMARKS, AND RACE. The risk rating system, as it related to the property and its location, was one in which the home under consideration was assigned to a particular housing market and rated against benchmarks within that housing market. These benchmarks were of two kinds: absolute and market-specific. The former established FHA standards for the property and location regardless of the specific market in which the evaluation was taking place; the latter established standards for the particular housing market in which the subject property was located. Most of the property ratings were made against absolute benchmarks, with some market-specific standards included,[21] and thus served to establish the FHA's minimum property standards. Locations within a given neighborhood were rated with respect to a benchmark property typical of that neighborhood.[22] The neighbor-

hoods themselves were delineated according to the uniformity principle
and rated according to their economic viability, with significant results.

One of the assumptions of the principle of uniformity is that the area
under consideration is a functional part of a larger whole. Without this
larger whole the uniform, spatially distinct area could not survive in that,
almost by definition, it does not itself provide all the services it needs.[23] In
the Manual this assumption was made explicit. The first task it set was to
establish the "Economic Background Rating" of the metropolitan area in
which the FHA was to operate. The chief valuator in the FHA's regional
office rated the present and future economic climate of the metropolitan
area (pt. II, para. 215). The FHA kept these ratings, and the criteria used
to establish them, confidential (para. 214). They were kept confidential
because of their sensitive nature as Babcock explained in the *Appraisal
Journal* when describing the rating system as a whole. There he listed 11
categories of factors which he deemed to be relevant to the risk rating of
mortgages. Category 3 covered factors related to the economic viability of
the metropolitan area as a whole, while category 4 covered those related to
the neighborhood. In a discussion of how these 11 categories were reduced to 5, he noted:

> It was discovered that the third and fourth risk categories were better han-
> dled if combined into a single category described as "The Neighborhood." It
> would have subjected the Federal Housing Administration to considerable
> embarrassment to establish any system in which the cities of the United
> States were rated according to quality as areas in which to do mortgage
> lending. The same difficulty does not apply when neighborhoods are rated.
> (Babcock 1935, 322)

And the Manual itself stated:

> The effect of the economic background upon the risk involved in mortgages
> has been recognized by mortgage lenders. Some companies have excluded
> entire cities from their lists of acceptable areas. Others have limited their ac-
> tivities to cities beyond definite population sizes and have favored selected
> locations within the accepted larger metropolitan areas. It is not the policy
> of the Federal Housing Administration to exclude entire cities and towns
> from the benefits of mutual mortgage insurance. It may well be, however,
> that within certain communities whose present-day and expected future sta-
> bility is exceedingly low, only certain favored locations which surpass the
> general average of the town or community may prove acceptable for insur-
> ance. (Pt. II, para. 216)[24]

54   In other words, the FHA considered it impolitic to exclude or redline whole cities, though it would still rate them secretly. Neighborhoods, on the other hand, were fair game.

There were three reasons why neighborhoods, even within the same city, were not rated the same. First, the "Relative Economic Stability" rating was contingent on "the extent to which owners and occupants of properties in the neighborhood may be expected to share in and enjoy the advantages attributable to residence in the economic background area" (pt. II, para. 212(2)). In particular this rating focused on the level of adaptability of neighborhood residents in the face of a loss of employment. It also gauged the extent to which residents were living within their means, especially with regard to housing expenses. The latter assessment was likely to result in lower ratings for lower-income neighborhoods, while both lower- and upper-income neighborhoods were considered vulnerable to adaptability problems (pt. II, paras. 220, 221, and 224).

Second, all neighborhoods were not rated the same because of the Manual's policy toward the "central downtown core of the city which can usually be outlined and considered as an ineligible area" (pt. II, para. 208). This "core" was defined as including "the business and commercial sections of the cities as well as the slum and blighted areas which almost invariably surround downtown sections of major cities" (ibid.). As residential neighborhoods these areas had reached the end of their useful "economic life." This had race and class implications. Inasmuch as minorities and lower-income people were confined to such downtown sections, or, as likely, such areas by definition included their neighborhoods, they were denied access to FHA insurance.[25] Here boundary-drawing resulted in the absolute exclusion of a part of many cities from access to FHA insurance.

Third, the Manual adopted an explicitly racist attitude toward minority neighborhoods. They were not deemed comparable to other, white neighborhoods. This was made apparent in an article titled "Techniques of Residential Location Rating" by Babcock, Massey, and Greene in which they explained the FHA's rating system. They discussed how it was important to divide the city into areas so that "competitive" locations could be compared for rating purposes (as outlined above). In doing so they argued: "With the minor exception of certain racial characteristics which render properties actually noncompetitive, residential accommodations within a metropolitan area are competitive when they may be acquired by families of similar income characteristics"(Babcock, Massey, and Greene 1938, 136). The meaning of noncompetitive was clear—such properties could not be compared to others with respect to the services they delivered to their owners. Thus properties owned by blacks did not even warrant a rating, because there was nothing to rate them against.[26]

To make it possible to conduct such a neighborhood rating analysis there had to be an adequate definition of a neighborhood. The Manual defined the neighborhood as: "a single area composed of locations separated only by publicly-used land, the residential portions of which exhibit a degree of homogeneity. In general, a neighborhood is available for or improved with dwellings of more or less similar character, age, and quality" (pt. II, para. 201(4)).

To facilitate the processing of loan applications the Manual suggested that each FHA regional office divide the city into "outlined" neighborhoods.[27] Each of these neighborhoods was then rated relative to the others through a comparison of the ratings of the best property in each area (called an "Established Rating of Location"), which was the benchmark property in the area. The ratings of the benchmark property in each neighborhood, with the reasoning and details of the rating included, were kept on file on a card.

This practice facilitated a second rating process whereby the appraiser rated the other properties in any particular neighborhood relative to its benchmark property (pt. II, para. 209).[28] This rating process related the factors considered to represent the risk inherent in any particular property within a neighborhood to the class of people living in that neighborhood. In other words, the level of risk associated with a particular feature of a property's location was contingent on the needs of the type of people who made up the market in the neighborhood. These were people with the same incomes and needs. For example, in the case of "adequacy of transportation" the Manual stated: "The Valuator does not rate transportation itself but rather the adequacy of transportation for the type of residents occupying the location" (pt. II, para. 234). Or, in the case of "need for housing," the Manual differentiated between newer and older neighborhoods. The important factor, in either case, was that there should be a group of financially able purchasers for the homes in question, with the added caveat in the case of older neighborhoods that they be able to compete with newer ones. In fact a high rating could not be given to older neighborhoods, in general, unless there was a "lack of new dwellings at the same price range at other locations" (pt. II, para. 247). Another factor, "appeal," was defined as "purely relative and . . . to be measured by the attitude of the income group or the social class which will constitute the market for properties near the location under consideration" (pt. II, para. 249). The same was true for "sufficiency of utilities" and "adequacy of civic, social, and commercial centers." Even in the case of "levels of taxes

56 and assessments" consideration was given to what "local residents have learned to expect" if taxes in a particular city were high (pt. II, para. 272).

The drawing of boundaries and the use of place-specific benchmarks within those boundaries led to the rating of locations in a way that was class-based, but at the same time respected the relative needs of different classes. In the case of blacks this boundary-drawing exercise led to their exclusion from FHA insurance. This was the root of what came to be known as redlining. But this static delineation of the city was only the start. The Manual was also highly conscious of the problems created by city dynamics.

CITY DYNAMICS—ADVERSE INFLUENCES, CLASS, AND RACE. The Manual's dynamic model of the city followed the reasoning Babcock laid out in 1932. The decline of residential neighborhoods was inevitable. This process was sufficiently slow that the resulting decline in property values in the future was not a problem. Two types of change could, however, accelerate this gradual decline: change in the type of land use; and change in the race of residents. In these two cases the vulnerability of the principles on which the whole of the FHA's valuation and risk rating system were based was apparent. Uniformly high land values were no guarantee of exclusivity. Uniform buildings on lots of uniform value could offer such a guarantee, so long as adequate precautions were taken. The FHA pursued this guarantee through the implementation of policies set out in the Manual under a section containing instructions about the rating of "Protection from Adverse Influences."

One recommendation was to use zoning, though Babcock was not a strong advocate of zoning as a source of protection for residential areas. The Manual was explicit in arguing that only zoning carried out with a good knowledge of the nature of the city's growth would be effective (pt. II, para. 227). Zoning could be effective against the accidental incursion of an incompatible use, but not against the inevitable progress of city growth (see also Babcock 1932, 90). The Manual recommended other forms of protection designed to maintain neighborhood uniformity. It recommended deed restrictions so long as they covered a wide area and were adequately enforced (pt. II, para. 228). The "geographical position of a location" offered protection so long as it was "in the middle of an area well developed with a uniform type of residential properties . . . away from main arteries which could logically be used for business purposes" (para. 229). A neighborhood "solidly developed in accordance with accepted good housing practices" (para. 230) offered protection, as did good "quality of dwelling construction" (para. 231).

A major goal of these "protections" was to prevent the mixing of people of different incomes. This was made clear in a letter from Frederick Babcock, as director of the Underwriting Division, to the chief underwriters of the Field Offices concerning the promotion of new subdivisions of smaller homes:

> There is a vital need in most communities throughout the country for decent houses in lower-priced classes. . . .
> When dealing with small properties it should be remembered that fewer amenities are required by lower-income groups and that the alternatives with respect to living quarters available to such groups are not overly attractive. It should be an endeavor of the Federal Housing Administration to make attractive living quarters available to these people and it is felt that if such quarters can be made available the degree of mortgage risk is materially reduced for this very reason. It follows that suitable locations for small homes will, in general, be segregated to some degree, from residential areas providing housing for persons in higher-income brackets. To a certain degree, the Federal Housing Administration should hold itself responsible to protect higher-priced areas from encroachments resulting from the construction of low-cost housing in the same area. The most critical need at the present time is for new subdivisions expressly for small homes. . . .
> The low-priced home represents desirable security for a mortgage when it is part of a rather extensive development of similar price range. For this reason it is obvious that such homes should be grouped and should not be intermixed with dwellings of higher price levels. (Letter to Chief Underwriters, May 21, 1936, Federal Housing Administration 1934–1940)

Here the logic underlying the FHA's Manual was clearly stated. The risk rating of the neighborhood was based on the suitability of its amenities to the type of buyer attracted to that neighborhood. A good rating was contingent on segregating neighborhoods by income to produce the best fit. As a result the FHA actively promoted the *income* segregation of new subdivisions, and was able to do so by advocating the construction of equally priced houses. Furthermore:

> The Valuator should investigate areas surrounding the location to determine whether or not incompatible racial and social groups are present, to the end that an intelligent prediction may be made regarding the possibility or probability of the location being invaded by such groups. If a neighborhood is to retain stability it is necessary that properties shall continue to be occupied by the same social and racial classes. A change in social and racial occu-

pancy generally leads to instability and a reduction in values. (FHA 1936, pt. II, para. 233)

The Manual also recommended avoiding *any* type of vulnerability:

> Where nuisances are present in the neighborhood little protection is offered to locations close to such undesirable elements. . . . A few nuisances may be listed: Presence of billboards, undesirable domestic animals, stables, chicken coops and runs, liquor dispensing establishments, rooming houses, zoos, *public playgrounds, schools, churches,* mercantile and industrial establishments, cemeteries, homes of an institutional character, offensive noises and odors, and poorly-kept unsightly properties. (Pt. II, para. 232; emphasis added)

As in Babcock's earlier works, and as in the minds of many of the country's real estate professionals and academics, there was an inherent tension in the Manual between, on the one hand, the desirability and theoretical "rationality" of the separation of people by race and class and, on the other hand, the reality of urban dynamics that continually sought to undermine this rationality. The Manual guided appraisers and, because of its focus on insuring homes in newly constructed subdivisions, builders on how to protect uniform neighborhoods from urban dynamics.

SUMMARY. The (misguided) genius of Babcock's solution to the problem of placing a value on owner-occupied homes was that he and his assistants created a system of market delineation and categorization that put the comparison sales approach to valuation on a sound theoretical and practical footing. Theoretically, the system the FHA imposed on the urban structure delineated markets made up of properties that had similar "amenity income" streams, which meant that they could safely be used as comparable properties in any appraisal of a property in that market, because they represented the same inherent value. Practically, it provided clear guidance to the appraiser as to how and from where to draw his comparables. This methodological aspect of the Manual's achievement should not be underestimated. The ability to buy and sell real property rights freely had turned lots and their improvements into differentiable commodities. But unlike mass-produced commodities, any two lots and their improvements were never alike, because of the exclusive nature of any particular site. This was highly problematic for both theorists and practitioners attempting to value a property through the sales comparison method. What the FHA did was give appraisers a way to see a number of different lots and their improvements as comparable, if not completely uniform, commodities.[29]

In establishing this system the FHA clearly articulated a class logic that, as I detail in chapter 4, persists today. The logic of the system demanded that lower-income home owners be segregated from their middle- and upper-income counterparts, regardless of race. Furthermore, the logic of the system ensured that lower-income neighborhoods would be the least likely to receive insurance, because the neighborhoods they occupied were considered to be near the end of their economic life. But over and above this class logic was a logic that was gratuitously unjust toward nonwhites. That logic stipulated that white and nonwhite neighborhoods were separate housing markets and, in the vocabulary of the Manual, the latter were "non-competitive." On this basis the FHA explicitly and categorically excluded nonwhite neighborhoods from the benefits of FHA insurance. What we have in the FHA Manual is a clear explanation of the relationship between race and class in the minds of the real estate industry at the time. Minorities and lower-income people suffered under the same logic of segregation, but minorities suffered the additional burden of pernicious, gratuitous discrimination.

During the 1960s and 1970s much of the reasoning in the FHA Manual came under attack, and, as we shall see, language that led to the redlining of minority and old neighborhoods has been eliminated from appraisal theory. What has not been eliminated is the underlying logic of uniformity. This will be explained more fully in chapter 4, but for now I want to pick up again the institutional story of what happened to appraisal theory and practice to show how we got to where we are now.

Toward Uniformity

The diffusion of an economic concept is an important part of its construction. Diffusion transforms the idea from a theoretical construct into an economic institution with a dynamic and power of its own, because diffusion means that a large number of people are using that idea to make decisions. We might assume that once the FHA had developed its systematic, "scientific" appraisal theory and procedures that others would follow suit. After all, the Manual had shown forcefully how a theoretically solid definition of value could be practically operationalized to generate economically sound valuations. But the road from the Manual to today's practices was not a straightforward one.

Uniformity and Diversity, 1945–1970

Much of the focus of studies of postwar appraisal practices has been on the effect that the FHA and VA had on the process of suburbanization and on reinforcing racial discrimination and segregation in the mortgage lending industry. Jackson contends that the neighborhood rating policies of the HOLC were adopted and extended by the FHA, which then influenced the VA. With regard to the impact of the FHA and VA his argument is twofold. First, their consistent bias against minorities and central cities had a direct impact on the market for properties available to minorities and in central cities. Second, these agencies' practices "embraced the discriminatory attitudes of the marketplace" and generally put a "seal of approval" on discriminatory practices (1985, 213–17 passim). This seal of approval included a "scientific" exposition regarding the link between residential real estate values and the structure and dynamics of urban areas, clearly outlined in the 1936 Manual. But it is important to keep in mind that the reason the market and the government were of one mind on this issue was because the government relied on the existing real estate profession for both its knowledge and its personnel. In doing so, it institutionalized as government practice the biases of actors in the marketplace.

There was no such consensus with regard to the definition of value or with regard to the preferred approach to valuation. This was true both within the government and in the private sector. In the postwar era the major new government program in the mortgage market was the Veterans Administration's loan guarantee program, established by the Servicemen's Readjustment Act of 1944. The legislation stipulated that any veteran using the program should not pay more than "the reasonable normal value" of the property "as determined by proper appraisal" (P.L. 78-346, Sec. 501(a)(3)). The congressional intent, as interpreted by the courts in cases involving the program, was to ensure that the veteran did not pay an inflated price for the home (*Sattler v. Van Natta*, Court of Appeal, September 24, 1953). Haar (1960) notes that the VA interpreted this as meaning the "willing buyer, willing seller" (market) definition of value. In 1945 an amendment to the Servicemen's Readjustment Act changed the definition of value to "reasonable value" of the property "as determined by proper appraisal made by an appraiser designated by the Administrator" (P.L. 79-268, Sec. 501(a)(3)). This was done at the urging of bureaucrats in the Veterans Administration itself, who argued before Congress that the program could not work while the phrase "reasonable normal value" was in

the statute.[30] Along with an increase in the maximum loan amount to   *61*
$4,000 and the delegation of loan approval to "supervised lenders" this
change opened a flood of capital into the VA program (Wilken 1956).
Though the VA did adopt the FHA's minimum property standards to evaluate newly constructed homes, it did not adopt the FHA's extensive risk
rating procedures. This reflected the very different concern that the VA
had with respect to the valuation process—it was there to protect the veteran.

In addition to differences within the government, the government and
the private sector and the various institutions within the private sector
were also not of one mind with regard to the definition and measurement
of value. This was particularly notable in the savings and loan industry,
which had vehemently opposed the establishment of the FHA.[31] In 1937,
the "Committee on the FHA" of the U.S. Savings and Loan League reported the results of a survey (500 sent out, resulting in 275 responses) in
which managers of savings and loans were asked "has the improved FHA
appraisal procedure been of benefit to the savings and loan industry?"
Thirty-four percent said "yes," 55 percent said "no," and 11 percent were
"non-committal" (U.S. Building and Loan League 1937, 566). A 1941
"Current Survey on Appraisal Practices and Policies" published in *The Review* of the Society of Residential Appraisers noted that "unfortunately . . .
no progress has been made in the manner of appraising over the past 20 or
30 years" (Society of Residential Appraisers 1941, 6).

In 1947, the Committee on Appraisal Policy and Building Practices reported on the deliberations of the committee with regard to having a consistent appraisal policy. The report indicated that "unfortunately the concept of 'value' cannot be clearly defined." As a result, the committee
advocated that the management of savings and loan associations should
simply define value in their own terms and make sure that the definition
was implemented consistently. And the committee concluded: "The committee does not intend to suggest to members of the United States savings
and loan league any one guide or to recommend a single policy on appraisals." Instead, it described the various practices of "leading institutions" (U.S. Savings and Loan League 1947, 281–83 passim). These practices ranged from the primary use of the reproduction cost approach, with
varying bases for establishing construction costs such as using current
costs or 1940 costs, to the primary use of market prices, to the use of a
number of different figures all of which the appraiser should report to the
loan committee (ibid., 284–87 passim).

This situation persisted into the 1950s. What brought uniformity to
the savings and loan industry was the increasing use of professional ap-

praisers, who were, in turn, brought into line by the efforts of the Society of Residential Appraisers (henceforth SREA, because it changed its name to the Society of Real Estate Appraisers in 1961). The SREA was initially sponsored by the U.S. Building and Loan League when it was founded in 1935, but its philosophy was heavily influenced in its early years by the AIREA and the FHA. The FHA's Manual was distributed to members of the SREA in the 1930s. In 1940 it adopted a code of ethics that replicated the code of the AIREA, including its definition of value, which had so influenced the writing of the FHA Manual. Frederick Babcock was a founding member of the SREA, as were two other prominent members of the AIREA, Herman Walther and Louis Ardouin.[32] In turn the SREA was instrumental in helping the VA develop a definition of "reasonable value." As a result, the AIREA, SREA, VA, and FHA were, to some extent, speaking with one voice in the early part of the postwar era. This voice advocated the three approaches to value, placed more or less emphasis on the "present worth of future benefits" concept in the actual definition of value, and distinguished this from "market value," which was value in exchange. The major standout in this group was the FHA, which, in addition to its valuation procedures, continued to use its risk rating procedures. In 1946 the SREA issued its first *Appraisal Guide*, which closely adhered to the Manual's "Principles of Valuation" in how the three approaches to valuation were related to one another, but did not include a discussion of risk rating.[33] In 1949 the SREA issued its first appraisal form (17-PRA, which came to be known as the "Green Hornet"). The Guide and the "Green Hornet" were both attempts to assist appraisal practitioners to develop consistent, sound appraisal practices. But the savings and loan associations were not quick to change. Only "a small proportion of the associations used professional appraisers" according to a survey by the League; they mostly used managers and board members (U.S. Savings and Loan League 1953, 186). As such their practices were far removed from the influence of any professional association.

As savings and loan associations began to rely more on professional appraisers, so the influence of the professional associations took hold. A survey in 1958 by the League showed that three-quarters of the members used the market definition of value (U.S. Savings and Loan League 1958, 318). The same survey also showed that there was an increasing use of professional appraisers—40 percent of the associations responding to the survey used staff appraisers, 20 percent used fee appraisers, while the remainder still relied on "appraisal committees" (ibid.). In 1962, the Committee on Appraisal Policies and Building Practices of the League endorsed a revised appraisal form, and agreed that "a form for universal use is an impossibility, but the consensus was that the 17-PRA is perhaps as close as we can come to that goal" (U.S. Savings and Loan League 1962, 278). In that same year the SREA changed its definition of value to one that was a purely market value definition, consistent with that used by the AIREA, except that the SREA made reference to the role of "typical financing" in determining values that could be relied upon. A further push toward standardization in the savings and loan industry's appraisal practices came with the opening in Los Angeles in 1967 of the Market Data Center of the SREA. The data center provided appraisers with data on comparable properties by type of building, neighborhood, and other factors, thus facilitating the comparable sales methodology.

The FHLBB, which regulated a large number of savings and loan associations, was not responsible for standardizing the industry's appraisal practices. Up until the 1960s the FHLBB took a laissez-faire attitude toward the regulation of associations in general, and made no effort to prescribe how associations appraised homes securing their mortgages, in particular.[34] The Board did send a sample loan application and appraisal report and an appraisal guide in the form of a letter to all members in September 1936, but it was not binding (Wagner 1936). As a result, up until the 1960s there was no government demand for a universal definition of value. All that mattered was that each individual association knew the type of valuation on which it was making its decisions as to whether to advance a loan or not.

It was only in the 1960s that the FHLBB, through its office of examinations and supervision, began to exert pressure on savings and loan associations to become more professional in their appraisals. In 1963 the FHLBB added section 563.17-1 to its regulations, which specified the requirements for an examination and audit, including under subsection (b)(iii) the requirement that the "record with respect to loans on the security of real estate . . . [include] [o]ne or more written appraisal reports, prepared and signed . . . by a person or persons duly appointed and qualified as an appraiser or appraisers by the board of directors of such institutions, disclosing the fair market value of the security" (28 FR 3473, 1963).[35] This new attention that regulators were paying to appraisals was troubling to the savings and loan industry, as indicated by concern the League's appraisal committee expressed in 1965 regarding examiners' reappraisals. But by 1968 members of the committee noted that reappraisals were no longer a problem. In that same year, the FHLBB, in direct response to a question asking "what is the meaning of the word 'value'?" in its regulations responded, noncommittally: "The value is not necessarily the purchase price but rather the fair market value as determined by a sound and fair appraisal" (Federal Home Loan Bank Board 1968). Even in 1970 the League's appraisal committee's minutes recorded a victory by the savings and loan industry in fending off FHLBB regulation of its appraisal practices. This time the victory was a result of a meeting with the Board regarding a "proposed change . . . pertaining to the market value definition" the Board used in its regulations, which resulted in the proposed regulation not being put into effect (U.S. Savings and Loan League 1970, 264–65).

The adoption of the market definition of value, the definition used today, gained supremacy in the lending market through the efforts of the appraisers' professional associations. The process by which this came about was not straightforward. In the 1930s the FHA laid the methodological groundwork for the comparative sales method, even though it grounded its valuation process in the "warranted value" definition.

Uniform Standards of Practice, 1970 to the Present

A new era in the push toward standardization of the real estate industry's appraisal practices began in 1970 with the reorganization of Fannie Mae and the establishment of Freddie Mac. Initially, there was an attempt to establish uniformity in the forms used by the two organizations. It is unclear whether this uniformity was supposed to extend to their appraisal forms, but in the early 1970s Freddie Mac and Fannie Mae used different forms. Only in 1975 did the two organizations jointly develop a uniform "Residential Appraisal Report," a revised version of which is in use today. In the same year, the SREA and the AIREA came to an agreement on a definition of market value, after many years of disagreement over whether the definition should include a "typical financing" clause. During this same period the FHLBB also tried to standardize the appraisal practices of its members, through two memoranda that established "Guidelines Regarding Appraisal Procedures and Management" (#R 41), issued in 1977, and "Guidelines Regarding Definition of 'Market Value' and 'Typical Financing' Valuation Policy" (#R 41a-1), issued in 1979. The latter memorandum brought the FHLBB's definition of value in line with that of the AIREA and SREA.

Though Fannie Mae and Freddie Mac contributed to the increasing uniformity of appraisal practices in the United States because of their growing presence in the mortgage market, the adoption of uniform standards and practices by the industry as a whole required a further coordination of efforts by professional associations and government agencies, under pressure from Congress. In 1984 the SREA and the AIREA began meetings with the VA, HUD, Fannie Mae, and Freddie Mac to develop common appraisal standards and practices. In 1986 they produced a Uniform Residential Appraisal Report that they would all use to appraise residential, 1- to 4-family properties. In 1987 the SREA and the AIREA joined with six other appraisal associations to form the Appraisal Foundation, which, in 1989, issued the first "Uniform Standards of Appraisal Practice." These standards included a definition of value that is a version of the many definitions of market value that have been discussed within the profession since the end of the Second World War.[36] In 1991 the SREA and the AIREA merged and became the Appraisal Institute.

The final effort toward uniformity took place against the background of scandals within the lending industry, especially savings and loan associations, many of which were the direct result of shoddy and fraudulent appraisals. A report by the House Committee on Government Operations based on hearings held in December 1985 documented the lack of oversight of appraisers by lenders, government regulators, and the professional associations. That the professional associations and various government agencies make efforts to create uniform standards in the profession was one of the recommendations of the House report (U.S. Congress, House, Committee on Government Operations 1986). The profession remained in the spotlight throughout the late 1980s, as problems resulting from both fraudulent behavior and a steep economic downturn in the "oil patch" states revealed the many deficiencies in its members' practices even by its own loose standards. In 1989 Congress charged the Appraisal Foundation with developing the licensing standards to be used by state licensing boards to certify appraisers and to develop uniform appraisal reporting standards, under Title XI of the Financial Institutions Reform, Recovery and Enforcement Act (FIRREA). The state licensing boards were themselves a requirement of FIRREA, because many states did not license appraisers at the time.

Ironically, as the process of standardization reached its zenith in the early 1990s with the implementation of FIRREA, the federal agencies that regulate financial institutions took a radical step away from standardization. Under FIRREA the agencies were charged with determining the threshold loan amounts under which an appraisal is not required. In the early 1990s different agencies adopted different amounts. In 1994 they uniformly promulgated regulations that did *not* require appraisals on loan amounts less than $250,000—82 percent of the dollar volume of mortgages on existing homes and 85 percent of the dollar volume of mortgages on new homes originated in the United States (59 FR 29482). The agencies based this regulation on research showing that during the savings and loan debacle of the 1980s faulty appraisals were not a problem on loans under $250,000 that were secured by 1- to 4-family residential real estate. It is only because the FHA, VA, Fannie Mae, and Freddie Mac, and the individual initiative of managers of financial institutions, require appraisals that they are used on loan amounts less than $250,000.[37]

The Unraveling of the Racist Consensus

The consensus in the appraisal profession that the most desirable urban structure was one in which people were separated by race and class remained in place up until the late 1970s. But the willingness of Congress, the executive branch, and many ordinary people to accept this consensus with respect to race began to unravel in the 1960s and 1970s. The erosion of the consensus took many forms. It included accommodationist policy responses that sought to fix the problems created by the FHA and the mortgage lending industry by creating new mortgage insurance programs for "special risk" areas, such as older urban neighborhoods and urban renewal areas. It also included legislation banning discrimination in federally supported housing initiatives (Executive Order 11063 in 1961, and Title VI of the Civil Rights Act of 1964), and legislation prohibiting discrimination in the sale and rental of housing and in the extension of credit (Title VIII of the Civil Rights Act of 1968, Equal Credit Opportunity Act of 1974). This was followed by a direct assault on the racist assumptions of the appraisal profession and a lawsuit against the AIREA and the SREA in the 1970s, which culminated in a consent decree with the Justice Department in 1976 in which the associations agreed to strike the racist language from their training materials for appraisers. Finally, the passage of the Home Mortgage Disclosure Act in 1975 provided public data on the distribution of mortgage loans by census tract, and the Community Reinvestment Act of 1977 provided a statutory imperative that depository institutions serve the communities from which they receive deposits. Today federal regulators, the FHA, the VA, and the secondary market make explicit policy statements in their rules and regulations prohibiting discrimination against neighborhoods based on the race of their inhabitants and/or the age of the structures. (See 12 CFR 528.9(c)(9) for OTS regulations, Fannie Mae 1995a, Freddie Mac 2002b, 44.6 and 44.15(b), and U.S. Department of Housing and Urban Development 1994, ML94-22 for the FHA's policy statement.)[38]

In their assault on the appraisal profession, community activists focused on explicitly racist attitudes and practices. They also highlighted the bias against urban neighborhoods, which did not suit the prevailing attitudes of appraisers because of their heterogeneity and their age. Despite their many successes the activists were not successful in overcoming the appraisal profession's bias toward uniformity. Chapter 4 will explain this in more detail by showing how contemporary appraisers conceptualize neighborhoods. But to give a brief illustration of the general attitude of the mortgage lending industry toward uniformity it is sufficient, for now, to quote Fannie Mae's current guidelines:

> Typically, dwellings best maintain their value when they are situated in neighborhoods that consist of other similar dwellings. However, some factors that are typical of a mixed-use neighborhood—such as easy access to employment centers and a high level of community activity—can actually enhance the market value of the property through increased buyer demand. Urban neighborhoods also frequently reflect a blend of single-family residential and nonresidential land uses—including residential multifamily properties, other properties that are used to provide commercial services (such as groceries and other neighborhood stores) in support of the local neighborhood, industrial properties, etc. (Fannie Mae 2002, XI, 403.08)

Despite the efforts to accommodate "urban neighborhoods" it is quite clear that the predominant attitude toward the analysis of the neighborhood is that it be homogeneous with regard to building type and land use.

Conclusion: The Construction and Diffusion of the Meaning of Value

Up until the 1920s the cost approach to valuation was the accepted practice of the industry. But an increasingly influential group of practitioner-scholars, prompted by an overarching concern with understanding the fate of real estate values in the face of the dynamics of urban growth, challenged the accuracy of this approach. The fact that this group "won" the contest, at least insofar as it wrote the rules for the Federal Housing Administration and dominated the two major professional associations, was a tribute both to the intellectual sophistication of its approach and to its self-conscious awareness that it actually was in a contest. It was Babcock and others who dominated the appraisal division of NAREB and then founded the AIREA and the SREA, because they had a real concern about the way appraisers practiced their profession.

In terms of their theories about racial segregation and discrimination and class segregation, these practitioner-scholars were in tune with their times. And though the FHA is blamed for the diffusion of systematic redlining practices, it is clear that these were already in place at the local level. But in terms of their definition of value and the methodology most appropriate for measuring it, these same practitioner-scholars had a more uphill battle. The savings and loan industry, which was a dominant player in the home mortgage lending industry, did not easily adopt the market valuation approach, and paid little attention to the theoretical problem of defining value. There was no need to do so on their part—the savings and loans were local institutions that had to worry only about local values, and their regulator, the FHLBB, had a laissez-faire approach to their supervision and examination. Their professional association tried to exert influence on their practices by providing them with the appropriate tools of the trade, but its success was limited initially by the fact that few institutions hired professional appraisers. As more and more did so, and the tools of the trade became more sophisticated, so the influence of the association spread.

The final drive toward uniformity that began in 1970 when Fannie Mae and Freddie Mac offered the whole industry the opportunity to sell their loans on the secondary mortgage market was completed 19 years later through FIRREA in the wake of scandals that tarred the appraisal profession as both incompetent and fraudulent, even though much of this incompetence and fraud had little to do with the everyday appraisal of 1- to 4-family homes. At the same time that the profession was trying to get its house in order, its racist consensus came under attack. This has resulted in a revised consensus, grounded in a uniform theory of value, that eschews racial and ethnic segregation, but still explicitly endorses income segregation.

The story of real estate appraising is one of tragic ironies. In the 1920s, and all the way up to the 1960s, there was a diversity of views on how to define and measure value, yet there was a consensus that the mixing of people by race, country of origin, and social class depressed real estate values. Theories of urban structure and dynamics that informed both private sector and government policies in the 1930s predicted land use uniformity, but urban reality showed that this could not be the case without government intervention or coordinated private sector action—market theories needed nonmarket coordination to make them work. The final irony of the 1994 regulations promulgated by federal regulators not requiring appraisals on loans of $250,000 or less reveals that, maybe, the whole issue of appraising homes has been, after all, "much ado about nothing."

The ironies highlight a key point of this chapter and the next. Lending rules are a reflection of their time and institutional place. Ironies happen because, within a specific time and place, people making the rules do not see the irony in what they are doing—their reasoning is logical given where they are. The fact that the ironies described here have tended to damage the interests of minorities and lower-income people illustrates that they are not something that we can simply shake our heads at, but, rather, are a warning against future tragic ironies and a call to action to alter the conditions that created them.

2

Rules for Assessing the Borrower and Managing Behavioral Risk

The value of the home is important to a mortgage lender because the value is an estimate of what the home can be sold for either voluntarily or involuntarily if a borrower becomes either unable or unwilling to make the loan payments. But a lender is interested in a continual flow of payments for a specified period of time and so prefers to make loans to borrowers who will not prematurely pay off the loan, whether it be voluntarily through the sale of the home or involuntarily through a foreclosure process. As a result, the lender is also interested in the willingness and ability of the borrower to make the loan payments. This chapter discusses the origins and logic of the rules used by the mortgage lending industry to evaluate the borrower. It begins with a discussion of the loan-to-value ratio, which, because it has relevance both to the collateral standing behind the loan and to the borrower's willingness to make payments, serves as a bridge between the previous chapter and this one. I then go on to discuss the borrower's ability to pay, focusing on the debt-to-income ratios used by lenders, and his willingness to pay, focusing on the origins and development of credit records and their changing association with the concept of "character." Finally, I discuss the absence of any underwriting criteria concerned with the willingness or ability of the borrower to voluntarily prepay a mortgage for reasons other than financial distress.

The data in this chapter show that the rules used by the lending industry are a product of the interaction between the federal government, the private sector, and professional associations, though the nature of this interaction varies across the different sets of rules developed for each risk criterion. In the case of the loan-to-value ratio Congress and federal regulations have set the maximum allowable ratios. The history of the criterion used to measure an applicant's ability to pay back a loan reveals a disagreement between the FHA and the VA, on the one hand, and the rest of the mortgage lending industry, on the other, that only changed beginning in 1972 and was not fully resolved until the 1980s. The disagreement revolved around the validity of the industry's rule of thumb, which relied on numerical ratios. Today the ratios approach prevails, though lenders apply it flexibly. The history of the criteria used to evaluate an applicant's willingness to pay back the loan shows that these developed out of a preexisting consensus about how to measure the "character" of a loan applicant and that this consensus was, and is, grounded in a national network of credit reporting agencies. And finally, the analysis of the prepayment issue reveals a complex history that has played out in the courts, in state legislatures, in the Congress, and in administrative hearings and negotiations involving bureaucrats, consumer advocates, industry representatives, and politicians.

As in the previous chapter, the history of the criteria lenders now use identifies both their institutional origins and the values they represent. What they show is that one cannot understand the criteria in their present form without understanding the institutions that constructed them.

Loan-to-Value Ratio

State legislatures, Congress, and federal regulators have routinely set the maximum loan-to-value ratio for lenders. When the federal government intervened in the home mortgage market in the 1930s it continued a practice that the states had engaged in for many years. The Home Owners Loan Act of 1933 stipulated an 80 percent ratio for the Home Owner's Loan Corporation mortgage refinancing program. The act also gave the Federal Home Loan Bank Board authority to charter federal savings and loan associations, and the Board promulgated regulations that set the maximum loan-to-value ratio for any loans secured by a home mortgage at 80 percent.[1] Section 203(b)(2) of the National Housing Act of 1934 set the maximum loan-to-value ratio for the FHA at 80 percent—the only specific underwriting criterion in the 1934 act. More recently, the Emergency Home Finance Act of 1970 established a loan-to-value limit of 75 percent for Fannie Mae and Freddie Mac in their charters (changed to 80 percent in 1974), though they did allow the two organizations to exceed that limit subject to certain conditions, the most important of which is the stipulation that the part of the loan in excess of 80 percent of value be insured.

The FHA

The tradition of setting the loan-to-value ratio at the governmental level has meant that any debate about the appropriate ratio has been a public one, and one in which the parties involved have clearly articulated their interests. Haar (1960) argues that in the postwar period the government manipulated the loan-to-value ratio as a means to control the flow of credit into the housing market. There is ample evidence to support Haar's case. For example, in 1957 Congress amended the National Housing Act to give the FHA commissioner discretion in setting the loan-to-value ratio of the FHA (below a congressionally prescribed limit), "taking into consideration (1) the effects of such ratios on the national economy and on conditions in the building industry, and (2) the availability or unavailability of residential mortgage credit assisted under the Servicemen's Readjustment Act of 1944, as amended" (12 USCS 1709a). But, even as item (2) of this part of the United States code suggests, there is more to the debate about setting loan-to-value ratios than simply determining the appropriate flow of capital into the housing market. It is also about "who gets what." The history of the FHA's 80 percent loan-to-value criterion is a case study in the multiplicity of policy roles a risk criterion can serve to meet the demands of one constituency or another. The main purpose of the FHA's 80 percent figure was to get rid of the need for a second mortgage when making a loan. As Frank Watson, attorney with the Reconstruction Finance Corporation and one of the authors of the bill, admitted, whether this figure was high enough was a guess: "It is necessary that you go high enough so that a workman can properly finance his home without going into the second-mortgage market. You cannot ask him to put up too big a stake. Now, whether 20 percent is too big a stake or too small a stake I haven't the experience to state" (U.S. Congress, Senate, Committee on Banking and Currency 1934, 127; see also the testimony of John Fahey, chairman of the FHLBB, ibid., 61).

But the 80 percent ratio was opposed by the U.S. Building and Loan League, as part of its opposition to the whole idea of the FHA because it threatened to introduce additional competition into the mortgage market. It attacked the 80 percent criterion as being overly aggressive for a nonlocal financial institution. Its representative, Morton Bodfish, argued: "they are going to lend to 80 percent of appraised value. That is pretty high, and the experience of the past 3 or 4 years has taught us that we can go that high where we know a man, and know him well, and we have the facilities for following every step of that loan and getting it paid off immediately, but I am not sure it is prudent for the Government to go that far" (U.S. Congress, House, Committee on Banking and Currency 1934, 264).

The proponents of the bill had an answer for these concerns. They had structured the FHA on an extremely conservative basis, actuarially. Proponents of the bill to set up the FHA were fond of noting that 25 percent of all loans insured would have to go into foreclosure and be sold at 50 percent of their appraised value before the insurance fund, financed by borrower contributions, was exhausted. This statement's validity, of course, was contingent on the timing of the defaults, but by tying a socially valid purpose, the elimination of the second mortgage, to a conservative projection of likely losses through the instrument of an 80 percent loan-to-value ratio the proponents of the bill were able to deliver a powerful message.

Beyond the aim of eliminating the second mortgage, the loan-to-value ratio criterion was manipulated to serve another purpose. The bill sent to the House and Senate by the Roosevelt administration restricted the 80 percent ratio to properties built after the passage of the act, while existing properties could secure mortgages only up to 60 percent of their value. The technical rationale for this was that appraisals on existing properties were supposedly more difficult and so such properties constituted a greater risk (ibid., 150). But the ratio differential also served a broader policy purpose, namely promoting employment in the building trades by stimulating the flow of credit into the new construction market—an explicit goal of the National Housing Act. A lower maximum loan-to-value ratio for mortgages on existing properties restricted the flow of credit into the refinancing of existing short-term mortgages that came due after the passage of the act—a flow that would create no new employment but simply allow home owners to restructure their mortgages as amortized loans. Congressman Franklin Wills Hancock Jr., of the House Committee on Banking and Currency, went so far as to argue that allowing any loans on existing properties was simply a ruse to bail out "some rotten mortgages held by big eastern companies" (ibid., 267). But there was opposition to the ratio differential from representatives of home owners and real estate interests because the 60 percent ratio disqualified many home owners with mortgages coming due from taking advantage of the FHA program by refinancing their loans. D. E. McAvoy, secretary of the Home Mortgage

Advisory Board of New York, and an advocate of the home owners' position, disputed the technical rationale for the ratio differential:

> Appraisals should be the determining factor between the new and the old. As an appraiser I regard that a higher percentage of loan in relation to value can be more safely made on an existing structure than a new one. This is because the existing house is the seasoned one, in respect to neighborhood and all characteristics upon which values are determined; while the new has yet to prove itself as to valuation established which has necessarily been predetermined. (U.S. Congress, Senate, Committee on Banking and Currency 1934, 337)[2]

Despite the seeming importance of the differential, it was eliminated in the bill reported out from the Senate Banking and Currency Committee. Furthermore, this amendment faced no objection from House members when the Conference Committee reported out the same measure as part of the final bill that became the National Housing Act—this despite the fact that it was in opposition to the interests of the United State Building and Loan League, which had proven its political muscle by temporarily winning a battle against the national mortgage associations proposed in the bill.[3]

In 1938, Congress amended the National Housing Act to allow a 90 percent ratio for loans on homes with an appraised value of $6,000. These loans carried only a ¼ percent insurance premium, as opposed to the 1 percent premium on larger mortgages. The homes purchased under these new rules had to be single-family, owner-occupied homes that had been constructed after July 1, 1939. This last stipulation reintroduced the bias against existing homes found in the original bill. It was not until the Housing Act of 1956 that the ratio differential between new and existing construction was eliminated (U.S. Department of Housing and Urban Development 1976, 21). The 1938 amendments prompted an interesting shift in the position of the U.S. Building and Loan League with respect to high loan-to-value ratios. The league's representative, I. Friedlander, argued that the date after which the homes had to be constructed to qualify for the 90 percent loan should be July 1, 1938 (U.S. Congress, House, Committee on Banking and Currency 1937, 257). The reason for this was that the thrifts were concerned that the FHA was stealing business from them through its refinancing of existing mortgages and its financing of the purchase of existing homes. As Friedlander himself noted, half the loans insured by the FHA since its inception were on existing properties—the sooner the FHA could be redirected into new construction the better. He provided a far less forceful or straightforward risk-based argument against a 90 percent ratio than Morton Bodfish had provided against the 80 percent ratio four years previously, because the 90 percent ratio clearly served the interests of his members.

The lesson of the fate of the 80 percent criterion in the National Housing Act during the 1930s is that a technical specification can come to represent a number of different policy goals, depending on the perspective of the advocate or opponent. In the eyes of some it was a great social benefit, especially to the "working man"; to others it was an inordinate risk for a government to take on, since it was operating without the benefit of local knowledge. The differential between a 60 percent ratio for existing properties and an 80 percent ratio for new properties also meant different things to different people. For some it displayed a patent disregard for the interests of home owners; for others it was a prudent device for limiting the risk exposure of the government based on a theory, albeit a disputed one, about the difficulty of appraising existing homes; and for still others allowing mortgages on existing properties at all was a needless concession to banking interests that did nothing to fulfill the goal of the act, which was to provide employment. The 1938 amendments reintroduced the bias against existing homes and, as a result, saw the opponent of the 80 percent ratio in 1934, the thrift industry, become the advocate of a more rapid introduction of the 90 percent ratio in 1938 because it would steer the business of the FHA away from direct competition with thrifts.

It is important to note that the drafters of the original bill that resulted in the National Housing Act were quite conscious of the important relationship between the loan-to-value ratio and the appraised value—the latter is essential for the former to have any meaning. Despite this they made no effort to define the appraised value that would form the basis on which the loan-to-value ratio would be calculated. This was also the practice of the Federal Home Loan Bank Board in its regulation of member thrifts. Though, as noted in the previous chapter, Congress focused a lot of attention on the appraisal process in the 1970s, little attention was paid to the value basis on which the FHA was making loan-to-value calculations at that time. This changed in the 1980s as Congress focused, almost for the first time since the 1930s, on the risk exposure of the FHA. In hearings in 1982 the FHA revealed that its "traditional" administrative practice was to calculate the loan-to-value ratio based on the sum of the appraised value and the closing costs paid by the borrower—referred to as the "cost of acquisition" (see "Supplementary Information" discussion in 48 FR 9300). As a result, despite rules restricting the loan-to-value ratio to under 100 percent and a downpayment requirement of 3 percent, it was possible to borrow more than 100 percent of the appraised value of the home under the FHA's 203(b) insurance program. The congressional response to this discovery was to allow the FHA to institutionalize this practice in its regulations governing the charging of an up-front mortgage insurance premium (MIP), which Congress approved in 1982 as part of the Omnibus Budget Reconciliation Act. It allowed the up-front mortgage insurance premium to be included in the "cost of acquisition" basis for the loan-to-value ratio calculation, and also allowed the borrower to finance the cost of the premium and closing costs up to 95 percent of their total (48 FR 28794). But Congress and the FHA defied the tradition the FHA had established by excluding the MIP from the "cost of acquisition" when calculating the statutorily required downpayment of 3 percent. The wrangling around the "cost of acquisition" concept was a political compromise—in exchange for paying a burdensome up-front premium, borrowers were accorded the most favorable loan-to-value and downpayment requirements possible without altering the statutes regulating loan-to-value ratios themselves.[4]

The legislative changes of the early 1980s set up a new political fight in the late 1980s and early 1990s. This new fight was prompted by the "oil patch" states' economic crisis, which resulted in massive home mortgage foreclosures, including FHA-insured home loans. These events and the long shadow of the savings and loan scandal prompted Congress to commission a study of the actuarial soundness of the FHA's insurance fund. The resulting study by the accounting firm Price Waterhouse showed that the insurance fund, though solvent, was losing money, possibly for the first time since 1934. The study was heavily oriented to an analysis of the impact of changes in loan-to-value ratio requirements on the soundness of the fund in the face of "adverse conditions" (Price Waterhouse 1990, 1–3). Based on the results of the study the administration introduced a proposal to charge risk-based premiums that varied depending on the loan-to-value ratio of the loan. The political battle waged over the administration's proposal was fierce, with community advocates and the housing industry joining together in opposition ("FHA's Insurance Fund" 1990). The debate was clearly framed by the Price Waterhouse study and the administration—the focus was on the configuration of loan-to-value ratio limits, closing costs, and the MIP, and the opposition's counterproposal also focused on that configuration. The protagonists in the debate couched their arguments in terms of risk. The secretary of HUD, Jack Kemp, took the position that he was protecting both the insurance fund and families, who should not be allowed to get into debt over their heads through FHA insurance that allowed a small cash commitment from the borrower. In opposition, community and industry advocates railed against the higher cash outlay the administration would require from borrowers and the fact that the risk-based premiums moved the FHA away from its "mutual" origins. The one major departure in this clearly delineated debate was the proposal from community advocates that the FHA fund counseling for first-time homebuyers to help them manage their financial obligations to avoid delinquencies and default, which they hoped would lower the risks of low downpayment loans.[5]

As in the 1930s, the political debates over the FHA in the 1980s and early 1990s were often about apparently technical issues concerning the appropriate loan-to-value ratio for the FHA insurance program. The language used in discussing these technical issues was that of risk. But in these cases, and many others not recounted here, the parties to the debate were taking overt stands in defense of their interests. This should come as no surprise to most students of politics, but it does demonstrate three important points. First, small technical changes can take on profound political, if not real, significance. The debate in the early 1990s revolved around hundreds of dollars worth of closing costs that, according to whom you believed, would result in either tens of thousands of families being shut out of the housing market or tens of thousands of families going through the pain of foreclosure. Second, because risk debates are about the future, the positions that different parties to the debate advocate are based on predictions, giving them wide latitude to generate data in support of those positions. On the other hand, it is clear from the debates in both the 1930s and the 1980s that the "risk talk" confines the debate to a particular set of issues and that the different parties attempt to provide at least the veneer of rationality to their arguments within this narrowed context. Finally, the debate over loan-to-value ratios has taken place in a public forum because of the tradition of setting ratios in the legislature and in agencies. This public setting has provided ample evidence of the distributive implications of risk debates and is symptomatic of the political content of technical issues that are often discussed behind closed doors.

The Federal Home Loan Bank Board, Fannie Mae, and Freddie Mac

The FHLBB and Fannie Mae and Freddie Mac have also changed their loan-to-value ratio to meet the demands of constituents, though these changes have taken place in less public settings than those affecting the FHA. Unlike the FHA, the FHLBB maintained a consistent loan-to-value ratio policy from 1937 until the early 1970s. The policy allowed associations to vote to raise their maximum ratio to 80 percent, and to go even higher if the loan was insured under the National Housing Act, to allow member institutions to take advantage of higher ratio FHA-insured loans (1938 CFR 203.10(b)).[6]

In the early 1970s the policy went through some dramatic changes. In 1971 the Board altered the regulations to allow 90 percent loans without mortgage insurance on single-family, owner-occupied homes where the borrower was also paying his taxes and insurance on a monthly basis, and the loan amount was less than $36,000 (36 FR 901). In 1972 the FHLBB allowed 100 percent loans for its Home Ownership Assistance Program (HOAP) (37 FR 14756). And in 1974 the Board introduced 95 percent loans, but rescinded the 100 percent loans because the HOAP had ceased to operate (39 FR 9429). None of these changes were subject to congressional oversight or public hearings.

In 1980, for the first time, Congress set statutory loan-to-value ratio limits for thrifts, through Title IV of the Depository Institutions Deregulation and Monetary Control Act. Taking its cue from the statute, the FHLBB raised the basic ratio again to 90 percent and allowed 95 percent loans on all types of homes so long as the loan contract required tax and assessment escrow payments, the property was owner-occupied, and the loan had mortgage insurance (45 FR 76099). In 1983 the regulations changed again, allowing 100 percent ratio loans, so long as those loans over 90 percent had mortgage insurance in the same way as the previous regulations required. Finally, in 1992 the Office of Thrift Supervision (the successor to FHLBB) issued regulations along with the other five regulatory agencies to establish a uniform set of rules covering all federally regulated depository institutions. This rule set no loan-to-value limit, but simply required that each institution set "prudent underwriting standards . . . including loan-to-value limits" and that for "any such loan with a loan-to-value ratio that equals or exceeds 90 percent at origination, an institution should require appropriate credit enhancement in the form of either mortgage insurance or readily marketable collateral" (57 FR 62890). So today federally regulated financial institutions no longer have to comply with a maximum loan-to-value ratio and are not required to have an appraisal on loans less than $250,000, as noted in the previous chapter.

Fannie Mae and Freddie Mac have moved in the same direction as the federal regulators, but to a more limited extent. The changes have not involved legislative action because, as noted above, Fannie Mae's and Freddie Mac's charters allow them to lend above the statutory limit of 80 percent so long as there is mortgage insurance in place, but the way they have introduced their high ratio loan products has been heavily influenced by their political position. They have done so under pressure from community groups who argue that the GSEs should do more lending in lower-income communities and to lower-income borrowers. In the early 1990s they both introduced a 95 percent loan-to-value product; in 1994 Fannie Mae rolled out a 97 percent product, and Freddie Mac followed suit in 1996. Fannie Mae's high ratio products are part of its overall "Community Home Buyer Program" (CHBP) strategy to target low-income and central city home buyers. The products include restrictions on the income that a borrower applying for a loan can have, though it waives these restrictions for homes purchased in central city locations. Freddie Mac's high ratio products are part of its "Affordable Gold" program, which has the same targets as Fannie Mae's CHBP. The populations at which the GSEs have targeted their high ratio loans match those specified in the 1992 Federal Housing Enterprises Financial Safety and Soundness Act.

The changes in policy with respect to loan-to-value ratio maxima made by the FHLBB in the early 1970s and by Fannie Mae and Freddie Mac in the 1990s are consistent with the long tradition of manipulating the maximum ratio to achieve explicit social purposes. The decision of the federal regulators to allow 100 percent ratios in 1992 was a break from this tradition because it was an effort to deregulate financial institutions — to let them set their own maximum ratio — rather than to use regulations to guide them toward serving some particular segment of the market.

Ability to Pay

In contrast to their extensive regulation of loan-to-value ratios, state and federal legislatures and regulators have been largely silent on the issue of the borrower's ability to make mortgage payments.[7] Despite this there has been, historically, an industry consensus about how to measure a prospective borrower's ability to make mortgage payments, though the exact criteria vary across different institutions. This consensus survived even though the FHA, from 1934 to 1971, measured a borrower's ability to pay using a completely different method that explicitly rejected the industry consensus.

The "rule of thumb" that a family should spend no more than a certain percentage of their income on housing originated in the 1920s when lenders first started looking more closely at a borrower's carrying capacity and borrowed the idea of calculating it as a ratio from lenders making loans to businesses (Feins and Lane 1981, 10). The ratio used by business lenders was a ratio of the loan amount to the annual income of the business, which was not to exceed 2.5. This rule of thumb or one which stipulated that the monthly housing payment not exceed 25 percent of the borrower's monthly income (a close equivalent depending on the term and the interest rate) was commonly used by mortgage lenders in the 1920s (ibid.).[8] In 1932 the Home Finance and Taxation Committee of the President's Conference on Home Building and Home Ownership conducted a survey of lenders in West Coast cities (President's Conference 1932a, 52–60). It asked what percentage of monthly income a borrower should pay toward mortgage interest and principle. The average of the answers was 23.8 percent (ibid., 55). The committee recommended that financial institutions adopt a 25 percent rule (ibid., 23). In 1977 Feins and Lane conducted interviews with ten real estate agents and found that all adhered to the rule of thumb that borrowers should not pay more than 25 percent of their *gross* monthly income for housing expenses — principal, interest, taxes, and insurance (1981, 105). In 1980 interviews with 18 lenders revealed that 16 of them used "some version of the rule of thumb to screen mortgage applications" (ibid., 103). This "version" closely adhered to that used by Fannie Mae and Freddie Mac which, in 1979, had changed from the 25 percent rule to a range of 26–28 percent.[9] The rule today is 28 percent, though lenders can exceed this for reasons discussed below and in chapter 4.

Despite this widespread acceptance of the rule of thumb the FHA "explicitly rejected the use of a fixed ratio to assess whether housing expenses were excessive in proportion to family income" when it began insuring mortgages in 1934 (ibid., 108). The 1936 Manual stated "Rules, such as the one that a man should not undertake to purchase a property when the price exceeds 2 or 2½ times his yearly income, cannot be applied blindly" (FHA 1936, pt. II, para. 320). The 1947 and 1971 Manuals were more categorical:

> The rules of thumb, monthly mortgage payment should not exceed 25 percent of a mortgagor's income and value of the property should not exceed two and one-half times the mortgagor's annual income, have been demonstrated to be unreliable as criteria and in fact, unsound in principle. Specific maximum ratios for all mortgagors are not practicable because of variations in local conditions, living standards, different family housing needs and other conditions affecting ability to pay. (FHA 1947, Section 1655, and 1971, Section 71693.4 quoted in Feins and Lane 1981, 108)

Instead the FHA provided data on previous *successful* applicants for FHA mortgage insurance to serve as a guide for underwriters. As a result the FHA established a range of housing expense/income ratios that became a self-reinforcing rule — data about past successful applicants informed decisions about new applicants (Feins and Lane 1981, 110). The heavily revised 1972 Manual adopted a fixed ratio of 30 percent for housing expenses to *net effective income* (ibid., 111), and the revised 1982 Manual fixed the ratio at 35 percent (U.S. Department of Housing and Urban Development 1982). Today the ratio is 29 percent of *gross income* (U.S. Department of Housing and Urban Development 1995).[10]

The rationale behind the FHA's initial rejection of the fixed ratio rule of thumb was akin to the rationale behind its property and location rating system. The purpose was to assess the borrower relative to her circumstances, acknowledging that those circumstances varied on an individual basis and by income and neighborhood. As a result, the number of dependents and the amount of other obligations had to be taken into account (FHA 1936, pt. II, para. 320), allowance had to be made for the fact that lower-income persons spent a larger proportion of their income on housing (para. 322), and, finally, assessment of applicants' ability to pay had to be guided by prevailing expense to income ratios, which varied across communities (para. 324).

In the case of the debt-to-income ratios the FHA, eventually, bowed to the industry norm. Feins and Lane observe that the FHA moved to a fixed ratio criterion as part of an "effort to allow more households to qualify for FHA-insured mortgages." The reasoning here was that the "risk rating system had disqualified some families who were willing and probably able to spend more on housing than most successful mortgagors" (1981, 112). In other words it was an attempt to break the mold set by previous FHA borrowers. Such reasoning was misguided because it moved the FHA away from a policy designed to take the circumstances of the poor into account. The original policy set out in the 1936 Manual seems to have been thwarted by the subsequent use of data on successful applicants as a guide for the assessment of new borrowers, instead of the use of data on the circumstances of the new borrowers themselves. The adoption of the fixed ratio did nothing to alter this faulty implementation of the original policy.

The one holdout against the debt-to-income ratio consensus was the VA's loan guarantee program. Up until 1986 it did not use ratios at all. Instead it required that the underwriter evaluate the applicant's "residual income." The purpose of the residual income calculation was to assess whether the veteran had sufficient income over and above what he spent on housing and long-term debts to cover his living expenses. The Veterans' Benefits Improvement and Health-Care Authorization Act of 1986 required that the VA adopt a debt-to-income ratio, though it left the setting of the ratio to the secretary of Veterans Affairs. The debate surrounding this statutory requirement reversed the arguments in the debate regarding changes in the FHA's ability-to-pay criterion 14 years earlier: opponents of the ratio approach, which included the National Association of Home Builders and the Non-Commissioned Officers Association, criticized the legislation because it would tighten the VA's standards and deny many creditworthy veterans the opportunity to own a home. Testimony from the Mortgage Bankers Association of America, which supported the idea of the VA using ratios but opposed a statutory requirement to that effect, showed that the VA's experience with foreclosures was slightly better than the FHA's, which was, by then, using ratios (U.S. Congress, House, Committee on Veterans Affairs 1986). The debate about ratios took place within a context of high foreclosure rates on VA loans and effort on the part of the Reagan administration to increase the origination fee on VA loans from 1 to 3.8 percent. There was general opposition from the housing industry to this fee hike. One way to view the legislative outcome, which saw no increase in the origination fee but did see a statutory requirement that the VA use debt-to-income ratios (and stricter residual income criteria), is as a compromise between Congress and the housing industry, on the one hand, and the Reagan administration on the other. The introduction of tighter underwriting criteria effectively cut the number of eligible borrowers, thus cutting the potential number of borrowers who might end up in foreclosure. Furthermore, this method of restricting the VA program served to divide opposition from the housing industry because traditional supporters of government mortgage insurance programs could not easily come out against a practice that the lending industry had traditionally endorsed.

The emphasis on ratios in today's underwriting does not preclude the type of reasoning that attempts to gauge what size housing payment a borrower can actually manage. The FHA, Fannie Mae, and Freddie Mac all recommend in their underwriting guidelines that the underwriter take into account the previous housing expenses and savings pattern of the applicant. If the applicant's housing expense-to-income ratio exceeds the guideline, the fact that the applicant has been paying as much or more for housing or there is evidence that she has been living within her means and saving money can be used as rationales for allowing her to exceed the guideline. In addition, as I describe in more detail in chapter 4, these institutions' automated underwriting processes have allowed violations of the debt-to-income criteria.[11] But the lesson of the history of the debt-to-income ratio criteria points, once again, to the power of established practice in the definition of underwriting criteria. Despite the efforts of the FHA, whose record for the years when it did not use ratios was that of an extremely conservative insurer, the industry never adopted its approach. The VA's residual income criterion, though still in place, has been overshadowed by the ratio criterion as a result of a foreclosure crisis and political battle that had little to do with the soundness of either as an underwriting criterion.

Willingness to Pay

The underwriter assesses the applicant's willingness to pay the mortgage by examining her credit record. This record is largely contained in a report that lists all revolving and installment debt accounts and information from court records concerning bankruptcies and judgments. Underlying this practice is the idea that how one has paid one's debts in the past is indicative of how one will pay them in the future. This idea seems to be mere common sense nowadays, but it was not always so, as this section shows. The focus here is not so much on the rules of underwriting as on the development of the credit reporting industry itself, because it is this industry that has shaped how lenders think about a borrower's willingness to pay and has provided them with the information they use to assess this willingness.

The Reconstruction of "Character"

Beginning in the early 1900s the private sector, composed of credit grantors, credit bureaus, and their national association, engaged in two activities that laid the foundation for the modern credit reporting industry. First, these groups transformed the traditional idea that a person's thriftiness was a measure of his "character" into the idea that a person's ability to handle debt was as good a measure of the same. As a result they made a person's credit record a key component in the assessment of that person's willingness to pay. Second, they established a mechanism by which local credit bureaus could exchange information about individuals and thus created a national credit reporting system that meant that no individual could escape their reach.

Though it may have been an ideal that the country failed to live up to, at the beginning of the twentieth century a strong ethic of thrift was deeply embedded in the culture of the United States. The "Victorian money management" ethic emphasized economy, thrift, planning and "living within your means" (Calder 1999, 91). A person of "character" lived according to this ethic and benefited from doing so according to the Victorians (ibid., 87) Being in debt was antithetical to this ethic, except insofar as the debt was incurred for productive purposes rather than consumption, was a result of hard times, or was a matter of convenience, such as keeping a tab at a local store (ibid., 98–103). The emphasis on thrift had both Christian roots, especially in the Methodism of John Wesley (Tucker 1991, 20), and secular roots, particularly in the writings of Benjamin Franklin, who "abhorred debt." "Think what you do when you run in Debt," Franklin wrote. *"You give to another Power over your Liberty. . . .* Be *industrious* and *free;* be *frugal* and *free"* (quoted in ibid., 9–10).

The notion of thrift as a virtue first came under attack in the late nineteenth century in debates over Chinese and Japanese immigration. These immigrants were accused of undercutting Americans' standard of living by working for lower wages. They were able to do so, it was argued, because of their thrifty ways (ibid., 99–112 passim). But the great debate about thrift occurred in the 1920s (ibid., 113–21), because of the expansion of the use of installment loans to buy consumer goods, largely promoted by the automobile industry. The debate focused on the impact of installment buying on the morality of the consumer. One outspoken opponent of the overuse of this form of credit was James T. Lynch, president of the International Typographical Union. He advanced his argument in a vein that recalled Franklin's admonition:

> Installment buying, carried to excessive lengths, is likely to affect the independence of the workingman in more ways than one. Debt entanglement inevitably reduces a man's dignity and self-respect. It also restricts his movements, socially and industrially. Discouragement and loss of ambition naturally follow. . . .
>
> Credit is a fine thing, of course. Purchase of homes, land, necessary furniture and certain kinds of merchandise of lasting quality on credit sometimes promotes thrift or helps in the formation of economic habits. The present evil lies in the indulgence of intemperate desires that are not essential to comfort or enduring in contentment. (Lynch 1925, 7)

Lynch was not totally opposed to the use of credit, but his support for it extended only to uses that would end up promoting thrift.

The credit-granting industry did not reject the idea that people should act responsibly even while it promoted the use of installment credit. There was no attempt to break with the financial discipline at the core of the Victorian ethic. The credit-granting industry needed its borrowers to act responsibly with regard to their debts to ensure the timely repayment of installment loans, and the Victorian money management ethic was a powerful tool for assuring this behavior. In defense of his industry, H. Nelson Street, a credit manager writing in the National Retail Credit Association's (NRCA) *Credit World*, argued that the extension of installment credit had not been excessive and had not had the adverse impact on savings that it was supposed to have had; in fact there had been an increase in savings deposited in savings banks. As a result he argued:

> It might not be far from the truth to interpret these remarkable records of increased savings as indicating that credit managers, working industriously, day after day, in thousands of retail stores, in all sections of the United States, and watching and regulating the operation of installment systems, have compelled or taught thousands, perhaps millions of people, to spend their money wisely, to look ahead, to plan and to budget, to regulate their living and to form habits of systematic spending which later on developed into systematic savings.
>
> They are making men square, straight, and on the level. (Street 1927, 8)

Thus he argued that all installment credit could serve the purpose of promoting good economic habits, so long as its extension was in the hands of "industrious" credit managers.

Street's defense of his industry was part of a broad effort on the part of credit managers to construct an alternative version of what it meant to be a person of "good character." Character was the most important factor that a "credit man" took into account when deciding whether to extend credit to an applicant, because a person of good character was one who could be relied on to pay his bills on time. What was meant by character? The standard text for training "credit men" identified character as the "barometer of a person's willingness and intention to pay his bills when due and discharge his obligations promptly.... The applicant's character may be revealed in his antecedents, in his standing in the community, his habits, and his moral principles" (Beckman 1930, 121).

In the same way J. A. Barnes, manager of the credit department of the National Commercial Bank and Trust Company of Albany, New York, stated in an address to a convention of credit grantors and bureau personnel: "Just what do we mean by character? Here is a good definition: Moral principles, business practices, and the estimate in which a company or an individual is held by the business world, constitute Character. We must include—in this definition of character—a willingness to pay, even though the payment may mean personal sacrifice and a lowering of living standards for a time (for a very brief time, let us hope)" (Barnes 1933, 22). And finally, the secretary of the NRCA noted the inextricable link between having a good credit reputation and one's character:

> To be rated as good credit, should be the aim of every honest man and woman. It is the stamp of character. It indicates uprightness and stability. Credit building and character are like the Siamese twins, you cannot kill the one without killing the other. They are a priceless possession which follow you

through life and will be your best friends in the hour of adversity. Business reverse may come, fortunes may fade, but if you possess a good credit reputation, which means character, it will help you begin anew, because you can look any man in the eye and command his honor and respect. (Woodlock 1926, 3)

This sentiment was captured in the association's logo (see Figure 2.1) and in a cover page illustration of *Credit World* (see Figure 2.2).

Despite the close association that representatives of the NCRA drew between character and credit, the organization's "standard report," which it promoted for use by local bureaus, still contained information on both the character of the consumer and his credit history, *as separate items*.[12] Truesdale identified the following categories of information as essential to a standard report: identity, history, reputation, resources, and credit record. Within the category of reputation he cited William S. Rauch's definition of what should be included under reputation: "His or her general commercial reputation, character and habits and how regarded in the community" (Truesdale 1927, 224). And Truesdale cited some examples of credit reports which asked for information such as "Is his general reputation as to character and morals good?" or "General reputation, habits," in addition to questions pertaining to the person's actual credit record (ibid., 212–13). So even though character and credit history had come to be associated, there was still a (formal) residual concern with the essential character of the credit applicant apart from her credit record. Nevertheless, the NCRA had established the ethical grounds on which it could make the case for the extension of credit for the purpose of consumption, most importantly by showing how going into debt could be good for one's character.

But this cultural reconstruction of character as it related to credit was not enough, on its own, to satisfy the credit managers of the day. They needed a record of an applicant's payment history to assess whether he paid his bills on time; they also needed a way to make known to others when a borrower failed to make his payments. Street advocated an organizational solution to ensure that debtors were kept in line—the use of the credit bureau. Information provided by the credit bureau allowed a credit grantor to see how the applicant had reacted to credit in the past and to make a credit decision about him accordingly:

> Let every merchant use his credit bureau; then, through it, installment credit will turn out to be the great stabilizer of retail business; through the credit manager's directing, the most practical strengthener and developer of character. . . .
> Installment credit is here to stay.
> Strengthen and develop it thru your credit bureau. (Street 1927, 30)

Credit bureaus were organized either as private companies or as merchant-owned cooperatives to provide a means by which credit information could be exchanged between retailers in a particular town or city. The bureaus solved a problem facing retailers who were not willing to share information with each other directly because they did not want to

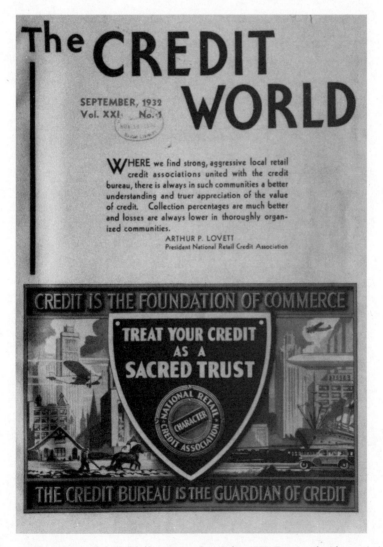

Figure 2.1. Front cover of *Credit World* magazine, September 1932. Reprinted with permission of the ACA International. © 2002 ACA International. All Rights Reserved.

88   help a competitor. The credit bureau allowed for the pooling of information, without this direct interaction. The organizations that formed or belonged to a credit bureau, known as its members, were "principally department stores, merchants, mail order houses, banks, finance companies, hotels, insurance companies and business and professional men" ("Gov-

Figure 2.2. Front cover of *Credit World* magazine, September 1930. Reprinted with permission of the ACA International. © 2002 ACA International. All Rights Reserved.

ernment Seeks Injunction" 1933, 16). They were required, as a condition
of membership, to submit credit information on all their existing customers and on all their new customers as new accounts were opened.
Once the credit bureau was in place, its purpose was to be the sole conduit
through which credit information in its locality was exchanged. Its neme-
sis in this regard was the "direct inquiry," whereby one retailer contacted
another to inquire after a credit applicant's payment record at that store.
To prevent this from happening credit bureaus required, as another condition of membership, that their members not make or respond to any direct
inquiries.

The result was an organization which served as a central depository
for the credit information provided to it by local businesses. The key to its
success was the cooperation of its members in providing it with complete
information. But this was easier said than done. The incentive for the
member was to provide information only on debtors who were past due on
their accounts or had defaulted. The provision of all positive information,
which was the majority of it, was costly to the member and did not provide
him with any benefit, but the posting of derogatory information served the
member by taking advantage of the bureau's most important service—that
of central recorder of all credit information. Derogatory information
posted with the bureau ensured that the debtor who was in trouble with
one creditor would be prevented from getting credit elsewhere—essentially punishing that debtor. The bureau served as a way to hold a debtor
accountable to his creditors. This was highlighted by the fact that many
bureaus also ran collection agencies: one of their tactics in gathering outstanding debts was to remind delinquent borrowers that their credit
record was in jeopardy if they did not either pay off their debt or provide
a convincing explanation of why this could not be done.

The influence of bureaus was extended beyond their localities through
the National Consumer Credit Reporting Corporation (NCCRC), a division of the NRCA.[13] The NCCRC served as an exchange which organized
information flows between credit bureaus whenever an inquiry required
information from somewhere outside of the local bureau's area. A credit
grantor in Houston requiring information on an applicant who had just
moved there from Chicago would call up the local Houston bureau, which
would then call the Chicago bureau for credit information on the applicant. Payment for this exchange of information was made only through
the use of tickets issued by the NCCRC. Each type of ticket, of a particular value, was associated with a standard report. As a result, member bureaus could exchange information only in the NCCRC-defined standard
format (*United States v. Associated Credit Bureaus, Inc.* 1972). The NCCRC

also provided information directly to national organizations, by drawing on the files of local bureaus. As a result a speaker from the Morris County Credit Bureau of New Jersey could boast to the students of a high school: "No matter where you are or where you may go, you cannot lose your credit record!" (MacEwan 1931, 32).

By the early 1930s this system for collecting and disseminating information on the paying habits of debtors covered 50 to 60 million Americans through 900 local bureaus. It also drew the attention of the federal government, which sued the NRCA under the antitrust laws. The result was a 1933 District Court order that prohibited the NRCA from assigning individual bureaus to exclusive territories, treating nonmember credit bureaus differently from members, and requiring that all member credit bureaus forbid member creditors from answering direct inquiries (*United States v. National Retail Credit Assn.* 1933). Nevertheless the basic infrastructure of the credit bureaus and the NCCRC (after 1937, the Associated Credit Bureaus of America) remained in place until the 1970s.

Despite its legal problems NRCA also began selling its services to the federal government. In the September 1934 issue of *Credit World* the association's legislative committee reported that it was campaigning for the widespread use of "credit and character reports" by the federal government. This campaign had begun three years before when the NRCA "was successful in convincing the U.S. Civil Service Commission of the value of such reports" (National Retail Credit Association 1934, 26–27). Another success it noted was that the Home Owners Loan Corporation had already ordered an estimated quarter of a million reports from credit bureaus (ibid.).

Credit Reports and the Mortgage Lending Industry

In the 1920s and early 1930s savings and loan associations (also known as building and loan associations) did not make great use of credit reports. For example, Piquet reported the results of a survey of New Jersey savings and loan associations in which less than 25 percent of 215 associations made a "credit inquiry" as a matter of practice (1931, 133–40). Piquet offered two explanations for this lack of inquiry. First he noted that concern for the borrower's credit was dampened in times of rising real estate prices (such as the 1920s), which led associations to rely on the property to provide them with security. Second, he remarked that often "the Directors are personally acquainted with the applicant and can vouch for his financial integrity," and that if cases in which this was so were counted as instances of a credit inquiry "the proportion of associations making such inquiry would be greater than one-third" (ibid., 136).

This familiarity of the lender with the borrower was a product of the cooperative principle upon which savings and loan associations were organized, the requirement being that the borrower become a member of the association, if he was not already one, before he could get a loan. Membership gave the borrower an incentive to meet his payments given that he was, in effect, a part owner of the lending institution (Dexter 1894).[14] Furthermore, associations confined their lending to a limited geographical area so that a borrower was likely to be held accountable to his neighbors if he failed to keep up with his payments (ibid.). As Morton Bodfish, vice-president of the United States Building and Loan League, argued in both House and Senate committee hearings, the success of the savings and loan industry, which made relatively high loan-to-value loans, was credited to these mechanisms.

The FHA was not a locally based cooperative, but it did want to make high loan-to-value loans. As a result its risk assessment placed some emphasis on the type of borrower it was going to insure. In 1935 it designated three prominent credit reporting agencies as acceptable sources for credit reports, though their use was voluntary (Federal Housing Administration, 1934–1940). The agencies the FHA selected were Dun and Bradstreet, the Retail Credit Company, and the NCCRC. Of these three organizations, the one most able to provide the FHA with the information it needed was the NCCRC.[15]

The FHA's 1936 Manual required that the underwriter examine the "Reputation" and "Attitude Towards Obligations" of the loan applicant. These should, according to the Manual, be "considered from the point of view of character" (pt. II, para. 310). Thus the examination of "Reputation" measured the applicant's "moral stability" (para. 311), and included observation of his behavior and associations, while the examination of his "Attitude Towards Obligations" dealt with "the borrower's principles, or the ethical side of his character" (para. 315). In addition to these analyses the Manual also had the underwriter look at the applicant's "Past Record" as part of the assessment of the *capacity* of the borrower to make the mortgage payments. This required the examination of data concerning the applicant's past experience with debt:

> Human beings are very largely creatures of habit. For the purpose of rating the feature "Past Record" information should be gathered which will disclose the nature and extent of financial obligations which the borrower has incurred in times past, and the excellence or poorness of his record in meeting them. If at some time in the past he became insolvent or was adjudged bankrupt, the cause of such conditions should be ascertained and his record in discharging his obligations to his creditors examined. If past failures have been occasioned by shortcomings on his part, and he has not become aware of his deficiencies nor attempted to correct them, it is likely that his future

experience will be similar to the past. In such a case a reject rating of this feature would be warranted. If, however, he has profited by his past mistakes, his experience need not constitute a cause for a reject rating. Inquiries which will be helpful in determining the proper rating in a given case include the following: What is the borrower's history as to real-estate transactions and his mortgage-loan record? Is he a "promoter" type of a questionable character? Has he met satisfactorily all his obligations in times past, or is his record satisfactory only as to certain classes of obligations such as mortgage loans or secured loans? Is he a chronic litigant? What inclinations have been reflected in his business and personal pursuits in times past? (Para. 332)

The FHA's treatment of character and credit history is essentially the same as the NRCA's — on the one hand they were highly connected; on the other hand it was still important to gather information about the applicant's character above and beyond his history of payments. This treatment was also captured in the FHA's first "Standardized Factual Data Report," which was produced in conjunction with the NCCRC. The questions on the report, shown in Table 2.1., highlight the continuity from a thrift-based definition of character to a credit history–based definition. Note also the biblical roots of the question, under the heading "Attitude Towards Obligations," as to whether "his wife lend[s] encouragement to him." It has its roots in Proverbs 31:10–31 of the Old Testament, which was used by the nineteenth-century journal editor and novelist Sarah Hale to promote the virtue of thrift in women in her nationally distributed *Godey's Lady's Book* (Tucker 1991, 25–28). Finally, it should be noted that the credit report includes information on the race or ethnicity of its subject.

The credit reporting system did not change much in the 30 years following the establishment of the FHA. Local bureaus multiplied in number, but their modus operandi remained largely unchanged. A 1965 Associated Credit Bureaus of America report and a 1964 Credit Bureaus Report, Inc. (CBR) report had almost the exact same questions as those on a 1938 ACB of A report.[16] The questions on the 1938 form are listed in Table 2.2. The 1968 FHA credit report was similar to those of the ACB of A and CBR except that it did not ask for the "racial extraction" of the subject of the report, nor whether the subject was well regarded by his employer or engaged in illegal activity. It did ask an additional question under the "character" section: "Did you learn of any domestic difficulties?" Regardless of these variations, the credit reports in the 1960s included both credit history data and information on character.

This stability in the credit reporting industry was disrupted by two de-

Table 2.1. Questions on FHA credit report, 1935

Identity
A. Is this person's name correct as given above? (If not, give correct name.)
B. About what is his age? What is his racial descent (answer whether Anglo-Saxon, Greek, Hebrew, Italian, Negro etc.)?
C. Is he married? (How many dependent on him?)

Character
Is he regarded as steady and dependable?
Is his general reputation as to character, habits and morals good? (If not, state nature of unfavorable reports.)
Did you learn of any domestic difficulties?
Is his personal reputation as to honesty good?

Attitude Towards Obligations
What is his general attitude towards contractual obligations?
Does his wife lend encouragement to him?
Does he have the reputation of living within his income?
Does his family have the reputation of living extravagantly?
Has he the reputation of willingness to pay, if able?

Ability to Pay
What is his annual earned income from his employment or business?
About what income, if any, has he from other sources? (From investments, rentals, or contributions of other members of family to household expenses.)
What would you estimate his net worth?
If married, does his wife follow a gainful occupation?
What is his wife's independent annual income, if any? Independent net worth?
If above person does not live in property, give its monthly rental.

Business History
What is the nature of his business, and what position does he hold?
About how long has he been in present connection?
Does he work full time steadily? (If not, how many days per week does he work?)
What is his reputation for real estate transactions?
Is or was he a "legitimate" speculator or promoter type of borrower?
Is he considered a chronic litigant?
Has he ever been insolvent? When? (Explain in remarks and give circumstances.)
Does the cause now exist? (Explain under Remarks.)

Prospects for Future
What are his prospects for future?
Is he making efforts to improve himself in his work?
Is he self-satisfied or ambitious?

Associates
What is class of his business associates?
What is reputation of his social associates?

Remarks
1. Amplify his business history.
2. Amplify fully all unusual and unfavorable information.
3. If a woman, cover husband's or father's reputation, business history, worth and income.

Source: Federal Housing Administration 1934–1940.

Table 2.2. Associated Credit Bureaus of America Inc., sample credit report, 1938

Identity

Number of years applicant has resided at address shown above and in city
(See remarks for previous address.)

Applicant's approximate age and racial extraction (if applicant is a minor verify and give
exact age if possible).

Is applicant single, married, widowed or divorced? Number and identity of dependents. (If
separated give particulars under Remarks.)

History

Name and address of present employer. (If applicant operates own business, so state and
give details under Remarks.)

How long has applicant been working for firm named above (or operated own business)
and in his position, occupation or trade?

Name and address of previous employer, nature of employment, for how long? Give details.

Character

How is applicant regarded as to character, habits and morals?

How is applicant regarded by employer?

Is applicant alleged now to be, or alleged ever to have been, engaged in any illegal practice,
or business?

Resources

What is applicant's income from present employment? Give amount paid and when. Salary
or commission?

Does applicant receive any income from other sources such as rentals, investment or earnings of others in household? Give amounts.

Does applicant own home, rent or board?

Source: Credit World, vol. 27, nos. 1, 3.

velopments: congressional concern with the way the industry operated, and the use of computers to process information. Congress's concern was with the accuracy, relevance, and accountability of the information contained in credit bureau files and reports. The result was the Fair Credit Reporting Act, which imposes regulations on the purposes for which a report can be used, the age of its contents, and the use of investigative reports, and increases the consumer's rights to have the contents of a file disclosed to him.[17] Though the Fair Credit Reporting Act did put a spotlight on the reporting industry and tried to regulate some of its more egregious practices such as the investigative report, it is the other development — computerization — that had the greater impact on the type of information that a bureau provided to a lender. The first credit reporting agency to use computers in a significant way was the Credit Data Corporation. It was also the first agency to attempt to organize a computer-driven reporting

service on a national basis (Rule et al. 1976, 143). In 1968, in testimony   95
before the House Special Subcommittee on Invasion of Privacy the president of Credit Data, Harry Jordan, stated:

> Credit Data makes no effort to, and does not place personal, noncredit in-
> formation with respect to individuals in its file. . . .
>   Credit information has to do with his actual performance in paying his
> credit liabilities. Noncredit information we would regard as . . . hearsay evi-
> dence . . . or evidence of people's qualitative opinion about a person's charac-
> ter. (U.S. Congress, House, Committee on Government Operations 1968, 67)

By Jordan's account, the type of information included in a Credit
Data report was decided on by representatives of subscribers to his service—banks, mortgage lenders, finance companies, retailers, and others.
Thus it was Credit Data's subscribers who decided to do away with any
information directly pertaining to character. What replaced it was a complete statement of a person's credit performance, both good and bad, as reported by the subscribers. This was a direct benefit of computerization: it
allowed for a far more efficient transfer of data from subscriber to credit
bureau, which obviated the problem that traditional bureaus faced when
their members sent in only derogatory information to avoid the cost of
sending all their ledger information.

What became of that all-important measure of credit risk "character?"
The nub of the matter was revealed at the birth of computerization. In the
same hearings cited above, Congressmen Benjamin Rosenthal of New
York and Cornelius Gallagher of New Jersey both expressed reservations
about a credit report that contained only "cold information." This concern
was summed up by Gallagher, who noted:

> It would seem to me an individual in this file is only as complete as the in-
> formation given by the subscriber (to Credit Data's reporting service).
> Therefore, there would be an imbalance under your system. . . . It wouldn't
> reflect the total credit character of the individual. (Ibid., 77)

Jordan's response goes to the heart of what constitutes character in the
age of computerization:

> That is correct. Our system represents the pool of experience of our sub-
> scriber companies supplemented by certain public information. We cannot
> provide any experience on companies that do not elect to become sub-
> scribers, and to that extent our information will remain incomplete unless
> and until all companies become subscribers. . . .

I think you would find in the markets where we operate that our penetration is sufficient that if . . . we had one bad data item (on a loan applicant) which was really contrary to his character, that there would be a number of offsetting good data items, and this would cause a prospective credit grantor to be quizzical [about the one bad item]. . . .

We do not assign a rating. Our report contains a series of data items, each one dealing with one transaction and how it went.

This is part of the input which a credit granter has when he sits down to make a loan. He may also have a credit bureau report. He may also have verified himself some of the references which the individual gave him on his application. He sits down with all these inputs and says, "All right, is it all consistent with my hope that this man is a good bill payer, because I want to make him a loan?"

If you have 10 or 11 items which are consistent with this and one which is inconsistent, then, the man becomes curious (and asks for an explanation of the anomaly).

On the other hand, if you have 10 or 11 data items which reflect nonpayment of bills, he is pretty certain that his bill is not going to be paid either. (Ibid., 77–78)

In this way the applicant's credit history has come to be the sole indicator of his willingness to pay. The consequences of this have been twofold. First, the reliance solely on payment history and the public records as indicators of a person's willingness to pay makes the structure and content of this information very important—each item provides the context for the other items and, as a result, items that are omitted or wrongly reported can become highly significant. The second consequence is that the connection between a credit applicant's "character" and his willingness to pay has become hidden behind the rhetoric of objectivity and the reality of a credit report without any overt character data. No longer is character an overt concern of the credit grantor.[18]

In 1969 Credit Data Corporation was bought by TRW, Inc. (now Experian), which, along with Equifax and Transunion, dominates today's credit reporting services. They are all computerized services that report the credit history of individuals in the same way. Though they have intermittently come under congressional scrutiny for the large number of errors in their reports, these three organizations have dominated the industry since the 1970s and have been the source of credit information for mortgage lenders. Lenders access the information of all three reporting services through the intermediary of a supplier of merged credit reports, which concatenates the information of all three and sends the lender one report.[19]

In the 1990s the rhetoric of objectivity was enhanced by the advent of credit scoring. Credit scoring is based on a model of the past performance of mortgage loans granted to borrowers with differing credit records. This model is used to rank individuals based on the likelihood that they will default if they are approved for a loan. The ranking is captured in a single number, the credit score—the higher the number the less likely is the prospective borrower to default. The dominant supplier of credit scores to mortgage lenders is Fair, Isaac and Company, which supplies credit scores (known as FICO scores) to the big three credit reporting systems. Fannie Mae and Freddie Mac have adopted credit scoring as part of their underwriting process.[20] They both use the scores in two ways: as an absolute requirement for certain loan programs; and as an initial screen that guides the underwriter as to the extent to which she needs to scrutinize the information on which the credit score is based.[21] High scores (over 660) require only that the underwriter verify that the information in the credit report is complete and therefore the credit score is based on complete information. Medium scores (620 to 659) require a full review of the credit report. And low scores (below 620) require a full review of the credit report with an eye to identifying information that would indicate that the credit score is not a good indication of the borrower's willingness to pay.

An underwriter who is faced with the prospect of fully reviewing the credit report must exercise her judgment in assessing the applicant's willingness to pay, with the guidance of the rules of the FHA, VA, Fannie Mae, and Freddie Mac. In particular they endorse two practices essential to a proper understanding of the credit report: the search for patterns of credit behavior; and the solicitation of letters of explanation from the applicant to explain instances of bad credit. Both practices enable the underwriter to place the information in context, by highlighting derogatory information that is relevant and seeking to understand the events that produced it. Thus, both Fannie Mae's and Freddie Mac's guidelines state that the underwriter should look at the whole credit report, not just items in isolation, and that she can take into account explanations of "extenuating circumstances" in assessing the significance of derogatory information. Fannie Mae defines such circumstances as "nonrecurring events that are beyond the borrower's control, and result in a sudden, significant, and prolonged reduction in income or a catastrophic increase in financial obligations" (Fannie Mae 2002, X, 803.02). Freddie Mac's definition is almost identical (Freddie Mac 2002b, 37.7). The purpose of identifying extenuating circumstances is to identify situations where derogatory credit is not the fault of the borrower. In essence, Fannie Mae, the FHA, and Freddie

Mac are asking the underwriter to interpret the credit report in a manner consistent with the original format of the credit report: what does the payment record say about the character of the applicant?

The significance of this determination for the treatment of the loan application is made explicit in a Freddie Mac "Seller Bulletin" that it sent to its lenders to inform them of a change in underwriting criteria (Freddie Mac 1999). The bulletin informs lenders of a change in the rules about the length of time that must have elapsed before an applicant who has previously been bankrupt or in foreclosure, or has transferred her deed in lieu of foreclosure, is eligible for a loan. The bulletin makes a distinction between those applicants whose past problems were a result of "financial mismanagement" and those that were the result of "extenuating circumstances." For the latter the length of time that must have elapsed before eligibility is reestablished is half that of the former (24 months instead of 48) except in cases of Chapter 13 bankruptcies, for which the two time periods are the same.[22] In other words, whether the problem was the individual's responsibility or not is a key factor in determining when an applicant is once again eligible for a mortgage loan. This is true even though as Freddie Mac acknowledges: "Whether a bankruptcy or foreclosure resulted from extenuating circumstances or financial mismanagement, a future default is more likely when a Borrower has experienced either event compared with a Borrower who has no significant derogatory credit in his or her history" (ibid.). There may be no difference, actuarially, between two applicants; it is just that one is more culturally acceptable than the other, in the same way that the Victorian money management ethic did not frown on individuals who were in debt because of hard times.

Summary

The credit report is an essential part of every American's financial life — it is taken for granted. But the institutional history of the credit report is another, though different, example of the development of an approach to underwriting mortgage risk that is embedded in a particular institutional context and supported by a particular cultural orientation. The NRCA was the institutional context in which the credit reporting industry developed. As a professional association serving business interests, it had as its mission to develop a comprehensive, legitimate infrastructure in which information of a known quality could be shared. It further sought to legitimize itself within the context of the Victorian money ethic by developing the close association between a person's credit reputation and his character. Though there are now three credit reporting systems active across the nation, the dominance of Fair, Isaac and Company in the credit scoring business shows the monopolistic tendencies of the industry that the NRCA displayed. In addition, though credit scoring has now reduced the credit reputation of an individual to a single number, the Victorian money ethic is still alive and well in the way in which underwriters are allowed to forgive the past sins of derogatory credit by putting them in the context of "extenuating circumstances."

Prepayment

A borrower prepays a loan by paying off some or all of the principal borrowed before the end of the term of the loan. Technically a borrower who defaults on a loan prepays it, involuntarily. Through the foreclosure process or a deed transfer in lieu of foreclosure, most or all of the balance on the loan is paid off out of the proceeds of the sale of the home. There may also be situations in which the borrower is either in danger of becoming delinquent on the loan or is in fact delinquent and sells the home to extricate himself from his financial difficulties. Prepayment also occurs when a borrower voluntarily pays off some or all of the loan because he wants either to refinance the loan or to sell the home.

Roberts (1993) identifies four costs to the lender resulting from prepayment: loss of yield; administrative expenses resulting from soliciting, processing, and evaluating loan applications; "matched funds" losses; and disruption of planned income flow. In the mortgage lending industry the first cost is very important, especially to investors in mortgage-backed securities. Purchasers of such securities are buying a future stream of payments that will result in a particular yield over a particular time period. If the loans underlying the securities are prepaid then the investor loses that income stream. This is a problem when prepayment is the result of refinancing a loan to take advantage of lower interest rates—those lower rates mean that the investor will not be able to earn the same yield elsewhere when the loan is prepaid. The second cost is also very important to mortgage lenders who retain the servicing rights on the loans that they sell. They are paid a premium by Fannie Mae, Freddie Mac, or Ginnie Mae for servicing the loan that they originated. Assuming that on average they do not make any profit or loss on the actual sale of the loan, the principal manner in which lenders who retain the servicing rights recoup the costs they incurred to originate the loan is through the servicing premium. The longer the loan stays on the books the greater the premium earnings. The other two costs are less important: the matched funds cost occurs if a lender has borrowed money with a prepayment penalty to fund the loan it made; and the disruption of planned income flow cost is one that results from the fact that the prepayment requires the lender to reinvest the money, which may disrupt its financial planning.

Lenders can manage prepayment risk by charging borrowers a penalty if they prepay the loan. Currently, though, such penalty fees are extremely rare in the mortgage lending industry. The debate about prepayment penalties has pitted lender against borrowers: those in favor of the fees are on the side of lenders; those against the fees are on the side of borrowers. In this section I show that this is not the only way that the sides could line up in this debate, and that the reason why the lender-against-borrower alignment predominates is a result of the debate's institutional origins.

Since the early nineteenth century the courts have asserted that, absent any specific language in the mortgage note to the contrary, a borrower has no right to prepay a loan (Alexander 1987, 290).[23] Until the early 1970s Fannie Mae, the FHA, the FHLBB, and state legislatures and courts allowed lenders to impose prepayment penalty fees on borrowers.[24] The first change in the consensus at the federal level occurred in the wake of the Emergency Home Finance Act of 1970, which set up Freddie Mac and authorized Fannie Mae to buy conventional loans. After its passage a committee met to develop uniform mortgage documents for the two organizations (Jensen 1972). One of the items on the agenda was the issue of prepayment penalty fees. After the initial draft paper describing the new uniform documents of Fannie Mae and Freddie Mac was released in November 1970, members of Congress and consumer advocates requested that there be a public meeting on the contents of the documents. That meeting was held in the spring of 1971, and again the issue of prepayment penalties was raised.[25] In their final form the new mortgage documents included a clear difference between Fannie Mae and Freddie Mac: the former did not allow prepayment penalties, while the latter allowed penalties on prepayments that exceeded 20 percent in the first five years if "the borrower prepaid with money borrowed from another lender" (ibid., 411). Jensen argues that the split between Fannie Mae and Freddie Mac over this issue was quite clearly a political one:

> The lender task force that FNMA assembled also indicated that it felt protection during earlier periods of the loan's existence was necessary in order to induce the secondary mortgage market to accept the forms and apparently FNMA itself felt this of some significance. However, the ultimate result of the consumer and some congressional complaints against any restriction on the right of prepayment apparently registered very clearly with the Secretary of HUD. (Ibid., 415–16)

At that time Fannie Mae, though a private corporation, was under the
regulatory authority of HUD (U.S. Congress, Senate, 1968, quoted in
U.S. Department of Housing and Urban Development 1976, 35) while
Freddie Mac was under the authority of the Federal Home Loan Bank
Board. Consistent with the political split between HUD and the FHLBB,
in 1972 the FHA changed its rules to forbid prepayment penalties (37 FR
8661, April 29, 1972), while the FHLBB maintained its policy of allowing
lenders under its supervision to impose prepayment penalty fees on their
borrowers. At the state level legislators responded to consumer pressure
and enacted laws limiting or prohibiting prepayment penalties (Alexander
1987, 327).

In 1979 Freddie Mac changed its policy regarding prepayment
penalty fees to bring it in line with that of Fannie Mae and the FHA. Despite the volatility of interest rates during the 1980s and 1990s, which resulted in masses of refinancings during periods when interest rates
dropped, the FHA, Fannie Mae, and Freddie Mac have maintained their
policy of prohibiting prepayment penalty fees. Only in May 2000 did
Freddie Mac develop a new loan product called the "Prepayment Protection Mortgage" (Freddie Mac 2000b, chapter B33.4, 7/10/00) that allowed
prepayment fees.

Though the FHA, Fannie Mae, and Freddie Mac have been operating
in consensus for the past 20 years, this does not mean that the prepayment
issue has been laid to rest. The Federal Home Loan Bank Board and its
successor the OTS have continued to support the lenders' position in
favor of prepayment penalties. The 1982 Garn–St. Germain Act included
the Alternative Mortgage Transactions Parity Act, which gave the
FHLBB the authority to promulgate regulations that preempted state
laws regulating the practices of nonfederally chartered "housing creditors"
with respect to "alternative mortgage transactions."[26] In 1996 the OTS issued an opinion on a Wisconsin statute which prohibited prepayment
penalties on loans secured by mobile homes and on adjustable-rate mortgages. The opinion stated that OTS regulations allowing prepayment
penalties on such "alternative mortgage transactions" preempted the Wisconsin statute (Office of Thrift Supervision 1996).[27]

Despite the FHLBB's willingness to allow prepayment penalties, they
are not generally used by lenders. Part of this can be explained by the particular institutional structure of the U.S. mortgage lending industry, in
which the secondary market for loans is dominated by publicly accountable agencies, the GSEs. In 1997 a Mortgage Bankers Association of
America committee investigated the viability of a standard loan product

with a prepayment penalty. It found that in order to entice consumers to accept a penalty (six months interest on 80 percent of the outstanding balance for the first five years of the loan), a lender would have to offer a loan at 0.375 to 0.5 percent below the rate on a loan without a prepayment penalty. But it also found that investors in the secondary market were only willing to pay 0.125 percent more for loans with a penalty. One of the reasons for the disparity is that the loans with a prepayment penalty would not be as liquid as those without, because of the GSEs' policy of not issuing mortgage-backed securities backed by loans with prepayment penalties. Either agency has the market power to make loans with prepayment penalties liquid but as the head of the committee, Larry Kershner, noted: "This is a very politically sensitive issue . . . because it comes across as an anti-consumer measure to support a prepayment penalty when they [the agencies] already make more money than God" (Bush 1997). It remains to be seen whether Freddie Mac's change of policy elicits the right market reaction and avoids a political reaction from consumer advocates.

Today prepayment penalties are back in the public spotlight because of their use by "predatory lenders." Consumer and civil rights advocates and state regulators have testified before Congress that unscrupulous lenders have used prepayment penalties to lock unknowing borrowers into high interest loans (see, for example, U.S. Congress, House, Committee on Banking and Financial Services 2000). These and previous efforts of consumer advocates to change the policies of lenders with regard to prepayment penalties stem from the egregious imbalance of power the courts have perpetuated in favor of lenders. Until the 1970s courts permitted lenders to charge a prepayment penalty even if the mortgage note was silent in regard to prepayment. Furthermore, lenders were able to charge a prepayment penalty to borrowers whose loan had been accelerated by the lender for lack of payment, because the acceleration meant that the loan was being "prepaid."[28] The debate today regarding the practices of predatory lenders is in the same vein—prepayment penalties are seen as just one more weapon in the arsenal of lenders intent on extracting as much money from borrowers as possible. In other words, the debate about the prepayment penalties has been structured by the attitudes of the courts on the one hand and the street-level practices of the lenders on the other. Both forces have caused a reaction among consumer and civil rights activists against prepayment penalties.

There is an irony in the position taken by consumer and civil rights advocates regarding prepayment penalties that comes from their particularistic approach to the politics of risk. In the context of the problem of predatory lending, it makes sense to advocate against prepayment penalties. On the face of it prepayment penalties benefit lenders, and in cases where consumers are either ignorant or have been misled it is clear that such penalties are a real and unfair burden. But, more generally, prepayment penalties have other distributional consequences. In the absence of prepayment penalties, lenders and investors who buy mortgage-backed securities do not lose out. They simply charge a higher interest rate to compensate for the prepayment risk they endure. In essence, prepayment risk has been passed on to borrowers and then socialized across all of them — those borrowers that rarely prepay subsidize those who prepay extensively. For example, an executive who moves every two or three years as she moves up the corporate ladder is subsidized by the postal worker who has lived in the same house for 20 years. Kelly (1995) in a study of VA-insured mortgages, which have the merit for the purposes of his study of being very low-cost and require no appraisal or credit check, finds that owners of lower-priced homes, indicating a lower income, are less likely to prepay on their mortgage than are owners of higher-priced homes. He also finds that black owners are less likely to refinance than are either Hispanics or whites (holding income constant). This study indicates that lower-income homeowners are subsidizing higher-income homeowners and black homeowners are subsidizing Hispanic and white homeowners under the FHA, Fannie Mae, and Freddie Mac prepayment penalty regime.

Prepayment penalties are a significant method for managing risk. The public debate about these penalties has largely focused on the balance of power in the relationship between the borrower and the lender. The courts, based on common law, have largely sided with the lender. The regulators, showing their sympathy with those they regulate, have also sided with the lender. In response, consumer advocates have worked through federal agencies and state law to shift the balance, on the face of it, in favor of consumers. But it is only on the face of it that the balance has shifted back to consumers, because lenders and investors in mortgage-backed securities compensate themselves for the prepayment risk to which they are exposed by the lack of penalties by charging a higher interest rate. So, in fact, all consumer advocates have done is to work out a way to socialize prepayment risk. It may be the case that this is a desirable public policy outcome, but it is an unintended one that is the result of the particular institutional structure in which the debate about prepayment penalties is embedded, and the way that the institutional structure has framed the debate.

Conclusion

Mortgage lenders in the United States operate under varying loan-to-value ratio regulations set at the federal level by Congress and regulators; despite credit scoring they still consider "extenuating circumstances" in underwriting the credit report; they use debt-to-income ratios to assess the ability of the loan applicant to make the monthly payments; and Fannie Mae, Freddie Mac, the FHA, and the VA do not allow prepayment penalties. Each one of these rules has a history, both in terms of their content and in terms of the institutional arena in which they have been debated. Along with the rules prescribing the definition of value and its measurement, these rules have had a largely successful track record in terms of delinquencies and defaults, though not in terms of prepayments. The success on delinquencies and defaults should not be interpreted as a sign that the rules are the best available; they are simply sufficient for the task at hand. Nor should this success be interpreted as a sign that the appropriate people have been involved in setting the rules; who has been involved has been a product of the interaction between their own interests and values, on the one hand, and the opportunities offered by the institutional context of the rules for the expression of those interests, on the other hand.

Before I draw out both the theoretical and practical implications of the institutional history of the rules of risk assessment, which I do in the final chapter, another piece of the argument needs to be put into place—how these rules are currently implemented. This is the subject of the next two chapters.

3

The Loan Application Process

The previous two chapters outlined the logic behind the rules that are used to assess a loan application. This chapter examines the process through which a loan application goes. The focus here is on the way the applicant herself is treated and assessed. I discuss the lending decision in terms of an interaction among the people involved: the applicant, the real estate broker, the loan officer, the processor, and the underwriter. The mechanisms of this process changed during the 1990s with the advent of credit scoring and automated underwriting. This has resulted in a change in the incentives facing the individuals involved, but the essence of the process remains the same.

Interviews with real estate and mortgage lending professionals show that the *process* of risk assessment itself generates the profile of an applicant as a good or bad risk.[1] This process takes place within a context characterized by spatially segregated housing markets (more on this in the next two chapters) and relational networks between loan officers and real estate brokers. And, despite the discretion that people involved can exercise, underwriting rules inform their actions every step of the way.

The Real Estate Broker and the Loan Officer

A buyer who chooses to look for a home in certain neighborhoods will contact a real estate broker who knows those neighborhoods well. Even at this stage the prospective applicant's credit characteristics are being formed and evaluated, often at the same time. The real estate broker will ask a prospective buyer the amount she wishes to pay for a home and/or her income. On this basis the broker can assess whether a buyer is looking in the right neighborhoods and can, if necessary, expose her to a different segment of the housing market and other neighborhoods. In addition, the price of the house chosen, along with the downpayment and interest rate, determines the buyer's debt-to-income ratios. As a result, at its initial stages the home buying process generates part of the credit characteristics of the home buyer.

The next step for a home buyer is a referral to a loan officer. Most of the real estate brokers I spoke to worked with two or three lenders to whom they referred their prospective buyers. One broker explained:

> We cannot stop a client going to certain people, but when we deal with certain lenders we know exactly what their requirements are with respect to financing . . . and more or less you work together with them . . . you follow the steps as the deal is processed. . . . When you deal with a strange lender you lose control of the deal. (Reb. 10)

I followed up on this information with structured interviews with 29 real estate brokers with offices located in a black neighborhood in Chicago, and structured interviews with 16 real estate brokers in a Hispanic and white neighborhood in the same city. Though the samples are small, they confirm the importance to the real estate broker of having a working relationship with a loan officer. I found that, when asked to list three lending institutions with which they worked, 26 out of the 29 brokers interviewed in the black neighborhood were able to name three, and that on average they said they referred about 65 percent of their clients to the institutions they named. Twelve out of the 16 real estate brokers in the white and Hispanic neighborhood listed three lending institutions and said that on average they referred about 87 percent of their clients to those institutions. Beyond the relationship with a particular lender, some brokers also stated that they worked with particular loan officers within each institution they named. In the black neighborhood there were 47 such broker–loan officer relationships, while in the white and Hispanic neighborhood there were 27. Of the 47 relationships in the black neighborhood,

17 began before the loan officer started working for his current lending institution, while of the 27 relationships in the other neighborhood, 6 extended beyond the term of the loan officer's current employment. Finally, in both neighborhoods the average length of the broker–loan officer relationship was about five years. In other words, there is evidence that loan officers and real estate brokers form long-term relationships that are interpersonal, rather than determined by the institution for which the loan officer works.

From the perspective of the loan officer, having established relationships with real estate brokers is a good marketing strategy. A guide to lenders states: "a recommendation by a real estate professional is the overriding reason why *80 percent* of mortgage loan applicants approach one lender over another" (Fannie Mae 1993a, 3; italics in original). Kulkosky (1996) describes a survey of home buyers conducted by Norwest, one of the largest lenders in the country, that put the referral share from Realtors at 85 percent.[2]

The loan officer will initially pre-screen the prospective applicant to establish the likelihood that her application will pass underwriting. Loan officers can, on the basis of information provided to them by the borrower, check to see whether the housing expense-to-income ratio (front-end ratio) is sufficiently low, check the adequacy of the applicant's liquid assets to cover the downpayment, closing costs, and reserve requirements, and check the applicant's credit history using an instant "in-file" credit report. The credit report also provides good information on the applicant's current debt payments and, as a result, can be used to calculate her total debt-to-income ratio (back-end ratio). During this process the loan officer also gets a sense of the type of person the applicant is — whether she would "eat macaroni" (len. 11a) in order to make her house payment if she ran into financial trouble. Or as another loan officer, who does a cursory credit check during prequalification, noted, if credit problems emerge she asks what happened, "and given the response I would go with it or not . . . you can tell from the response whether it is b.s. or not" (len. 6).

On the basis of this pre-screening the loan officer can either encourage or discourage an applicant from applying for a loan. The loan officer has a strong incentive to let only creditworthy applicants apply. Taking an application is, in and of itself, time consuming. Many loan officers are on commission and get paid only if the loan is approved. The real estate broker involved in the deal does not want a property tied up by a lengthy application process if the ultimate outcome is likely to be a denial. It is better for the broker, and therefore the loan officer who wants to keep good relations with the broker, that the property be taken off the market only if there is a high likelihood of approval.

If the applicant chooses to apply for a loan, the loan officer will assist her in putting together the most effective loan application package in light of his knowledge of the underwriting criteria. For example, the applicant can write letters to explain blemishes on her credit report. These letters have a particular purpose. They shift the blame for the blemish away from the applicant to another party or to circumstances outside the applicant's control. Medical problems and divorces are two common reasons for bad credit. So long as the applicant can verify that the timing of her medical problem or divorce coincides with the timing of the credit problem, then the underwriter is likely to discount the negative information conveyed by the blemishes. In addition to such letters of explanation, an applicant can pay down outstanding debts to reduce her back-end ratio. She can also demonstrate how she will be saving toward closing so as to have sufficient cash to cover closing costs, the downpayment, and the reserves requirement. These activities, for the most part, are ones which ensure that the application package conforms to the requirements of the underwriting guidelines. Yezer et al. (1994) describe other ways in which a loan officer can affect the likelihood that a loan application will be approved. Choice of loan product, the use of co-signers, and increasing the size of the downpayment all actively improve the applicant's risk profile. As a result, the loan application package is carefully constructed by the loan officer and the applicant to best reflect the latter's conformity to the underwriting criteria.

Two processes are at work here: one of inclusion, the other of exclusion. Both real estate broker and loan officer use pre-screening as a way to draw the prospective homebuyer/applicant into the buying/borrowing process. They do this with the rules of underwriting that their lending institution uses in mind. This leads to the exclusion of those who do not fit the bill. Real estate brokers and loan officers have a lot of discretion at this stage, and what happens to the prospective home buyer/applicant depends on their willingness and ability to see her go further in the process. Real estate brokers can always "lose" a client if they feel that there is something "fishy" about her, for example, by not calling them (reb. 2). Loan officers have to make decisions about the qualifications of the applicants at pre-screening based on limited information, and so have to make a judgment call about the accuracy of the information being given and how it stands up against the underwriting rules.

The loan officer is only the entry point into the application process. The application goes next to the loan processor, who verifies the informa-

tion supplied. This verification process gives the loan officer more oppor- 109
tunities to work the file. He can expedite the production of additional information the processor requires to generate a complete package. The
loan officer or the processor also has to deal with problems that emerge
because the verification procedure reveals a discrepancy. Most commonly
this discrepancy has to do with information on the credit report, which is
of two sorts. First, the report may show that the applicant has more debts
than she declared on her application. This can add to the monthly expenses that the underwriter takes into account when she calculates the applicant's back-end debt-to-income ratio, taking it over the prescribed limit
and thus leading to a rejection of the application. Second, the credit record
shows in detail the way in which the applicant has handled her credit in
the past. If there is a problem with the ratios, a loan officer can try to submit the file in such a way as to establish that, though the applicant may be
over the ratios, she has other compensating factors that qualify her. Or, if
possible, the loan officer can get the applicant to pay off the debt. If there
is a pattern of slow pays then the loan officer can get the applicant to write
a letter of explanation. The important point stressed by the loan officers
interviewed is to get all the problems squared away before the file hits the
underwriter's desk.

As in any process, the willingness and ability of those involved to act
in a beneficial manner can affect its outcome. Whether the information in
the file the underwriter receives is put together correctly and in a manner
which best represents the applicants depends on the efforts of the loan officer, the processor, and the applicants themselves. As one loan officer
likes to tell her applicants: "I need so many bullets in my gun and you need
to provide the bullets" (len. 11a). This has two implications for our understanding of the interaction between potential applicant and lender. First,
the nature of the loan application process itself dictates that the real estate
broker has a vested interest in dealing with a loan officer that he knows
and trusts. To the extent to which the potential applicant relies on the broker to guide her in choosing a lender, the choice will be structured by the
existing relationship between loan officer and broker. The second implica-
tion is that the application process itself contributes to the construction of
a loan applicant as a good risk. This is done by both exclusion and inclusion. Both brokers and loan officers exclude those who they anticipate will
not fit the rules. But once they decide to include them in the process they
make every effort to represent them in the best possible light. In doing so
they pull together information according to the requirements of the underwriting guidelines. They also include or omit additional information in
order to construct a file that presents a good risk according to their read-

ing of the guidelines. Then it is up to the underwriter to review that information and come up with a final decision based on those same guidelines. As a result a rejection is an indicator of a disagreement between the loan officer and the underwriter, based on either the discovery of new information during the processing of the loan or a difference in their readings of the file.

Underwriting before Automation

The underwriter assesses the loan application to determine the applicant's ability and willingness to pay off the loan and the soundness of the collateral provided by the property. Here I will focus on the first two bases of assessment. Standard practice stipulated by the secondary market and the FHA provides this information by way of the application form (FNMA Form 1003), the verification forms (FNMA Forms 1005 and 1006), and the credit report. This information is assessed according to numerous guidelines, the main facets of which were outlined in the previous chapter. But these guidelines are not supposed to be set in stone and are designed only to guide the underwriter to her conclusion. Fannie Mae's "Welcome to Fannie Mae" aimed at its lenders, first written in 1993, but still in use today, captures the essence of the underwriting process:

> Fannie Mae provides guidelines for underwriting investment-quality loans—a task that demands that you maintain the delicate balance between the science of gathering information and analyzing risk and the art of making a judgment that gives the borrower every consideration. Your ability to originate loans that can be delivered to Fannie Mae will be greatly enhanced by using Fannie Mae's standardized documentation and appraisal forms and implementing a quality control system that meets our requirements. You will find that our guidelines represent basic sound business practices that have become industry standards. (Fannie Mae 1998, chapter 5)

This is a reminder to underwriters that the guidelines are just that, guidelines. It advocates the use of discretion by underwriters. The following analyzes how underwriters make decisions in the context of: the information with which they are provided; the guidelines they follow; and the mandate to use discretion.

The underwriter's decision-making process has three facets: investigation, interpretation, and treatment. The first requires that underwriters check the information with which they are presented in the file. This is the only information they use. They do not meet the applicants, and never directly communicate with them.[3] They check to see that all the information

makes sense. They do this for individual pieces of information—is the documentation sound? And they do it for the information as a whole—does
everything hang together? In the case of the former the underwriter is
often looking for straightforward fraud or whether those who have dealt
with the file before her have done their job properly. In the case of the latter, she may also be looking for fraud or omitted information, but more importantly, she is looking to see whether the documentation tells a coherent
story. One facet of this is to check to see if the information on the application form is different from that on the verification forms and credit report.
Fannie Mae requires that any such omission of a "significant debt" from an
application that is revealed by a credit report be explained, "to ensure the
borrower is not attempting to conceal liabilities to qualify for a mortgage"
(Fannie Mae 1993b, 67).

A situation I encountered during my interviews is another example of
the way in which the coherence of a loan application can come into question.[4] The applicants, who were at the time living rent-free in a condominium unit as part of their contract to manage the condominium complex, were buying a two-flat and counted the potential rental income from
both the units as part of the overall income with which they would make
the monthly mortgage payments. The underwriter queried this application
because it was for a loan on an owner-occupied home, yet the fact that the
applicants anticipated income from both units put in question their stated
intention to occupy the property. This was significant to the underwriter
because properties bought for investment purposes (i.e., that are not going
to be occupied by the buyers) require a different, more strict, set of underwriting criteria to be applied to them (len. 2).[5]

Thus part of the underwriter's job is to check that the information is
correct in that it has been collected in the appropriate manner, and that it
makes sense as a whole. This latter task is the first step in the underwriter's attempt to interpret the information. Part of the process of judging
whether a set of information hangs together is interpreting the meaning of
that information.

This interpretation is done at three different levels: applying the basic
guidelines, applying other guidelines when the basic guidelines do not
work, and looking beyond the file to see if the loan makes sense. The basic
guidelines underwriters follow are numerous and often detailed. They
cover the maximum housing expense-to-income and total debt-to-income
ratios allowed, they define what credit problems may jeopardize a loan,
they stipulate the source and size of downpayment and cash reserves
needed, they stipulate the methodology of the appraiser and so on. If the
applicant fits within these guidelines then the underwriter has to do very

little work. Such a file described to me as being a very easy one to approve was:

> a $48,000 VA loan for a single man, 79 percent loan-to-value, use of credit is minimal (only two trade lines), good savings, high residual income, good cash reserves and 22 percent ratios. (Len. 2b)

But most loans are not so easy and underwriters often need to make some assumptions about the lifestyle of applicants to make sense of the information. Underwriters' statements about lifestyle were forthcoming when we discussed, during the interviews, what are called "compensating factors" and letters of explanation. These are factors an underwriter takes into account when she finds that the numbers in the file do not conform to the basic guidelines she is following. There was a high level of consistency across underwriters in terms of the type of compensating factors they said they use, and types of letters of explanation they deemed acceptable. This is not surprising given that most lenders have guidelines related to these. For example, if the applicant's debt-to-income ratios are over the stipulated figure then an underwriter may look for a pattern of savings, a stable employment record, or a demonstrated ability to handle high housing costs, often reflected in past high rent payments, as indicators of responsibility and stability.

Over and over again I was told by underwriters, and loan officers, that what they are looking for is a pattern of debt mishandling. If the applicant was late on a store charge card one time four years ago, there is no problem. But if there was a period when the applicant had a series of late pays then this needs to be explained, and the underwriter is looking for an explanation that shows it was not by choice that the applicant got herself into a mess. The most often cited explanations are divorce, and illness with resultant medical bills. If the explanation is adequate, and there has been no indication of credit mishandling within the past two years, then the credit record is likely to be deemed acceptable.[6] But an underwriter will also want to see documentation supporting the explanation, which takes us back to her investigative role. Thus if an applicant explains a pattern of late pays as being the result of an ex-spouse's profligacy and unwillingness to pay the bills at the time of the divorce, then the underwriter will at least want a copy of the divorce decree to see that the dates of the late pays and the date of the divorce coincide.

But the reading of a file, including letters of explanation, can drift into a deeper reading of what the information indicates. And how those underwriters and others who were interviewed articulated this deeper reading varied.

One underwriter stated that "the final decision goes beyond the rules" (len. 11b). I asked how this was so and she cited the following example:

> a retired couple on social security who are over the ratios. You know they are going to make their payments, as they have been doing so all their lives, so you do it.

The same was suggested by this conversation I had over the telephone with a bank officer: He was reluctant to grant me an interview because he had had a previous experience in which a study on lending had used data he had provided to come to conclusions with which he disagreed (with respect to issues of lending discrimination). He noted that you can use data to support any conclusion you want. So I asked, "is this true of underwriters?" He answered:

> No, the regulators would not allow them to get away with making decisions in such a way. . . . For example, it is easy in this neighborhood to look at a credit bureau report and deny the loan—that's easy. But that means you are not doing your job. In this neighborhood there is 35 percent unemployment and you may have someone who was laid off from a low skill job at U.S. Steel six years ago, and for four years had a series of off-and-on jobs. . . . You have to take this into account when you look at the credit report. Though you also have to document things and basically cover your arse. This is where the individuality of the underwriter comes into play: if he doesn't know what it is like for his father to be unemployed then he may not go that step beyond. . . . Individuality is very important in underwriting. (Len. 6)

Another underwriter talked about using "common sense" (len. 2b), and another, in two marginal cases that he cited, explained how he looked at the resumes that the applicants sent in before approving the loan (len. 3).

Again this deeper reading of the file returns us to the investigative role of the underwriter. Part of the point of trying to look beyond the file is to see if the story told in the file is a credible one. There are considerable difficulties in ascertaining this. Loan officers will coach the applicant in the writing of letters of explanation. One underwriter skeptically suggested that it was very unusual to see a bad credit problem that did not end in divorce (len. 11b). Another who actually interviews the applicant cast doubt on the ability of underwriters to distinguish between credible and incredible explanations of credit problems (len. 9). Finally, an underwriter re-counted a situation in which his institution was having problems getting a private mortgage insurance (PMI) company to approve a loan. The dispute was over evidence that the applicant had not been paying his previous mortgage on time. The applicant said that he had been paying the mortgage *early,* and brought in canceled checks to back himself up. The underwriter believed this account. He described it as a "gut feeling type of situation. . . . I had a feeling that this guy was telling me as it was." In contrast the PMI company "did not get the same feel" and wanted further documentation from the servicer of the previous mortgage, which was not forthcoming. The deal eventually went through as a portfolio loan, without PMI, with a higher downpayment (len. 1).

In Garfinkel's account of the way jurors make decisions he stated:

> As a person underwent the process of "becoming a juror" the rules of daily life were modified. It is our impression, however, that the person who changed a great deal, changed as much as 5 per cent in the manner of making his decisions. A person is 95 per cent juror before he comes near the court. What did the change consist of, and how does the change characterize a person acting as a juror?
>
> Jurors' decisions that sort fact from fancy do not differ substantially from the decision that he makes in this respect in his ordinary affairs. Nevertheless, there is a difference. The difference bears on the work of assembling the "corpus" which serves as grounds for inferring the correctness of a verdict. (1984, 110)

The underwriters I interviewed were consistent in the basic structure of the "corpus" of information on which they based their decisions. But just as the loan officer and processor use their discretion to try to present the underwriter with a coherent, plausible story, so the underwriter uses her discretion to try to understand that story. Unlike the juror, the underwriter is not involved in a one-off situation — the decisions she makes are her job-of-work and so are part of her everyday life. Hence when going beyond the basic corpus of information, as presented relative to the basic guidelines, the underwriter is still following guidelines about how to go beyond the basic guidelines. And once these are exhausted the underwriter has appeal to "what makes sense," "a gut feeling," or the like, which is based on experience on and off the job. But these different levels of interpretation are not isolated from one another: documentation is required in order to back up discretionary decisions; and the very decisions based on experience must in some way be structured by the guidelines which are a part of that experience.

Finally, the way underwriters treat an application can have an impact on the final outcome. Underwriters are quite capable of rejecting a file and then failing to adequately articulate the reasons for that rejection beyond the pro forma statements required by law. On the other hand they are also quite capable of assessing a file and, if it is marginal, detecting the aspects of it which require further elucidation before it can be approved. This was highlighted during my research when two underwriters underwrote the same file. The file had been rejected by one underwriter and was on the supervisor's desk awaiting the supervisor's review, but it was, instead, given to a second underwriter. The file was the one cited above concerning the condominium managers and their new two-flat. It was rejected by the first underwriter because he had deducted the rental income from one of the units of the two-flat off the applicants' total income. He had also deducted the $500 a month the applicants were receiving from the condominium association, in addition to the rent-free unit, without giving a reason for doing so—though one can assume that it was because their moving out of the condominium complex was a sign that they would no longer be managing it. In a separate note to himself the underwriter had mentioned that the owner-occupancy status of the two-flat was in doubt, but on the form which showed his reasoning to the supervisor he merely stated that the loan should be rejected because of insufficient income due to the deductions off the applicants' income that he had made. The second underwriter read the file in very much the same way—most notably deducting the rental income from one unit off the applicants' income. But instead of rejecting the application she decided to approve it subject to two conditions: that the applicants sign a written affidavit to the effect that they were going to occupy one of the units of the two-flat; and that they provide evidence that their monthly earnings from the condominium association would continue once they moved out of the complex. This gave the applicants the opportunity to make their case, and get the loan if they met the conditions set out by the underwriter.

Another case described to me by a black loan officer, who cited it as an example of blatant discrimination, shows both how an underwriter can treat a file and the difference the perseverance of a loan officer can make. The following is a paraphrase of her account:

A nurse had recently begun contract work at a hospital for 24 hours per week. She was also working an additional 16 hours for an income of $30,000 a year. She had other contracts which increased her income to $55,000 a year. She had no credit problems. She was in school getting an M.A. The property was selling for $32,000—the appraisal came in at $46,000. She had a gift to cover the three-month reserve requirement. The condo assessments and her car payments pushed her payments high. The underwriter rejected the loan because of the nurse's change of employment status from full-time to contracted part-time. The loan officer had not put the contract with the hospital in the application because she did not think it would be needed. Furthermore, the loan officer did not let the nurse show that she had worked a couple of days at another hospital, because it would have given a poor impression—the client's ability to move around in her profession would be seen to be unstable. The loan officer had to bring in newspaper advertisements to show the underwriter the special programs with which nurses were being enticed by hospitals. When the loan officer showed the underwriter the employment contract, she found fault with it. Eventually, the underwriter adjusted the applicant's income upward in order for her to qualify, but only after the loan officer threatened to quit and the client wrote a personal letter of guarantee that she would continue to work the number of hours she was working then (len. 16).

Generally, underwriters can ask for more information as a method of looking for ways to make the loan work, but they are often also required to limit the number of files they place in pending and the number of conditions they attach to any given file. So though their ability to read a file in a sensitive manner and give the applicant an opportunity to respond to questions may be a product of their own experience and training, their willingness to do so may be the product of their institution's policy.

How Underwriters Read a Loan Application File: A Quasi-Experiment

In an attempt to understand more clearly how underwriters make decisions on loan applications I returned to the underwriting department of one lender to conduct an additional set of interviews. In these interviews I asked five underwriters, individually, to lead me through the same two loan application files. These files had been underwritten in the department in the past 12 months. The specific purpose of the interviews was to pin down what these underwriters used as their basis of comparison when assessing the loan applicant represented by the file. In essence I was in search of the grounding for the decisions made by underwriters based on "common sense" or "gut feeling." But because the underwriters went through the whole file with me, explaining what they were looking for as they went along, the interviews also yielded information on the intricacies of the process they go through. "I'm looking for patterns of behavior I guess," one said, "kind of maybe what you're doing too" (len. 2f).

The Set-Up

These interviews were conducted over two days. I was given a selection of seven files which had been picked out by the processing staff on the basis that they considered them to be hard files to underwrite. In part this meant that the files were selected on the basis of the amount of work that the processors had put into trying to get them approved. Thus in some cases the issue that had initially caused problems at underwriting had been resolved by the processor's and loan officer's work in gathering further information, which resulted in either a firm approval or a denial. All the files were from the Chicago metropolitan area.

I selected the two cases used in the interviews for different reasons: in one instance I simply disagreed with the final decision on the file; in the other instance I was puzzled by the fact that it was even considered marginal, given its weakness. I decided to use the latter because it contained an example of bad (by the FHA's underwriting rules) credit history. The first application included a co-borrower who had a bankruptcy in the past as a result of his quitting his job and not being able to find a new one. The credit report showed that since then the co-borrower had two accounts open which he had kept paid consistently. But it also showed that he had two accounts, opened before the bankruptcy, which were in collection. Otherwise the application was routine in the eyes of the underwriters. The other application showed a series of collections on charge card accounts, though the size of the debts incurred was small. There was one loan account with a credit union that had been paid consistently. The applicants' explanation of their problems referred to disputes with the store where they charged a purchase and with the credit card company itself, on the one hand, and to problems created by one applicant's recent divorce, on the other. They were also short of funds for closing, with very few savings in the bank. In both cases the loans were denied. Both loans were FHA.

Each underwriter was asked to go through the first file as if she were underwriting it herself. Their reviews of the second file were far more cursory, and focused on the credit history. They were asked to ignore the written comments by the actual underwriter of each file, though all eventually consulted the declination sheet on which the underwriter stated her reasons for rejecting the application. In fact, some of the more fruitful discussions of the files emerged after the interviewees had consulted the declination sheet. This was because the comments made there by the initial underwriter pointed to details in each file which the interviewees had overlooked. Further, the comments prompted a direct discussion of the issue at hand including points of disagreement with the initial underwriter.

Results

In discussing what the interviews yielded I will focus in on the concept of "common sense." Common sense is grounded in the rules in the underwriting manual, the information before the underwriter, and the information that the underwriter is prepared to pull in from outside the file based on experience. Its use manifested itself in the interviews in the way the underwriters told stories in the face of the information before them—both what was included and what was excluded. Underwriters know that they are being told a story about the applicant by the processor and the loan officer—that is what the file is. But as well as reading that story, they tell their own story/stories to make sense of the file. The following illustrates how stories are told, and what the underwriters consider to be a coherent, justifiable story. Let me begin with their statements about how they approach a file. One underwriter (len. 2d) introduced the fact that she liked to use her imagination when underwriting. I asked how she used her imagination. She replied:

> Oh I don't know. First of all, when I look at the credit reported and I see what the problem is, it's not just logical thinking, imagination has to do with common sense: is what somebody is telling me believable or is it just extremely creative? . . . So does it match the facts that are in the file? I can get a better idea from some of these people's letters on what type of individual they are and not by just what they say their reason is, but what their thinking is as far as when are they going to write out their check for their bills? Or maybe how they feel about whether they really should have paid something or not. I can tell . . . if somebody likes to fight about little things like Hickory Farm cheese, you know they just don't want to pay the bill because the cheese didn't taste good or something, or whether there's someone that is a procrastinator and just doesn't get around to it; and whether it's something they're procrastinating on is just little things that they're not concerned about and the big things they're real good about or whether they just do that on everything, or they're poor budgeters, depending on what their reason is. I can never tell for sure if it's the truth or not, but sometimes I have a pretty good idea when nothing matches . . . they could be anything. I guess I like to imagine the file as real people and not just papers, that they are human beings, they are people making mistakes, that things do happen to them but . . . is it a problem that always happens to them? Or a problem that just happens to them one time and probably isn't going to

happen to them again? . . . and of course I have to look at the appraisal. (Len. 2d)

Another underwriter stated:

I go by common sense and then look up the rules . . . is it a logical sequence of events? . . . It's very easy, I'm a numbers person, so I work the numbers I see, the percentages . . . then I go back and personalize it and say all right, does it make sense? . . . The critical issues for me are the history of income and the appraisal. Credit's going to work into it, either they have good credit or they don't, there's some issues that are real black and white for me. I look at credit explanations too. Sometimes I feel like the loan officers tell them what to say, you know because it's the same explanation you hear . . . but the ones with severe credit problems—if it was like on lay-off or medical problem I'm more sympathetic, as long as they've reestablished their credit and they've shown that it was an isolated incident, period of time. Divorces I'm more sympathetic to although a lot of times you get "it was my ex-husband's fault." . . . I always do read the divorce decrees. A lot of times . . . they won't tell you who was in charge of what debt. Ultimately I feel whether you're going through a divorce or anything, your credit's your credit. I know that divorces can get real messy, but it's a real important thing. Installment loans, maybe the revolvings have two 30 days late—they forgot to mail it, that kind of an excuse, but on an installment loan I don't buy it. The same as a student loan, student loans always seem to be late. (Len. 2f)

Later the same underwriter noted that with installment loans "you know they're going to be there every month," implying that there was, therefore, no excuse for being late in paying them.

Or again:

All you can do is to read all these papers, to look at them and then you have to develop a feel for that borrower. It's kind of like, you know, I'm reading this book and the book is telling me all these things, this is a book, we're reading a book, and this book then gives us right or wrong a feel for this customer and that could be a feeling of deep sympathy, it could be a feeling of "oh, o.k.," it could be a feeling of near hostility (laughs). Everybody is human right? But what comes through here by the processor and the loan officer, they on their own can make or break a deal because they know far more about that customer than we do, and if all they send in are the rough edges that's the only interpretation we're going to get. (Len. 2b)

And finally:

You try to get to know these people. . . . I'm sure that we don't see them probably in the way they really are but you get a feel for the file, it gives you more of an insight into whether they're going to be able to make it. (Len. 2c)

In looking at the information before them and filling in the gaps, the underwriters engaged in a series of storytellings. Each piece of information in the file had a story behind it, which often could be checked by reference to another piece of information there. Much of this was mundane. When looking at the verifications of employment and deposits they checked not only on income, employment stability, and account activity, but also on the way that information was generated and how it hung together. This was apparent in the comments they made as they went through the files. For example, they noted the applicants' employers, the type of job they were in, and what that meant for their economic prospects and the reliability of their information: some skills are transferable, others are not (len. 2f); verification of employment forms need to be checked against paystubs because the former are handwritten by the personnel department while the latter are computer generated; recent large changes in income need to be explained (len. 2c and len. 2b). Len. 2b described a file that showed a new employee getting a large raise after only a few months on the job, but this was explained by the fact that he had been in the field for a long time and had been receiving a lower income during an initial trial period. In the same way a big increase in the applicant's bank balance was investigated — it prompted a search in the file for documentation of the receipt of a gift or a secured loan. Finally, when looking at the credit report the underwriters reacted differently to different types of account. One of the applicants had a number of reported late pays at Sears, which prompted one underwriter to note, "Sears is notorious for dinging people instantaneously" (len. 2b); another underwriter had much the same reaction (len. 2f).

This is not to say that the underwriters do not follow the rules — many of their ways of reading the information were prompted by rules, such as those concerning fraud. Nor does the mundane quality of the storytelling mean that it is not important. It is important for two reasons. First, it is an essential part of the construction of the larger story. And second, the storytelling itself can have a direct impact on the reading of a particular part of the file which happens to be crucial in the decision to approve or decline the loan.

For example, it was clear in the case of the bankruptcy that all the underwriters thought it was foolish of the co-borrower to have quit his job. None of them held this against him. But they did disagree on what decision they should make about the file. Two said they would have approved the loan, one said she did not have sufficient information to make a decision, and two said they would decline the loan though they indicated they would reconsider it subject to being supplied with certain information. The issue that divided the underwriters was in their reading of the story behind the applicant's credit record since the bankruptcy, with particular reference to the outstanding collection accounts. In explaining their reasoning, all but one provided a story to justify it. These stories reconstructed what they assumed had gone on with these collection accounts.

The two that would have approved the file read the outstanding collection accounts as belonging to the period before the bankruptcy. Each accounted for the fact that they did not appear on the bankruptcy's schedule of debts in a different way: one suspected that the creditor wrote the loan off and did not bother to go through the bankruptcy proceedings (len. 2c); the other suggested that it was the result of an attorney's error—not putting all the debts on the bankruptcy schedule (len. 2b). The undecided underwriter suspected the credibility of the credit report as a whole (which she explained as being the result of recent experience with faulty reports) and was very careful in checking the court's schedule of debts in the bankruptcy papers to see if the accounts reported as being in bankruptcy on the report appeared on the schedule. She was not willing to assume what the status of the two collection accounts actually was and wanted more information before making a decision (len. 2d). Of the two underwriters who said they would have rejected the file, one had seen and considered it before. Both were unwilling to assume that the collection accounts were the result of spending before the bankruptcy. When I challenged them on the fact that there was no evidence that these accounts had been run up and put into collection since the bankruptcy, both admitted that this was true. The underwriter who had seen it before left the issue at that (len. 2e). The other noted that one of the accounts had recently been reported and that this was a sign that there had been recent activity on the account; further she pointed out that if the accounts had been run up before the bankruptcy then they should have been included in it (len. 2f).

What this case highlights is the way underwriters string together mundane information by telling a story about it, filling in any missing information with a reasonable assumption that they can support. But it is not as if the underwriters make things up as they go along, far from it. Their reasoning is structured and prompted by the information in the file. The key point here is that in order to make sense of the file the underwriters have to string the information together in a way which makes them feel com-

122 fortable, and which they can justify. In doing so they tell a coherent story about the applicants' financial behavior.

So what counts as a coherent, justifiable story? It has to be consistent with the reasoning behind the underwriting rules. For example, the underwriters paid attention to the extent to which the applicants would experience "payment shock." All were interested to see what the increase in monthly housing expenses was going to be as a result of the applicants' having to make the mortgage payments. They were concerned that the shock be not too great, and they liked to see an earlier pattern of savings as an indication that the applicants had previously been living within their means and could accommodate an increase in their living expenses. This reasoning goes beyond the formulaic application of ratios but was consistent with recent changes the FHA and the secondary market had made to the underwriting guidelines that allowed borrowers to exceed the ratios under certain circumstances.

Another example of how the underwriters reason within the rules manifested itself in the way they gauged the responsibility of the applicants, with particular emphasis on their handling of credit as shown in the credit report. This was consistent with the underwriting guidelines. The emphasis on responsibility was highlighted when I challenged their assessment of the second application. I noted that most of the problems concerned small amounts of money and could hardly be used as an indicator of how the applicants would behave with respect to their house payments. The response of the three underwriters to whom this was put directly was that the applicants had shown a level of irresponsibility toward credit which raised concerns about their willingness to make the mortgage payments:

> We don't want to make loans to people who are not creditworthy. What if they are in a position where it is even going to be difficult for them to make either the car payment or the house payment, which one are they going to make? They're going to make that car payment, that has to get them to work. They can always go out and rent a house and walk away from this one, or rent an apartment and walk away from this house, but that car they have to have to get to work, or they have no livelihood. You know where we're going to be sitting, we're going to get a house back because they don't take responsibility, they don't show responsibility for their debts and their obligations. . . . I would agree with this reject. (Len. 2c)

And:

I think it is more serious to me when I look at someone who has been stably employed on a job for quite some time but is a limited credit user, hardly borrows any money—most of their high credit isn't very high—and can't manage to make sure that their bills are properly taken care of. Let's say if they came up with all the evidence [the divorce decree] . . . there's still only to me one car loan with 7 months rent, which is not sufficient to prove to me that they make timely payments, but they've got ratios, really low ratios. . . . They've been on the job a real long time, to me that says that there's something seriously wrong here. Somebody really just isn't too concerned about when the check is going to get to their creditor in the mail; not that it might get there late, but according to most of their history, except for their car for the past year, it might not get there at all. (Len. 2d, who was the original underwriter on this loan)

And finally:

Yeah but no, it's the general disregard. . . . no, you can't say it that way [responding to my challenge]. Credit is credit, it's like gold, when you don't have it you don't get it anymore . . . unless she can prove that this guy. . . . When did she get divorced? they should have a divorce decree. (Len. 2f)

In the same way len. 2e noted, without being challenged:

What it looks to me like [referring to the second file] is that these people are pretty much delinquent on everything they pick up, and that doesn't make me feel as if we won't have a collection problem were we to give these people a loan. They can't say that it is because they didn't have the income because they've been on their jobs for the last 3 years, that apparently hasn't presented any kind of a problem.

Another aspect of this emphasis on responsibility manifested itself in the underwriters' willingness to forgive blemishes on the credit report if they were a result of a situation out of the applicants' control. If the situation was beyond their control, irresponsibility was not at the root of their problem. This provided the underwriters with some reassurance that the problem would not recur as a result of the applicants' own actions.

Much of this reasoning is explicitly endorsed by the underwriting rules, and they are what undergird the underwriters' feelings about what makes a good file. But in applying the rules in the assessment of a file the underwriters have to be able to tell a story that goes beyond them, not in the sense of breaking them, but in the sense of their utility as guides for action. In other words, common sense is grounded in and structured by the rules because they dictate the types of information that are gathered, and underwriters are held accountable to them. But the information provided needs to be woven together with any holes patched, and related to the model of a responsible and stable mortgage payer, which is the pattern that the weaver of the story has been using all along.

Automated Underwriting—the Late 1990s and Beyond

The underwriting process I have described, based on interviews conducted in the early 1990s, is one in which the decision-making process involves human judgment and a lot of paperwork. Since those interviews the process has become increasingly automated; the rest of this chapter discusses the state of the industry as of the end of 2000.

As described in chapter 2, automation began with the spread of Fair, Isaac and Company's credit scoring process, and got a boost in 1995 when both Fannie Mae and Freddie Mac sent letters to their lenders encouraging the use of credit scores. The guidelines Fannie Mae and Freddie Mac have set up for the use of credit scores are instructive as to how new technology has affected and will affect the underwriting process. Both organizations stipulate three different score ranges to categorize the risk associated with a particular loan application's credit report. Those ranges determine not only how an underwriter should evaluate the loan application as a whole, but also the level of review—the amount of time spent on it—that the credit report warrants. Fannie Mae's and Freddie Mac's guidelines with respect to credit scores highlight what they see as the dual purposes of new technologies in underwriting: more accurate assessment; and lower cost through a decrease in the amount of human review of information. Accuracy in this situation stems both from the predictive power of the credit score itself and from the time it frees up for experienced underwriters to review files that do not have scores greater than 660 (less experienced underwriters can be used to verify the integrity of the data on the better-risk applications). The assumption here is that underwriters will choose to, and their employers will allow them to, exercise their discretion on the lower-scoring files.

Fannie Mae and Freddie Mac have gone one step beyond credit scoring and developed their own automated underwriting systems, Desktop Underwriter (DU) and Loan Prospector (LP), respectively. They also serve the dual purposes of more accurate assessment and lower cost. The "black box" nature of these systems makes them hard to evaluate with respect to how they interpret the data entered into them by the loan officer and the underwriter. But interviews with underwriters and a review of their guidelines about the use of DU and LP provide a fairly clear picture of how these systems are used and how they affect the underwriting process. The automated systems are still highly dependent on the data entered into them; they rely on data gathered from a wide variety of sources, principally the applicant's employer, bank statements and investment accounts, and the appraisal and sales contract. The loan officer may gather much of this information and enter it into the system at the point of application, but the processor or underwriter has to verify that information with supporting documentation and with a careful review to make sure it has been entered correctly. For example, the applicant's bank statements must be reviewed manually because the current automated system does not have online access to those statements. As a result, assessment of an applicant's past savings patterns is still a manual underwriting process.

The automated underwriting system is not simply a "decision machine" that spits out an "accept" or "deny" answer when the lender submits a loan application to it. Both DU and LP differentiate among loans that they have approved according to the level of documentation they require. For example, LP categorizes approved applications as either Accept Plus, Streamlined Accept, or Standard Accept. In addition, Fannie Mae's DU evaluates the loan not only in terms of whether it is an acceptable risk, but also whether it is eligible under Fannie Mae's guidelines. It lets the lender know of cases where the loan still constitutes an acceptable risk even though it is ineligible for sale to Fannie Mae (Table 3.1). In addition, any loan application the system does not approve comes with recommendations on how to make it pass muster. Freddie Mac's LP Feedback Certificate uses 104 different codes to provide the underwriter with information about the major risk factors that the application presents. Fannie Mae's DU version 4 provided three broad "referral reasons": insufficient funds to close, expense ratios, and bankruptcy/foreclosure. These three categories were designed to guide the underwriter to the areas of greatest risk in the loan application. DU version 5 provides a more sophisticated set of feedback messages, including suggestions on alterations in the terms of the loan that might improve DU's recommendation.[7]

In cases where the automated underwriting system has rejected an application there are two strategies that an underwriter can use to generate an approval, beyond altering the terms of the loan. One is to gather further information that can be added to the automated file, resulting in an approval. The other is to manually underwrite the application to assess whether there is sufficient justification to override the automated decision. The most common example cited by underwriters of situations where the former strategy works is in the documentation of additional assets that the

Table 3.1. Fannie Mae Desktop Underwriter Version 4, decision categories

Approve/Eligible	Application is approved and is eligible for purchase by Fannie Mae.
Approve/Ineligible	Application is ineligible for purchase by Fannie Mae but meets Fannie Mae's underwriting guidelines based on the eligible parameters.
Refer/Eligible	Application is eligible but does not meet Fannie Mae's underwriting guidelines.
Refer/Ineligible	Application is ineligible and does not meet Fannie Mae's underwriting guidelines.
Refer/Caution	Application does not meet Fannie Mae's underwriting guidelines and represents a greater risk than those loans in the "refer" category.
Out of Scope	Applications that DU cannot evaluate because it lacks the rules or models necessary to do so.

Source: Fannie Mae 1999, chapter 2.

loan applicant can use as reserves, most commonly IRA and 401(k) retirement accounts.

To manually override the automated decision, the second strategy, underwriters have to justify their decision with compensating factors and other explanations and support it with additional documentation, in much the same way as they would if manually underwriting the loan. If the credit score is part of the reason why the system rejected the loan application, the underwriter has to underwrite the application manually to generate an approval—changing the credit score in the system is not allowed. If the underwriter can document errors in the credit report or extenuating circumstances, then she can override the automated decision, but this exposes the decision to the potential of additional scrutiny because, as noted above, the credit score is a key determinant of which loans Fannie Mae and Freddie Mac review as part of the postpurchase quality control program.

Currently we are only part of the way on the road to full automation. Fannie Mae and Freddie Mac are beginning to use automated appraisal information as part of their automated underwriting; and there is room for further data integration such as bank account, tax, salary/wage, and investment account information. Furthermore, thanks to the Internet, it has become possible for loan officers taking a loan application in someone's home to generate a loan decision on the spot—all they need is a laptop, a modem, and a telephone line. They enter the data into the laptop, and then submit that information to either Fannie Mae's Desktop Underwriter or Freddie Mac's Loan Prospector to get a decision. Both systems make the decision based on the data entered and the credit report they have requested using the applicant's name and social security number. But these decisions are only prequalification decisions because the data entered must be verified through paper documentation. For example, the applicant's income must be verified by requesting that information from the applicant's employer. It is only when there is a fully automated data gathering process (which would require the use of a digital signature of the applicant to authorize the release of the information) that the loan decision will be instantaneous.

Automated Underwriting and Risk-Based Pricing

Risk-based pricing is a system whereby applicants with different risk ratings pay different interest rates. The old FHA mutual insurance system was a version of risk-based pricing in that borrowers with different ratings were placed in different insurance pools. Though borrowers in all the different pools paid the same insurance premium, borrowers in some pools received a premium reimbursement if there were sufficiently few losses on the loans in their pool. The private mortgage insurance system is also a crude form of risk-based pricing in which the loan-to-value ratio is the only risk parameter measured and priced. But risk-based pricing whereby there is an explicit connection between one's risk profile and the interest rate is a relatively new phenomenon. Since the early 1990s specialized mortgage lenders have offered "subprime" or "B," "C," or "D" paper loans to home buyers who do not qualify under the mainstream underwriting guidelines. These loans are at interest rates that are higher than those offered by prime (A paper) lenders, with the interest rate increasing from B paper to D paper loans.

The next step in risk-based pricing is one in which it is integrated into the decision-making processes of mainstream lenders and, in particular, into the automated underwriting systems of Fannie Mae and Freddie Mac. Such integration will largely eliminate the need for manual underwriting — those who do not make the cut for a particular loan at a particular price will simply be offered a different price rather than being given the opportunity to have someone manually review the file to determine what sort of compensating factors might put them "over the top." Both Fannie Mae and Freddie Mac have the beginnings of a risk-based pricing policy in their current automated systems. Fannie Mae's DU version 5 has a risk-based pricing system called "Expanded Approval" that approves loans at different levels (1 to 4, with the last being a "refer with caution" recommendation) with different prices, depending on the risk (Fannie Mae 2002, X, 202.06).[8] Freddie Mac offers an "A-minus" product that comes with a higher interest rate than a regular loan (one that falls into one of the Accept categories) and, in return, can accommodate borrowers with poorer credit histories and/or low cash reserves to put toward a

128   downpayment. Its Feedback Certificate instructions regarding "credit warranties" that a lender may have to perform in order to get a particular loan application to qualify gives some insight into the fundamental choice the lender faces in a risk-based pricing system—in this case between approving an application as a regular loan and approving one as an A-minus loan. For example, one message states:

> Credit Warranty: Required to determine borrower's willingness to repay and an acceptable credit reputation is evidenced. You may elect to obtain relief from this warranty under the A-minus offering. Refer to your Freddie Mac S/S Guide for details. (Freddie Mac 2002a, Sec. 8)

In other words, the underwriter can gather the information necessary to document the borrower's willingness to repay, at a cost to the lender, or he can simply bypass this requirement and offer the borrower a higher priced A-minus product. This choice is the crux of a major policy issue confronting the lending industry as a result of automation. At its heart is the relationship between cost reduction and increasing accuracy, the twin benefits of automation. In the current system we still have a process in which those who are easy to underwrite are cross-subsidizing those who are more expensive to underwrite, but who are still A paper risks. To put this in terms of Fannie Mae's categories of applicants, those applicants who are "Approve/Eligible" pay the same loan costs as those who are "Refer/Eligible" or "Caution" but who, through manual underwriting, are approved for an A paper loan. The latter two categories of applicants are more expensive to underwrite, but are charged the same price as the former. In the brave new world of risk-based pricing the "Refer/Eligible" category no longer exists; it has been replaced with the categories "Level 1," "Level 2," and so on, and those who fall into them are charged a higher interest rate accordingly (where Level 1 borrowers pay the lowest interest). As a result, a lender can approve a loan that would have been a "Refer/Eligible" or "Caution" *without further manual underwriting* by simply offering that applicant a higher interest rate. There will be some applicants who, on the basis of their profile *as it is presented in the automated system*, will look the same as other Level 2 applicants, and look different from all Level 1 applicants, but their likelihood of defaulting is no greater than the Level 1 applicants. It is unclear whether the applicant who ends up in the Level 2 category will be worse off than she might have been before—the cost savings resulting from automation and the ability of the lender to differentiate between risks may mean that this category of borrower pays less than an A paper borrower paid in the past.

The key point to note is that in a risk-based pricing model, with auto-mated underwriting, all the incentives for the lender point to minimizing manual underwriting. Furthermore, if the decision process is put in the hands of the loan officer, his incentives also point him toward simply ap-proving the deal at whatever interest rate he is allowed to offer, rather than working the deal. So long as the loan is approved, the loan officer re-ceives his commission. Furthermore, in an environment where interest rates are fluid, the loan officer has a better opportunity to charge what is known in the lending industry as "overage." Overage is an additional in-terest rate charge, or points payment, that the borrower pays simply be-cause the loan officer quotes the borrower a rate higher than the amount stipulated by the lender in its rate sheets. The borrower has no knowledge of the rate on the rate sheet and so does not know she is paying overage. This situation is the same as the one faced by car buyers who seek financ-ing. A car dealer submits the buyer's credit information to a credit grantor through an automated system and is quoted an interest rate based on the automated system's assessment of the credit risk the buyer represents. The dealer, in turn, quotes the buyer an interest rate that cannot fall below but may be greater than the rate the system quotes. The lender gives the dealer an incentive to quote a higher rate by giving him a share of the ad-ditional profit the lender earns from the higher rate (Henriques 2000, A1).

The Impact of Automation on the Construction of Risk

The benefits of automation are supposed to be more accurate decisions at a lower monetary cost in a shorter amount of time. Leaving aside the issue of greater accuracy for the moment, let us look at how the cost and time savings affect the loan application process. In the manual world the process began with a dynamic of inclusion and exclusion. In an automated world, without risk-based pricing or the availability of products other than A paper loans, the loan officer simply has a more accurate pre-screening device, but is still left with the decision as to whether to "work the deal" or not. If the extent of automation is the availability of a credit score that the loan officer knows the underwriter will use in assessing the applicant's credit record, the fate of the applicant is still contingent on the loan offi-cer's willingness and ability to put a low credit score in the context of ex-tenuating circumstances that would allow the underwriter to manually override the score. But the loan officer has a greater incentive to submit the loan application regardless of the score because the time it takes for the underwriter to reach a decision is less. If risk-based pricing is avail-able, or the loan officer can shift the borrower from one product to an-other based on his assessment of the borrower's likelihood of being approved, then the inclusion/exclusion dynamic breaks down—the loan officer simply fits the borrower into whatever product he chooses. The loan officer is still party to the construction of risk in this process—he can choose to work the deal to put a borrower in a better risk category so she can secure a lower interest rate. But the loan officer has no incentive to do this, other than the incentives his conscience provides.

In the same way, automation does not fundamentally alter the choices facing an underwriter. The automated system may deny a loan that an underwriter must then look at manually. The manual process may simply be a matter of providing the automated system additional data, or it may involve fully underwriting the file to see whether a manual override is feasible. In doing either the underwriters follow the underwriting guidelines and use the same approach I described for manual underwriting. The questions facing the underwriter are still the same: How much effort should I put into securing additional information to see if this file will work or not? What story is the file telling? The one difference is that the underwriter faces the additional burden of justifying her decision contrary to the automated decision. Of course, a financial institution can decide that it is simply not cost-effective to allow manual overrides—the marginal cost of retaining experienced underwriting staff is greater than the marginal revenue that the manually underwritten loans will yield to the lender. The assumption here is that a lender can underwrite and approve enough loans through the automated system to cover its fixed costs that it has no real need for underwriters. As of now, this does not seem to be the case.

Risk-based pricing changes this situation. Under risk-based pricing the automated system has a far wider range of loans that it can approve. Loans that it previously denied can now be approved at a higher rate. Underwriters are far less likely to be needed and the process of manual underwriting is likely to become redundant. Furthermore, risk assessment itself becomes secondary; the loan application process becomes one in which the goal of the lending institution is to charge as high an interest rate as it can. This is the logic that has led to the association between subprime lending and what is known as predatory lending. Subprime lending is the precursor of risk-based pricing in that it does not apply one standard to all applicants, but puts the applicants in different risk categories and charges them different interest rates. Predatory lending is the logical extension of this: the practice of loading the borrower with the highest fees and interest charges possible, where the bounds of possibility are defined by profit maximization.

Competition between lenders is supposed to take care of predatory lending abuses—borrowers are supposed to shop around and compare interest rates. But this assumes that borrowers can gain access to good information. Such access is contingent on the networks in which they are embedded. It is unclear what impact automation and risk-based pricing will have on the networks in which the loan application process will take place. On the one hand, the loan officer–real estate broker relationship gives the loan officer the opportunity to be the first point of contact the borrower has with the mortgage market, and so long as a loan applicant needs the help of another person in filling out an application form, this first-contact advantage may be critical. On the other hand, risk-based pricing and automation combined with Web-based loan application forms should give a loan applicant with access to the Internet the opportunity to find the lender willing to offer her the lowest interest rate, thus destroying the importance of the real estate broker–loan officer relationship. In such a scenario, the process of constructing a risk profile comes down to the applicant's own willingness and ability to take advantage of networks, particularly the Internet, that offer the most information.

Conclusion

The loan application process involves the application of rules in the context of networks of relations between loan officers and real estate brokers. Within this structure are individuals making decisions contingent on their willingness and ability to see the applicant as a good risk. The individuals have good reasons to obey the rules: it is their job, and they are held accountable to them. The real estate broker and the loan officer attempt to anticipate those rules so as to avoid unnecessary work. In doing so they both exclude potential loan applicants and work to fit those they accept into the rules. It is these practices that undergird the relationship between particular brokers and particular loan officers. The underwriter is also held accountable to the rules. They organize the information the underwriter assesses and they serve as a guide in that assessment. But the rules are insufficient—the information they require to be gathered is never enough, and can never cover all situations. So underwriters have to do more than just implement rules—they have to tell a coherent financial story about the loan applicant in order to justify their decision, both to themselves and to those who review their work. Automation has not changed the essential choices that individuals within the process face. But automation in combination with risk-based pricing will. Risk assessment will become secondary; the focus of lenders will be to charge as high an interest rate as they can.

Understanding the loan application process as one in which a risk profile is constructed has important public policy implications, particularly
with regard to the issue of racial discrimination. It also has theoretical implications for understanding how credit markets and markets in general
work. To round out this theoretical picture, though, and to fully understand the policy implications of the construction process require an analysis of the construction of housing markets and their boundaries. It is in this
context that the application process takes place.

4

Constructing Housing Markets

The process described in the previous chapter takes place in a particular spatial context. We have various ways of demarcating space, which allow us to put boundaries around the context of a particular event. For example, we have the categories of city, suburbs, and rural or exurbs. These categories have generally accepted meanings derived from both the essential qualities of the places they describe and their relationship to one another. A city connotes a relatively higher population density and centrality within an urban mass. Suburbs connote places with lower population densities on the periphery of a city, most often with separate political jurisdictions. And rural connotes places away from large concentrations of population. Within these categories, and sometimes cutting across them, are townships, towns (though not within cities), various planning and municipal service-delivery districts, political districts, and neighborhoods. All but the last of these categories are defined by government, which delineates their boundaries and gives them a name. City and town governments may also define neighborhood boundaries and either give neighborhoods their names or adopt the names used by residents within each delineated space. But even absent such official delineation and naming, the idea of a neighborhood is still common currency in the everyday conversations of people in the United States. And it is the neighborhood, especially in cities, that is the most important component of "location" in the buying, selling, and financing of residential real estate.

This chapter explores the concept of the neighborhood. The focus here is on the way people draw neighborhood boundaries, because this activity is both important to how people identify neighborhoods in general and essential to the appraisal process. The analysis is based on data from Chicago, and builds on research that already exists on that city, as well as adding new data from interviews conducted there. It begins with an exploration of what a neighborhood is from a resident's point of view and then examines how real estate brokers and appraisers think about neighborhoods and their boundaries. It finishes with an analysis of how people produce and reproduce new neighborhood boundaries in situations where old boundaries have been breached—in cases of ethnic resegregation and gentrification.

What Is a Neighborhood?

On the face of it, what a neighborhood is seems to be obvious. But try articulating a definition, concisely. Where does one start? With the people? With physical boundaries? With the types of buildings or activities that take place in an area? Or does one cheat, by simply giving examples of neighborhoods? In Chicago the task, at least initially, has been made easier by the work of the Social Science Research Committee of the University of Chicago in the late 1920s. Under the leadership of the sociologist Ernest Burgess the committee divided up Chicago into 75 different community areas, based on physical divisions, the location of commercial centers, and local lore (Hunter 1974). These were first used in *Census Data of the City of Chicago, 1930*, and have remained the same since, with the addition of area 76 through the annexation of the land for O'Hare Airport, and area 77, which was created when Uptown was divided into Uptown and Edgewater. These community area delineations have had a profound influence on the way Chicago describes itself. The city government, academics, commercial interests, and community activists all use the community areas to organize information that they present to the public. The city organizes much of the data on Chicago's housing and population according to these areas. The *Local Community Fact Book*, which publishes the decennial census data, organizes its data in this fashion, and the business community does the same. For example the *Chicago Sun Times' Pocket Guide to the Chicago Market, 1990* presented its data by community area, and its

Chicago House Hunt Book, 1990 used many of those areas' names in its guide to housing in metropolitan Chicago, though it went beyond the broad strokes painted by the University of Chicago sociologists to provide more detailed neighborhood descriptions. Local telephone books are organized by clusters of community areas, with each book having a map on the back depicting the districts covered. Finally, community activists use the community area names to organize data and, sometimes, to delineate the areas they represent and serve. The Chicago Rehab Network, a nonprofit community development organization, uses the community areas for its *Chicago Affordable Housing Fact Book*, as does the Woodstock Institute, a nonprofit research organization, for its *Community Lending Fact Book*, which provides data on lending in Chicago.

But Hunter notes these community area definitions do not identify all the different neighborhoods in Chicago. The reason for this, he argues, is twofold. First he notes that "the Burgess areas may be somewhat 'artificial' in that he explicitly tried to define areas of equivalent size and population" (1974, 72). Second, Hunter maintains that a process of differentiation and fusion led to a greater variation in area size by the time of his study in the late 1960s than existed in Burgess's day. Thus Hunter lists 206 different neighborhoods that he identified in the 801 interviews he conducted with Chicago residents in 1967 and 1968, in his conversations with neighborhood leaders, and in his own visits to the neighborhoods. His questionnaire asked both about the name of the community in which the interviewees lived and about its boundaries. He found that 86 percent of the people he interviewed were able to name their local community and 69 percent were able to name its four boundaries (author's calculations based on Tables 9 and 10, ibid., 97–99).

> The name, then, is a symbol of communication that is a shared collective representation about the community itself. In the interaction and communication of individuals both within and without the local community, community names convey properties of both physical and social space.
>
> Names are also significant for identity. The ability to name an area gives an unambiguous status to those living there. (Hunter 1974, 68)

In the same vein, Suttles argues that neighborhood designations are a functional response to the decision-making problem an individual faces in a city. Again, separating the physical from the social, he writes:

> These cognitive maps, then, are a creative imposition on the city and useful because they provide a final solution to decision making where there are often no other clear cutoff points for determining how far social contacts

should go. The actual structure of most cities is best described as a series of gradients, and there are very few clear boundaries or sharp junctures which cannot be crossed by a simple decision to do so. In order to regulate one's spatial movement and locational possibilities, then, one needs a simpler model, because in the final analysis most decisions must be answered "yes" or "no." The utility of a more qualitative map of the city is that it permits this type of decision making, whereas the physical structure of the city leaves one in an eternal state of ambiguity. (1972, 23)

Suttles raises an important issue about the nature of boundaries that is reminiscent of the ontological ambiguity that Babcock and others expressed regarding the order, or lack thereof, of the city. People need boundaries to help them make decisions, but the city does not provide them with "clear boundaries or sharp junctures." As a result, they have to invent them—they have to impose order on a city that lacks it.

It may seem as if Suttles is exaggerating the lack of boundaries. Railroad lines, parks, rivers, expressways, and wide boulevards can act as physical barriers that prevent communication between people on either side of them, and there are plenty of these in cities. But these barriers are not absolute; rather, they are contingent on how people perceive and experience them. Parks can divide or unite people, acting either as a physical barrier to interaction between those on different sides of the park or as a meeting point where people from all sides come to play and relax. In the same way, rivers can divide neighborhoods or, if they are clean, they can serve as a recreational focus. And bridges over rivers can serve as meeting places for people who live on either bank, and so on. Suttles may also seem to be exaggerating because social differences between people, especially racial and ethnic differences, can create "clear boundaries and sharp junctures." In Chicago there are clear racial boundary lines: for example, parts of South Western Avenue separate black and Hispanic communities. The boundary line is there because people have chosen to use racial and ethnic differences in how they draw their boundaries. But the extent to which this boundary line prevents the free movement of people across it is unclear.

How do people generate their cognitive maps of cities? Jonathan Raban's account in *Hunting Mister Heartbreak* gives us an idea:

Within a few weeks I found that I had instinctively constructed a *neighborhood*. The word itself was old fashioned, warm and reassuring. It summoned echoes of the Whitewashed Puritan township, built around the meeting house, of borrowing twists of salt and pats of butter from the family next door. In New York, the reality was more like the enchanted circle cast around oneself by a primitive tribesman to ward off evil spirits. Here, you had to will a *neighborhood* into being in order to dare go out on the nearest street.

So I laid down my own magical grid lines, enclosing an arbitrary space that was nine blocks long and two blocks wide. It held everything necessary for survival—a Polish bistro, a Korean supermarket, a laundry, a cigar store that sold the *Nation* and *New Republic* as well as imported pipe tobacco, a good florist, two bars, a proper butcher, a diner. I could address the doormen on my block by name, and I had two beggars to whom I regularly gave alms.

At two in the morning, dropped from a shared cab on Seventh Avenue, I would march, sidewalk-craftily, along Eighteenth Street until I gained the eastern side of Broadway, which was where my neighborhood began. Here my shoulders would unhunch, my pace slow, and I'd start nodding to strangers.

The curious thing about New York was that your neighborhood was always "safe"; it was only places where your friends lived that were dangerous. (1992, 89–90)

Raban's account is instructive because it shows how he actually went about generating a neighborhood. He did need to feel safe out on the streets, and the construction of a recognizable neighborhood with set boundaries was a response to this need. But the neighborhood that he "willed" for himself did not just appear out of nowhere—it was produced by his everyday practices, and reconfirmed by them. Implied in his listing of stores is that he visited them on a regular basis. To get to know the doormen's names he must have passed by them sufficiently often that he could engage them in conversation. Raban identified a neighborhood that was particular to himself—an "ego community."

It is unclear from Hunter's research the extent to which people in the same neighborhood agreed on its boundaries. His map showing the 206 neighborhoods identified in his interviews implies some agreement on the part of his respondents, but he also acknowledges that neighborhood boundaries are often ambiguous, in part because individuals define such boundaries relative to their own location (Hunter 1974, 86–87).

Thus there are two ambiguities in the status of neighborhoods in cities. One is the ambiguity created by, on the one hand, the lack of order in a city and, on the other hand, the need people have in their own everyday decision-making to impose an order on the city. The second ambiguity is created by the fact that the construction of neighborhood boundaries is an individual act, resulting from everyday activities, though it informs and is informed by generally accepted boundary delineations. The real estate industry, however, has no truck with these ambiguities. We have seen how, in the past, it defined and delineated neighborhoods. How does it do so now?

Neighborhoods, Housing Markets, and Real Estate Values

Real estate brokers and appraisers both have to delineate neighborhood boundaries to do their jobs. In addition, real estate brokers like to be able to name neighborhoods. To earn a living, a broker has to match a buyer with a property, whose location is a key selling point. At the same time a broker has to secure listings from sellers. She can do these two things more effectively using neighborhood designations. First, by giving an identity to a particular group of houses she can match a buyer with a property according to her assessment of the buyer's identity. In other words, the neighborhood name allows her to categorize areas of the city according to the type of buyer to which they are likely to appeal. Second, when securing a listing, the broker uses neighborhood boundaries to determine a good selling price for the property, based on the previous sales in the neighborhood.

An appraiser is engaged in much the same practice as a real estate broker. Appraisers use the sales comparison approach today. An essential first step in using this approach is to identify the neighborhood in which a property is located. Defining the neighborhood defines the area from which the appraiser draws comparable sales data to determine the value of the property. Fannie Mae's *Selling Guide* states the importance of this very clearly:

> An appraiser must perform a neighborhood analysis in order to identify the area that is subject to the same influences as the property being appraised (based on the actions of typical buyers in the market area). The results of a neighborhood analysis enable the appraiser not only to identify the factors that influence the value of properties in the market area, but also to define the area from which to select the market data needed to perform a sales comparison analysis. (2002, XI, 403)

And if the neighborhood cannot provide the right comparables then, as Freddie Mac's regulations state:

> Comparables may be taken from a competing neighborhood if the appraiser has established that the neighborhoods are comparable and compete for the same buyers, and comparables taken from the competing neighborhood are better indicators of current market trends in the subject neighborhood than the existing comparables available in the subject neighborhood. (2002b, 44.16)

But what is the neighborhood? The Appraisal Institute defines it in this way:

A neighborhood exhibits a greater degree of uniformity than the larger surrounding area. Obviously, no group of inhabitants, buildings, or business enterprises can possess identical features or attributes, but a neighborhood is perceived to be relatively uniform. Many shared features may be evident in a neighborhood, including similar building types and styles, population characteristics, economic profiles of occupants, and zoning regulations that affect land-use. (1996, 190)

Appraisers whom I interviewed gave a variety of different answers as a first response to the question "What is a neighborhood?" They cited schools, similar land uses, amenities, and zoning, natural boundaries, socio-economics, and the economics of the area. But the reasoning was consistent across appraisers. What it boiled down to is that a neighborhood is an area of similar housing structures occupied by residents of similar incomes and tastes, resulting in similar housing prices within the area identified. One appraiser stated this directly:

GS: What sort of aids do you use to define neighborhood boundaries?
Ap. 1: Mostly visual.
GS: What sort of things are you looking for?
Ap. 1: Comparability, number one. You look for . . . different cl— I don't say class, but you look for like wages, if they're in the same economic thing, you know; same likes and dislikes, same social—that's a very important factor too. I could say same taste.

Another appraiser, who specializes in properties in the gentrified market, responded in the following manner:

A neighborhood is defined in several different ways. It does have boundaries. Sometimes they are blurred boundaries. They may be boundaries that are socio-economic. North Avenue is a good example of that. Within a one block area of North Avenue, let's say between 300 and 1200 block, we can see as much as a 50 to 60 percent difference in a one block area based upon socio-economics. In other words, the amount the properties sell for. (Ap. 7)

A third appraiser, who cited a property's location with respect to schools as the basis on which he identified a neighborhood, provided the following reasoning:

If you're going to move into a neighborhood, and you have children. There's no way you're going to have a house unless you have kids. So your kids are associated with the same kids that represent the same family background. (Ap. 2)

A fourth, who began by looking at an area's zoning and amenities, later on described how he identified neighborhood boundaries. Using the neighborhood in which we were sitting, he said that the railway tracks nearby were a good natural boundary, and that it was likely that the areas on the two sides were zoned differently. But he then noted that houses on either side of the tracks were of the same value and so they should all be treated as part of the same neighborhood for the purpose of the appraisal.

Finally, I had the following interchange with an appraiser who could not define a neighborhood for me:

> Ap. 9: A neighborhood is an area that. . . . How to define a neighborhood. I know what a neighborhood is, I know. . . . A neighborhood is normally a small area. . . . How can I define a neighborhood for you? A neighborhood normally has some natural boundaries: railroad tracks, major thoroughfares, things like that. The Institute defines a neighborhood like "homogeneous use of land," so forth and so on. I don't necessarily agree with that. Have I answered that question?
>
> GS: I'm going to push you . . . [I asked about subneighborhoods within a community area, something he mentioned earlier].
>
> Ap. 9: How do I determine the neighborhood? Well I determine the neighborhood on my experience and knowledge, and the market. In other words if I see houses in a certain area selling for 100,000 dollars . . . two streets away they are selling for 50,000 dollars then I think it is safe to assume that I am in a different neighborhood.
>
> GS: What creates that difference?
>
> Ap. 9: The neighborhood. . . .

So the neighborhood consists of properties within a similar price range—a product of demand-side and supply-side uniformity. The appraisers' answers to my question are consistent with the underwriting criteria of the secondary market and the FHA. Fannie Mae's guidelines state:

> VII, 404.01: Conformity to Neighborhood (12/31/94)
> The improvements should generally conform to the neighborhood in terms of age, type, design, and materials used for their construction. If there is market resistance to a property because its improvements are not compatible with the neighborhood or with the requirements of the competitive market—because of adequacy of plumbing, heating, or electrical services; design; quality; size; condition; or any other reason directly related to market demand—the lender should underwrite the mortgage more carefully and, if appropriate, require more conservative mortgage terms. However, the

lender should be aware that many older neighborhoods have favorable heterogeneity in architectural styles, land use, and age of housing. For example,
older neighborhoods are especially likely to have been developed through
custom building; this variety may be a positive marketing factor. (2002, XI,
405.01)

This follows the passage I quoted earlier, in chapter 1, which is worth re-
peating:

Typically, dwellings best maintain their value when they are situated in
neighborhoods that consist of other similar dwellings. However, some factors that are typical of a mixed-use neighborhood—such as easy access to
employment centers and a high level of community activity—can actually
enhance the market value of the property through increased buyer demand.
Urban neighborhoods also frequently reflect a blend of single-family residential and nonresidential land uses—including residential multifamily
properties, other properties that are used to provide commercial services
(such as groceries and other neighborhood stores) in support of the local
neighborhood, industrial properties, etc. (Ibid., 403.08)

Despite the efforts to accommodate "urban neighborhoods" it is quite
clear that the predominant attitude toward the analysis of the neighborhood is that it be homogeneous with regard to building type and land use.
Freddie Mac's rules state:

When the subject property does not conform to its neighborhood in terms of
type, design, age, and the materials and techniques used in its construction,
the appraisal must evaluate the effect the nonconformance has on the property's value and marketability. The appraisal must not improperly take into
consideration the age of the dwelling. (2002b, 44.15(d))

Finally, the FHA in its section titled "Conformity of Property to
Neighborhood: *Relation of Ownership Expense to Family Incomes*" is most explicit about the class implications of the conformity of a property to its
neighborhood:

Families usually select homes in neighborhoods where typical occupants
have financial means similar to their own. A home that is too costly for these
families to purchase or maintain will have limited marketability. (U.S. Department of Housing and Urban Development 1999, 3–3 D)

The appraisal profession no longer sticks religiously to the idea that a
neighborhood must be uniform in order for the properties within it to re-

tain their value. As described in chapter 1, much of the credit for the more catholic tastes of the profession is due to community activists who exposed the racist and anti-urban biases inherent in the appraisal process. Nevertheless, it is clear that neighborhood uniformity and class segregation are the norm, from which appraisers are allowed to deviate to accommodate the heterogeneous physical structure of urban areas. The persistence of the idea of uniformity and class segregation is a tribute to the power of the logic underlying today's appraisal practices—a logic grounded in the very way that appraisers and the real estate industry in general think about real estate value.

Though the appraisal industry does not explicitly endorse racial and ethnic segregation anymore, the logic of its reasoning points the appraiser toward using neighborhood delineations that follow existing racial and ethnic dividing lines. As one black appraiser explained it to me:

> Ap. 3: There again, it's location again. It says "people make value" and based on the income level and like that. So I couldn't use those comparables like that. You see the price range would be so much different—it's not a competing neighborhood, people have different incomes there.
> GS: A lot of those neighborhoods have roughly the same income levels.
> Ap. 3: Fine, but will the same people buy over there? I have to weigh all those factors. . . . We're not supposed to consider race at all. But it's something you just know as a fact, you just can't include it in the paper here though. Would this person go there to live or could they? That's the deciding factor you look for. It says "a similar user group for the neighborhood. . . ."

Ethnic Succession

For neighborhood ethnic succession to occur there has to be a neighborhood. The delineation of a neighborhood is therefore an essential first step. Schelling (1978) describes two kinds of neighborhood delineation, one individual and one collective, in his modeling of the ethnic succession process. The individual type is one in which every person constructs his own neighborhood around his home. The collective type is one in which there are generally agreed-upon neighborhood boundaries, what Schelling calls the bounded-neighborhood model. There is no doubt that people construct and use individually constructed neighborhoods to organize their day-to-day activities. But this does not preclude the development of an agreed-upon boundary, and, as I have discussed already, such boundary-drawing is an essential part of the social construction of housing markets.[1]

Also essential in the construction of a housing market is the mix of buyers who are exposed to and buy into the market. Most empirical analyses of ethnic succession focus their attention on the composition of the neighborhood they are studying. Part of this focus is a result of a lack of data—they have only census data describing who is already in the neighborhood—but part of it is also a stress on the search for a "tipping point," the point at which enough residents, with particular preferences, begin to leave and in doing so trigger the departure of ever-more residents, people who may be more accepting of new entrants but find themselves increasingly in the minority. This focus on who is in the neighborhood at a particular time does not take into account a process that is the precursor to the dynamic they describe, namely the changing mix of movers into or within the neighborhood. If the movers into or within the neighborhood increasingly become of one race or ethnicity, then that race or ethnicity will eventually come to dominate the neighborhood, *even if those who move out of the neighborhood do so for reasons other than its racial composition.* The change in the mix of movers could be characterized as a process in which individuals choose, based on their racial preferences, to buy in one neighborhood over another. But it is also contingent on the activities of real estate brokers, who have considerable discretion in what properties they show to whom.[2]

A case in point is the Southwest Side of Chicago, where ethnic succession is proceeding apace. A detailed look at the community areas of West Elsdon and Gage Park shows how the mix of home buyers (I have no data on renters) changes in neighborhoods undergoing succession (Figure 4.1).[3] In Gage Park, which began the 1990s with a population that was 39 percent of Hispanic origin (Chicago Fact Book Consortium 1995, 184), the percentage of home buyers who were Hispanic during the 1993–98 period varied from a low of 84 percent to a high of 91. In West Elsdon, which began the 1990s with a population that was 8 percent of Hispanic origin (ibid., 182), the percentage of home buyers who were Hispanic increased from 43 to 77 percent from 1993 to 1998 (Figure 4.2).

West Elsdon is itself divided into submarkets by Pulaski Avenue, a wide, four-lane commercial street that runs north-south through the middle of the community area. On the east side of Pulaski, the part of the community area that neighbors Gage Park, the population was 13 percent Hispanic in 1990. Hispanics' share of the home buyer market was 60 percent in 1993 and 90 percent in 1998. On the west side of Pulaski, the community area began the 1990s with a population that was 4 percent Hispanic, while Hispanics' share of the home buyer market was 18 percent in 1993 and increased to 64 percent in 1998 (Figure 4.3). Note that the succession process has not been characterized by the same steady increase in home buyers with lower incomes.[4] Though Gage Park's home buyers are

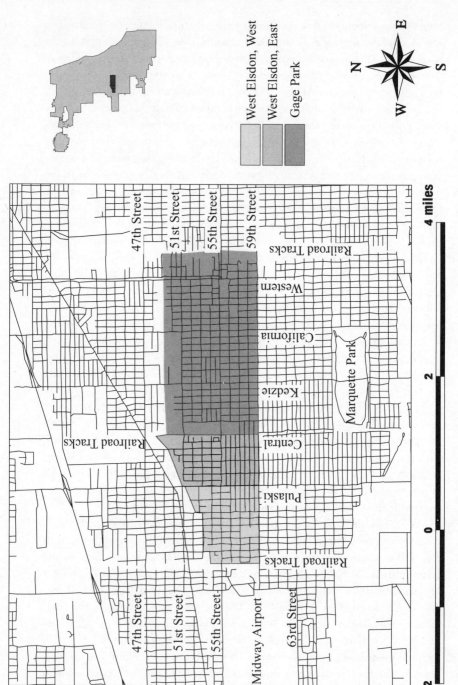

West Elsdon, West

West Elsdon, East

Gage Park

47th Street
51st Street
55th Street
59th Street

Railroad Tracks

Western

California

Kedzie

Central

Pulaski

Railroad Tracks

Marquette Park

Railroad Tracks

47th Street
51st Street
55th Street

Midway Airport

63rd Street

N E S W

2   0   2   4 miles

Figure 4.1. Southwest Side neighborhoods, Chicago, 1990s. Source: U.S. Census Bureau, TIGER/Line Files, 1995.

more likely to have low or moderate incomes than those in West Elsdon, the difference is not great, and the succession process in West Elsdon has not resulted in a rapid increase of low- and moderate-income home buyers (Figure 4.4).

It is clear from these data that the community areas of West Elsdon and Gage Park are not completely segregated housing markets—one area has not completely undergone succession while another remains all white. Rather, as one market becomes dominated by Hispanics so another market begins its rise in Hispanic market share. But it is also clear that market boundaries are having the effect of concentrating Hispanic home buying activity in particular areas, in Gage Park and the east side of Pulaski Avenue. Furthermore, the speed at which Hispanics have come to dominate the home buying market in all these different areas is remarkable. They

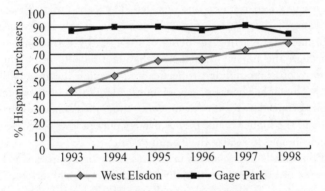

Figure 4.2. Ethnic change, Gage Park and West Elsdon home purchasers, 1993–1998.
Source: Federal Financial Institutions Examination Council 1993–1998.

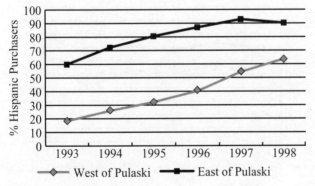

Figure 4.3. Ethnic change, West Elsdon home purchasers, 1993–1998.
Source: Federal Financial Institutions Examination Council 1993–1998.

146   constituted well over a majority of the home buyers in both Gage Park and West Elsdon in the mid-1990s, despite being a small percentage of the population in 1990.[5] In other words, housing market boundaries coordinate and concentrate ethnic succession, resulting in its seeming inevitability. To the extent that appraisals accept the market boundaries that segregate people by race and ethnicity, they endorse the succession process. In addition, they can fuel it because they exaggerate value differences across racial boundaries, reinforcing an assumption that neighborhood succession will result in lower values.

Gentrification

Gentrification is the process by which wealthy individuals and families buy homes in an area which, up until that time, was occupied by lower-income owners and renters, or consisted of vacant buildings and land. Gentrification is largely an urban phenomenon. The wealthy in-movers often displace the existing residents of the area by raising house prices both through the impact that their rehabilitation efforts on their own homes have on surrounding properties and through the speculation that they fuel. The higher house prices encourage landlords to raise rents or to sell their properties to the in-movers, thus displacing lower-income renters; and the higher house prices also encourage lower-income owners to sell their homes to realize their equity gains.

As Elijah Anderson recounts in *Streetwise*, the first steps toward gentrification may be taken unintentionally by middle-class whites looking to escape high-priced, "high-status" neighborhoods. They are in search of the use-value that the urban environment can provide through proximity to

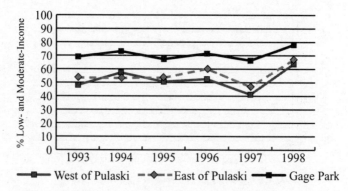

Figure 4.4. Class stability, Gage Park and West Elsdon home purchasers, 1993–1998.
Source: Federal Financial Institutions Examination Council 1993–1998.

work, the appeal of history, and the variety the environment brings to everyday life. But in the world of real estate investment and mortgage lending these middle-class whites are doing something else: they are "pioneers" securing "territory" for other middle-class whites to move in to. In the West Town community area of Chicago this is exactly what has happened. This was captured in a *Chicago Tribune* report on Wicker Park and Bucktown, two neighborhoods within the area. As the report described it, Wicker Park was first gentrified in the 1960s and 1970s in the area around the park of the same name. In the 1980s artists moved in because "the large spaces they needed . . . were relatively cheap" (Lauerman 1992, 14). In the early 1980s they began to move in to the area and spread out into Bucktown. The next significant date was 1986, when a developer bought a block on which he constructed new townhouses.

The *Tribune* report was titled "There Goes the Neighborhood. Will Wicker Park and Bucktown Survive Gentrification?" and explored how resentment was growing among long-time Hispanic residents and the artists' community against the influx of money. One artist was quoted as saying:

> I like the way this neighborhood is—mostly Puerto Rican—and I wish it would stay that way. . . . All these families have been here for years, and they're going to be pushed into another low-income-neighborhood [*sic*]. I've got to have a place to live, too, and it has to be cheap and large. I'm telling you this, but look, I moved here, and I'm part of the problem. (Lauerman 1992, 18)

In contrast to the angst of the artist regarding his role in the gentrification process, those who come into the neighborhood later have a different view of the artist's role. A vernacular account of how the white "pioneers" are viewed by those who move in behind them appeared in a 1992 special supplement to *Apartments and Homes*, a guide to just that. This was written in reference to gentrification along the north lakeshore areas of Buena Park, Sheridan Park, and Margate Park, three neighborhoods within the Lakeview and Uptown community areas:

> "The pioneers are the ones lying down with arrows in their backs." That's a very old joke but it embodies many painful truths about the reality of investing in Chicago's "hot neighborhoods."
>
> Pioneers, after all, often find themselves alone in the wilderness. Many of them, even when they survive, wish they hadn't. The only thing that mitigates the isolation and the loneliness (and the terror) is the knowledge that they have no peers to witness their suffering or ridicule their poor judgment.
>
> Savvy investors and homebuyers don't pioneer: they sit back, yell "Charge!" and only set foot on the field of battle when the smoke has

cleared and the good guys have won. The psychic and financial rewards of pioneering are still available—in part because the pioneers are bloodied and lack the strength to capitalize on the opportunities they created—without the pain. (Zekas 1992, 1)

The angst of the artist and the profit-motivated callousness of t'. ᴐse that come next into a gentrifying market are stereotypical of the gentrification process. The angst and the profit would not exist without effective boundary-drawing. In both statements cited above the focus is on a particular set of neighborhoods. These neighborhoods have established borders that serve to constrain the gentrifying housing market and thus constrain the supply of houses and allow gentrifiers to capture the externality effects of each other's actions for themselves. Note that the artist values the externality effects of the Puerto Rican presence in the neighborhood, but these are not valorized. In fact, the very concept of the "pioneer" implies that the artist or other first movers in the gentrification process are entering either a hostile or an abandoned "plain." In contrast, the externality effects of other gentrifiers are valorized, setting in motion a self-fulfilling dynamic.

The role of the appraiser is critical in this process. For gentrification to succeed home values must rise. Rising values justify the costs incurred by individuals and developers in rehabilitating the homes in a gentrifying area. Without rising values, mortgage money will not flow. When an appraiser goes into a new neighborhood he has to work out where to find the comparable sales on which he will base his estimate of value. One place to look is the immediate vicinity of the property. But if the subject property is one of the first to be rehabilitated, there may be no properties nearby that it can be compared to—it has had too much done to it, it appeals to a different market. So the appraiser is forced to look for comparables in a competitive market. Such a market is a previously gentrified neighborhood of similar structures, often adjacent to the new neighborhood. The appraiser's role is to acknowledge, in his valuation analysis, that a "pioneer" neighborhood is competitive with previously gentrified neighborhoods and act accordingly. This is how one appraiser described the process:

If a person is a pioneer. I'm sure the people who first moved into Bucktown were the pioneers. And the comps were being pulled at that point from what was happening east of Ashland Avenue [a street separating Bucktown from an already gentrified neighborhood]. Although there was only like a two or three block difference, but you had the expressway that divided that whole section. So they were still going east of Ashland Avenue to get their comps, to bring them into Bucktown [the newly gentrifying neighborhood], as we know it. Someone had to take that risk and possibly a lender with some forethought and foresight said "Wait a minute. The seams of DePaul (the already gentrified neighborhood) are bursting, let's take a look at the housing stock west of the expressway and see if its similar to what DePaul is." Now they go over there and they said "Oh yeah, right, you have Victorian buildings. Small bedrooms, big living rooms 'cos that's the way things were built in the early 1900s." But now you've got a low-level stockbroker who can't afford DePaul right now, but can afford just over the expressway. (Ap. 6)

On what grounds does the appraiser acknowledge this? It is a matter of judgment. If an appraiser can identify a trend toward gentrification in the "pioneer" neighborhood, then he can justify his use of comparables from the gentrified market: "You follow who's going where" (ap. 6). Another appraiser identified the same process and listed what she looked out for:

when you see a trend going in rehab in the inner city, and its a trend where the neighborhood, it appears that developers are buying, the purchase of 6-flats—you see that going on, you sees signs out "newly rehabed two-bedroom, three-bedroom condos" and yet the rehab is just beginning and they sell before they have a product ready for the market, you're seeing a trend. (Ap. 7)

This process results in the perpetuation of segregation because the new "pioneer" neighborhood must itself have a boundary which divides it from the territory beyond. So long as the "natives" are of a sufficiently lower income than the "pioneers," then the former will be forced out, for the reasons cited above. The key point here is that the decision-making process of brokers and appraisers requires boundary-setting, and it is only in this way that they can generate support for gentrification from lenders. This boundary-setting creates a "hot" market within a specific area and so results in displacement and resegregation.

The West Town, Humboldt Park, and Logan Square areas on the Near Northwest Side of Chicago provide a clear illustration of how boundaries work. The area stretches west from the Chicago River to the railroad tracks just east of Cicero Avenue, between Chicago Avenue on the south and Diversey Parkway on the north. Between Armitage Avenue and Diversey Parkway, the area goes only as far as Pulaski Avenue on the west (Figure 4.5). The distance between the river and the western railroad tracks is three miles. According to various sources, including Hunter (1974), this area is divided into a number of different neighborhoods.

At the easternmost end of the area are the neighborhoods of Wicker Park, Bucktown, Ukrainian Village, and East Village. This area stretches

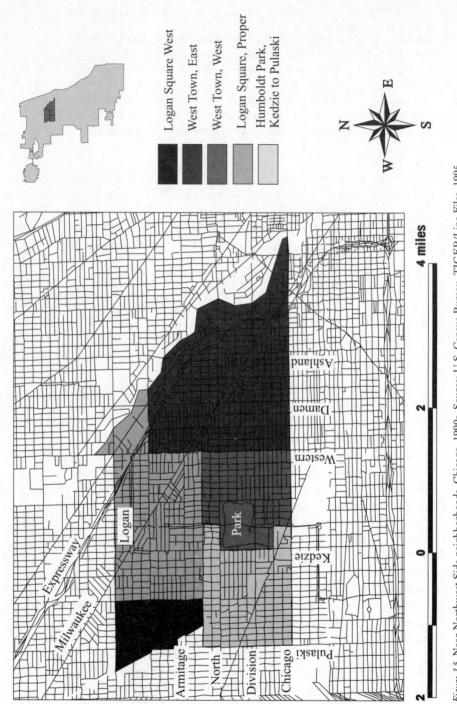

Legend:
- Logan Square West
- West Town, East
- West Town, West
- Logan Square, Proper
- Humboldt Park, Kedzie to Pulaski

Figure 4.5. Near Northwest Side neighborhoods, Chicago, 1990s. Source: U.S. Census Bureau, TIGER/Line Files, 1995.

for about 1.5 miles between the river and Western Avenue. It is an area of intense gentrification. Between 1993 and 1998 the percentage of home buyers in these neighborhoods that were upper-income increased from 40 percent to 60 percent (see "West Town, East" line in Figure 4.6).[6]

Just west of this area, continuing between North Avenue and Chicago Avenue, are a number of blocks that make up the remainder of the West Town community area. Though it is just across the street from Wicker Park and Bucktown, and is hemmed in on its west side by a railroad yard and a very large park (Humboldt Park), the number of upper-income home buyers here was only 10 percent of all buyers in the area in 1993 and 20 percent of buyers in 1998 ("West Town, West" in Figure 4.6). Going west of the park and the railroad yard we see a further drop-off of upper-income buying activity. In Humboldt Park, on both sides of Pulaski Avenue, upper-income home buyers constituted about 10 percent of buyers in 1993 and less than 10 percent in 1998 (Figure 4.6). Note that the gentrification process is also an ethnic succession process. White home buyers dominate the housing market in the eastern part of West Town, and are an increasing presence west of Western Avenue (Figure 4.7). Not all the white home buyers are in the highest income category—37 percent of whites buying in the eastern part of West Town have either low, moderate, or middle incomes, and 68 percent of whites buying in the western part of West Town are not in the highest income bracket (Federal Financial Institutions Examination Council 1993–1998, author's calculations).

North of Humboldt Park and West Town is the Logan Square community area. According to one real estate map, published by Kahn Realty, the Logan Square/Palmer Square neighborhood begins at the western edge of Bucktown and ends just short of the western edge of the boundary line given to the Logan Square community area by Burgess and his research associates in the 1920s. According to *Living in Greater Chicago* (Meyers 1999–2000), Logan Square is the fifth largest community area geographically. It creates problems for the real estate market because of its large size and because its major features are its squares linked by boulevards. It is around these squares and along these boulevards that upper-income people are most likely to buy homes. As a result of this linear pattern of "gentry" settlement, Logan Square does not manifest the same sort of intense market activity as its neighbors to the south and east. And the part of Logan Square identified by Kahn Realty does not show as stark a difference in the level of upper-income buying activity from the rest of Logan Square to the west (Figure 4.8).[7]

Western Avenue clearly plays a significant role in concentrating the buying activity of upper-income home buyers between North and Chicago

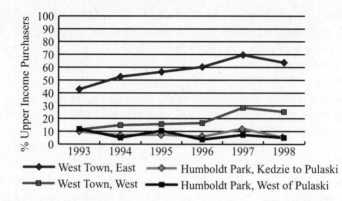

Figure 4.6. Class change, Near Northwest Side home purchasers, 1993–1998.
Source: Federal Financial Institutions Examination Council 1993–1998.

Avenues. It is also clear that though Western Avenue by no means constitutes a major physical barrier for anyone who wishes to cross it, it is a
well-accepted boundary that even Hunter's research in the late 1960s recognized. There is then a very rational story that could be told about Western Avenue and the neighborhoods on either side of it. The neighborhoods
east of it are recognizable communities with a certain history and culture,
and a certain building type, all of which are very appealing to an upper-
income home buyer. But why all the focus on the neighborhoods to the
east of Western Avenue? The answer lies deeply ingrained in the culture
of the real estate industry. Homogeneity, even in a physically diverse

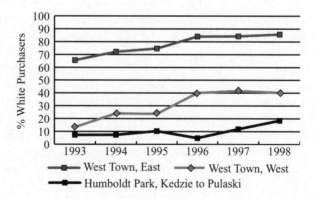

Figure 4.7. Ethnic change, Near Northwest Side home purchasers, 1993–1998. Source: Federal Financial Institutions
Examination Council 1993–1998.

urban area such as the Near Northwest Side, is paramount. And homogeneity requires boundaries, especially in a physically diverse urban area. Without boundaries one cannot create a homogeneous area, or the illusion of a homogeneous area, because only boundaries can serve to exclude and include. Additionally, to get the support of loan capital, buyers seeking to rehabilitate a home in an impoverished area can justify the expenditure only if it is a part of a general process in which structures in the neighborhood are becoming "competitive" with already gentrified neighborhoods. To be deemed competitive, a neighborhood must appeal to the same set of buyers to which a gentrified neighborhood appeals. Thus, by definition, loan capital assumes gentrification when it supports home buyers in their efforts to improve a particular home.[8]

Conclusion

Real estate brokers and appraisers both require neighborhood boundaries for what they do. The evidence from the Near Northwest and Southwest Sides of Chicago suggest that in the turbulence of ethnic succession and gentrification there is a consensus on what the boundaries of a particular neighborhood are. In essence, the market for homes is not one in which each home is treated as an individual unit on a particular plot of land, it is one in which the home is treated as part and parcel of and an entrée into a neighborhood.[9] The practice of demarcating a neighborhood is, therefore, a form of market coordination—the greater the consensus on the boundaries the greater the coordination. And the greater the coordination the greater the ability of the real estate industry to promote what it values—homogeneity.

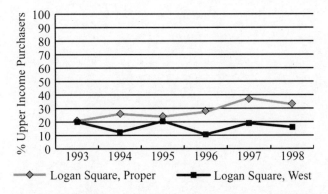

Figure 4.8. Class stability, Logan Square home purchasers, 1993–1998. Source: Federal Financial Institutions Examination Council 1993–1998.

But one could always argue that the real estate brokers and appraisers are simply describing and acting on what they observe. This account assumes a passive role on the part of brokers and appraisers. Yet the evidence is clear that they are active agents in the process. In the case of gentrification on the Near Northwest Side it was up to the appraiser to come up with the comparables from the DePaul neighborhood to justify a loan in Bucktown. In the case of ethnic succession we saw that neighborhoods on the Southwest Side with a very small Hispanic population in 1990 nevertheless had home buyer markets dominated by Hispanics in 1993; can we attribute this solely to home buyer preferences, particularly the preferences of whites? Furthermore, the fact that people do not, in their everyday lives, necessarily stay within prescribed boundaries belies the neat order of the city that brokers and appraisers impose on it. But it *is* likely that, through the way the processes of ethnic succession and gentrification play out, people will end up being more likely to conform to the boundaries drawn for them, because the processes exacerbate the differences on either side of them. This is not to say that brokers and appraisers completely control and structure the market, but they do have an active role. And that active role is informed by the way the real estate professionals think about neighborhoods in general. Thus, even if they are in the process of exploring a market to understand what is happening in it, the focus of their exploration is explicitly for class signals, and implicitly for racial and ethnic signals. It is those signals that lead them to draw the boundary lines that they do. To put this in terms of social and abstract space: people produce social space along a number of dimensions through their everyday activities, but real estate professionals abstract from that social space along class, race, and ethnic dimensions.

5

Lending Discrimination

W e now have a clear picture of how the rules, networks, and space in which lenders are embedded inform the way they construct risk, in terms of risk assessment, management, and self-fulfilling prophecies. One purpose of elaborating this framework is to provide an alternative approach to understanding the persistent phenomenon of racial disparities in the distribution of home mortgage loans. In this chapter I employ the framework I have developed to explain these disparities, once again using Chicago as my example. I begin by delineating Chicago into broad submarkets, go on to describe the way networks of relations between real estate brokers and loan officers structure the flow of mortgage applications from the different submarkets, and then focus on two issues that arise from a close examination of racial disparities in application approval and denial rates. Before embarking on this analysis, however, I want to summarize the current state of the debate about lending discrimination in more detail than I have previously, and reiterate the way in which my approach cuts across this debate.

Discrimination Studies and Theories of Discrimination

Racial or ethnic discrimination in the mortgage loan application process occurs when an employee of a financial institution makes a decision about the application that takes into account the race or ethnicity of the applicant or the neighborhood in which she is buying a home. Numerous quantitative studies have attempted to detect and/or explain lending disparities between white home buyers and minorities. Up until the 1990s these studies were plagued by inadequate data—though they showed patterns consistent with discrimination they could always be criticized for not taking into account factors correlated with race that a lender could legitimately consider in making a decision.[1] But in the 1990s the evidence showing discrimination became much stronger as a result of the 1989 amendments to the Home Mortgage Disclosure Act. This act required lenders to provide the federal government with information on the race, gender, income, and census tract location of all the home loan applications they received each year, beginning in 1990. The amendments also required that the lenders report the disposition of each application—whether it was approved, approved but not accepted, denied, withdrawn, or closed out because of incomplete information. The data have consistently shown that minority and lower-income applicants are more likely to be denied a loan. Nationally during the mid-1990s, the period for which the best data are available, the black denial rate on applications to prime lenders for conventional home purchase loans was over 2 times that of whites. The denial rate for Hispanics was about 1.75 times that of whites during the mid-1990s; and the denial rate for low- and moderate-income applicants ranged between 2.3 and 3.2 times that of high-income applicants (Scheessele 1999, author's calculations).[2] The data have been especially striking with regard to blacks—even the highest-income applicants are denied at rates higher than those for lower-income whites. For example, during the mid-1990s, the average denial rate for high-income blacks was 1.6 times that for low- and moderate-income whites.[3]

The data have sparked a cottage industry of analysts who have argued back and forth over the validity of any conclusions drawn from them. In 1992 the Boston Federal Reserve attempted a conclusive test of whether minorities suffer discrimination during the loan application process. Its analysts examined the decisions of mortgage lenders in the Boston Metropolitan Area using additional data, not available under HMDA, which included information on a large number of variables that lenders normally considered when underwriting a loan application. Their analysis showed that even after controlling for these variables, blacks and Hispanics were

more likely to be denied a loan than whites. For many the study was conclusive evidence that lenders discriminate. For others it simply raised more
questions about missing variables and the integrity of the research itself.

One of the consequences of the Boston Federal Reserve study has
been to prompt economists to pay more attention to the ways discrimination might occur. There are two prevalent hypotheses about why discrimination can take place: (a) the lender prefers to discriminate; (b) the
lender has less relevant information about minorities than it does about
white applicants, and this affects the outcomes of its decisions about minority applicants.

A corollary of the first hypothesis, attributable to Becker (1993), is
that lenders who indulge their preference for discrimination will make less
profits than those who do not because the preference will lead the former
to miss profitable loan opportunities. One line of research resulting from
this reasoning is the investigation of whether minorities default on their
loans at a greater or lesser rate than whites, where the hypothesis is that
minorities default at a lower rate because discrimination restricts lenders
to making only the most profitable loans. There are numerous problems
with these studies, but, most important, the direct, negative correlation between minority default rates and discrimination against minority loan applicants is not valid. As Ferguson and Peters (1995) and Tootell (1993)
argue, it may be the case that lenders discriminate against minorities, but
minority borrowers default more than whites because, on average, approved minority borrowers are less creditworthy. This lower average
creditworthiness says nothing about the creditworthiness of the marginal
minority applicants in contrast to the marginal nonminority applicants,
which is where discrimination is most likely to take place.[4]

The second theoretical approach to discrimination is to think of it as
resulting from information problems. Conventional definitions of statistical discrimination posit that a lender, lacking complete information about
a borrower, will resort to cheap proxies for the missing information, such
as the race of the applicant. Minority applicants suffer because their racial
status is correlated with information that demonstrates that they are less
creditworthy than whites. The cultural affinity hypothesis, which is also
premised on the idea of imperfect information, identifies a different mechanism by which discrimination takes place: employees of a lender who
have a cultural affinity with the applicant have more information about
that applicant than they do about an applicant with whom they do not
have an affinity, given the expenditure of the same screening costs
(Calomiris, Kahn, and Longhofer 1994; Ferguson and Peters 1995 and
1997; Hunter and Walker 1996; Longhofer 1996).[5] The variation in the ac-

curacy of the information available to the decision-maker about the applicants leads to variation in the results of decisions he makes about those applicants. For discrimination to occur on the basis of cultural affinity it is
not necessary for the decision-maker to know the race or ethnicity of the
loan applicant (Ferguson and Peters 1997, 157); it simply must be the case
that the information in minority loan application files is different from that
contained in the files of white applicants.

Whether minorities experience a disparate impact as a result of a
lesser cultural affinity between a loan applicant and a decision-maker or
not is contingent on three factors: the extent to which the decision-maker
makes more or less errors in his decisions about different racial and ethnic
groups; the distribution of creditworthiness within the different groups;
and the relationship between the average creditworthiness of each racial
group and the cut-off point the decision-maker applies to applicants (ibid.,
160). It is possible for minorities to benefit from greater decision-making
errors owing to a lack of cultural affinity between the decision-maker
and the applicant if minorities have a lower average credit score than the
decision-maker's cut-off point (assuming a normal distribution of applicants across the range of credit scores).[6] It is also possible that the cultural
affinity effect counteracts the effects of either a straightforward preference for discrimination or statistical discrimination (ibid.).

The statistical discrimination and cultural affinity theories both identify the problems that incomplete information can create for minority loan
applicants. They offer critical insights into how the cost of gathering information can undermine a lender's ability to make a good decision. One
point they do not address in any detail is where the lack of affinity comes
from and, as a result, where the information problems that plague the underwriting decision come from.[7] This is because their focus remains on the
screen of the lending decision rather than the process by which a loan application is put together and how it affects and is affected by the working
of the screen.[8] Furthermore, they do not question whether the screen the
lender is using is valid—it is assumed to be so.

I have argued that the only way to understand the loan decision is to
understand the context in which it takes place, described in terms of the
concepts of rules, networks, and the production of space. This argument
applies directly to the issue of racial disparities in loan approvals. There is
no assumption here that there are objective decision-making criteria, but
there is an assumption that such disparities are indicative of a failure of the
loan process, and of the social structure of which it is a part and which it
helps to construct. What I try to show in the next section is in what ways
the lending industry fails to serve a large segment of the population.

Chicago's Housing Submarkets   *159*

To organize the analysis of how lenders fail minorities in the loan application process, I have divided Chicago up into seven distinct housing submarkets: White ethnic, Core Hispanic, Expanding Hispanic, Gentrifying,
Black middle-class, Black working-class, and Devastated black (Figure
5.1). These submarkets contain a number of complete community areas
and neighborhoods. The delineation of submarkets is based primarily on
race and ethnicity. The white, black, and Hispanic areas were over 80 percent white, black, and Hispanic respectively in 1990 according to the U.S.
Census Bureau. The areas identified as "Expanding Hispanic" were white
areas which experienced an increase in Hispanic population of over 20
percent between 1980 and 1990. The gentrifying market is racially more
heterogeneous, and the definition of its borders is based on various real estate sources (including interviews) which clearly identify them as encompassing a distinct housing market. The distinction between different black
neighborhoods is based on real estate sources, and income and land value
differences.[9] As is apparent in Figure 5.1 the market delineations listed are

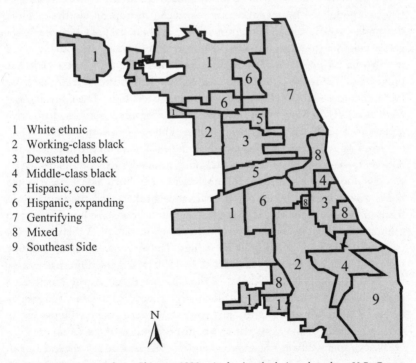

1 White ethnic
2 Working-class black
3 Devastated black
4 Middle-class black
5 Hispanic, core
6 Hispanic, expanding
7 Gentrifying
8 Mixed
9 Southeast Side

Figure 5.1. Housing markets, Chicago, 1990s. Author's calculations based on U.S. Census
Bureau, 1990.

not necessarily one continuous area—some are two areas sharing common characteristics.

The figure shows two sets of neighborhoods, the Southeast Side and "Mixed" areas, that I have omitted from the analysis that follows, though I have included data on them. I chose to classify the Southeast Side as an entity unto itself because it is a microcosm of the city at large, encompassing black, Hispanic, and white neighborhoods, but geographically separated from the rest of the city. The neighborhoods classified as "Mixed" are stable, integrated areas where there is microlevel segregation that cannot be captured by census tract–level data. The Hyde Park–Kenwood neighborhood on the south lakefront is an example of the former, while the Bridgeport, Canaryville, and Chinatown neighborhoods southwest of downtown are examples of the latter. Included in the "Mixed" category is downtown, which is dominated by commercial buildings.

Table 5.1 contains demographic data from the 1990 census on each submarket as well as 1990 land value data.[10] A short description of each submarket as it was in 1990 follows.

White ethnic. These are areas on the Southwest and Northwest Sides of Chicago populated by recent and not-so-recent European immigrants and descendants of European immigrants. They are both part of Chicago's "bungalow belt," located near airports—Midway and O'Hare respectively—and in 1990 had a predominantly white population. The Northwest Side has higher land values, ranging from approximately $500 to $1,200 per front foot as compared to $500 to $700 on the Southwest Side. The *Chicago House Hunt Book, 1990* (Meyers and DeBat 1990) identified both as distinctive areas and described a variety of specific neighborhoods within each.

Gentrifying. The area is bounded by the city limits on the north, by the lake on the east, by the Loop on the south, and, with exceptions, by Western Avenue on the west. In defining these neighborhoods I have relied most heavily on the definitions of real estate brokers and the land values maps. The reason for this is that these neighborhoods are less likely than others to be homogeneous in terms of race or income.[11] A distinguishing feature of this area is its high land values. These were as high as $10,000 per front foot right on the lake front in 1990, though within a very few blocks dropping below $700 east of the Chicago River. At the North End of the city where the Northwest Side market borders the gentrifying market, land values dipped slightly just west of Western Avenue before rising as they neared the lake. Further south, just northwest of the Loop, they increased dramatically as one moved from the Hispanic areas around Logan Square and Humboldt Park to those that were gentrifying just to the east.

Black. The black areas of the city are delineated solely on the basis of

Table 5.1. Chicago housing markets demographics, 1990

Markets	Population	% Black	% Hispanic	% White	% Other	Land values (per front foot)
Black						
Devastated	255,133	96	3	1	0	$100–$250
Working-class	477,991	96	2	2	0	$100–$250
Middle-class	170,901	95	2	3	0	$200–$600
Hispanic						
Core	213,245	10	79	11	0	$150–$300
Expanding	298,747	5	43	45	6	$200–$750
White ethnic	526,366	5	7	84	4	$500–$1000
Gentrifying	626,721	14	23	56	7	$700–$10,000
Other						
Mixed	125,636	27	8	53	11	n/a
Southeast Side	88,986	40	31	29	0	$100–$250
TOTAL	2,783,726	39	19	38	4	

Note: Black, other, and white are non-Hispanic.
Source: U.S. Bureau of Census 1990; Olcott and Co. 1990.

race. This is because, in 1990, the areas in which blacks constituted over 80 percent of the population were heterogeneous in terms of income, land values, and whether they were recognized as viable housing markets by real estate specialists. At least three different types of market exist within the predominantly black areas of the city. First, there are the most devastated areas, plagued by vacant lots and abandoned buildings. These are the city's poorest neighborhoods. They are also home to the Chicago Housing Authority's very large housing projects, which were built in the postwar era in a manner designed to segregate blacks and whites, and are now in the process of being torn down. The second type of black housing market encompasses the neighborhoods identified as being the bastions of the black middle class. Third, there are those neighborhoods not fitting into either of the other two categories that constitute the working-class market area.

The middle-class submarket is distinct from the working-class and devastated areas in two ways. First, it generally has higher land values. In 1990 land values ranged from $200 to $600 per front foot east of the Dan Ryan Expressway on the Southeast Side. In South Shore, which is included in the middle-class market area, values went up to $600 for lots overlooking Jackson Park. The Douglas Park/The Gap neighborhood, which is surrounded by the most devastated part of the South Side, has values of $200 to $500 per front foot as a result of low-level rehabilitation and the presence of the middle-class high-rise buildings of Prairie Shores and Lake Meadows. The other black areas had land values ranging from $100 to $250. There are two exceptions to this: the northern part of Austin, on the Northwest Side, where land values were almost $400; and the Kenwood-Oakland area right on the lakefront, which has been the subject of speculation for years. The other distinguishing feature of the middle-class areas is that they were recognized as being distinct in the CHHB (1990) — each neighborhood was named and described. The rest of the black South and West Sides were not deemed to constitute a housing market.[12]

Hispanic and Expanding Hispanic areas. There are two types of area in which Hispanics live: the core areas where Hispanics make up a majority of the population, and those areas into which they moved between 1980 and 1990. This pattern exists on both the Southwest and Northwest Sides of the city, with the cores being respectively Little Village and Pilsen on the one side, and Humboldt Park and parts of Logan Square on the other. The areas I have designated as Expanding Hispanic are those that experienced an increase in the proportion of the population that is Hispanic to over 20 percent from 1980 to 1990. These extend northwest and southwest from their respective core areas. I distinguish these areas from others in the city predominantly on the basis of ethnicity, though it is striking to note that land values drop sharply as one moves from white or gentrifying blocks to those where Hispanics live.

Market Boundaries and Lender Networks

These different housing submarkets are served by different mixes of lenders and different mixes of loan product. For a start there is a large difference in the number of branches of depository institutions located in each submarket (Figure 5.2 and Table 5.2). For example, despite a net gain of 6 branches in the black devastated market between 1993 and 1998, the number of people per branch in this market was still almost 7 times as high as the number of people per branch in the white market in 1998. Overall the black markets had fewer branches for their population size than did the Hispanic markets, and the white and gentrifying markets had the most branches for their population size. Historically, mortgage banks, which do not take deposits and are largely unregulated (especially at the federal level), have served the black markets (Dunham 1991). In the

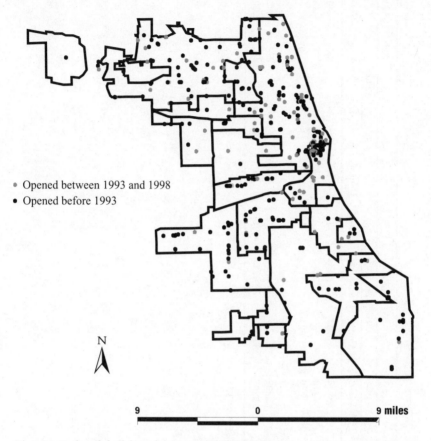

● Opened between 1993 and 1998
● Opened before 1993

N

9   0   9 **miles**

Figure 5.2. Bank and thrift branch locations, Chicago, 1998. Source: Federal Deposit Insurance Corporation 2000.

1990s the black housing submarkets were disproportionately served by mortgage banks making prime loans and by subprime lenders (Table 5.3). About 40 percent of loans for home purchases for owner occupancy made by prime lenders in the devastated and middle-class black markets were made by mortgage banks, and 53 percent of loans made in the working-class black market were made by mortgage banks, as compared to a city average of 29 percent. In recent years, especially in 1997 and 1998, subprime lenders have targeted the black markets disproportionately. In the 1993–96 period, 4 to 6 percent of loans made in the black markets were made by subprime lenders; in the 1997–98 period, such loans rose to 12 to 16 percent. These figures compare to 2 percent for the whole city in the

Table 5.2. Distribution of bank and thrift branches, Chicago, 1993–1998

| | Markets | | | | | | | | | |
| | Black | | | Hispanic | | White ethnic | Gentrifying | Other | | Total |
	Devastated	Working-class	Middle-class	Core	Expanding			Mixed	Southeast	
1993	3	9	14	23	39	115	98	84	17	402
1998	9	14	14	25	38	125	121	93	17	456
Gain/loss 1993–98	6	5	0	2	−1	10	23	9	0	54
Population per branch										
1993	85,044	53,110	12,207	9,272	7,660	4,577	6,395	1,496	5,234	6,925
1998	28,348	34,142	12,207	8,530	7,862	4,211	5,180	1,351	5,234	6,105

Source: Federal Deposit Insurance Corporation 2000, author's calculations.

Table 5.5. Distribution of home purchase loans by market, loan type, and lender, 1993–1998

| | Black | | | Hispanic | | White | | Other | | |
Loans	Devastated	Working-class	Middle-class	Core	Expanding	ethnic	Gentrifying	Mixed	Southeast	Total
Loans by type										
Conventional	1,755	4,916	2,421	2,997	8,739	33,476	48,511	7,771	1,900	112,486
	52%	40%	56%	53%	51%	78%	94%	91%	52%	75%
FHA	1,485	6,504	1,693	2,640	8,123	8,749	2,961	681	1,639	34,475
	44%	54%	39%	46%	48%	20%	6%	8%	45%	23%
Other	122	722	205	52	209	885	230	103	143	2,671
	4%	6%	5%	1%	1%	2%	0%	1%	4%	2%
TOTAL	3,362	12,142	4,319	5,689	17,071	43,110	51,702	8,555	3,682	149,632
Loans by lender										
Prime										
Depository	1,828	5,124	2,441	3,512	10,121	29,656	42,039	6,380	2,164	103,265
% of prime loans	60%	47%	61%	64%	61%	71%	83%	76%	62%	71%
Mortgage bank	1,226	5,889	1,578	1,999	6,512	12,170	8,547	1,965	1,307	41,193
% of prime loans	40%	53%	39%	36%	39%	29%	17%	24%	38%	29%
TOTAL	3,054	11,013	4,019	5,511	16,633	41,826	50,586	8,345	3,471	144,458
% of total loans	91%	91%	93%	97%	97%	97%	98%	98%	94%	97%
Subprime										
Depository	40	152	49	36	109	430	358	62	32	1,268
% of subprime loans	13%	13%	16%	20%	25%	33%	32%	30%	15%	25%
Mortgage bank	268	977	251	142	329	854	758	148	179	3906
% of subprime loans	87%	87%	84%	80%	75%	67%	68%	70%	85%	75%
TOTAL	308	1,129	300	178	438	1,284	1,116	210	211	5,174
% of total loans	9%	9%	7%	3%	3%	3%	2%	2%	6%	3%

Source: Federal Financial Institutions Examination Council 1993–1998, author's calculations.

1993–96 period and 6 percent in the 1997–98 period. Within the prime market, black markets disproportionately receive FHA-insured loans. In the 1993–98 period, 44 percent of loans made in the devastated, 54 percent of loans made in the working-class, and 42 percent of loans made in the middle-class black markets were FHA-insured, while the city average was 24 percent.

The Hispanic markets, which are home to a large number of depository institution branches, are also more likely to be served by mortgage banks, but have not been targeted by subprime lenders. In the 1993–98 period mortgage banks made 36 percent of the home purchase loans in the core Hispanic market and 39 percent in the expanding Hispanic market. FHA loans also figured heavily in these markets: 46 percent of loans made in the core Hispanic market and 48 percent of those made in the expanding Hispanic market were FHA loans. In contrast, the white and gentrifying markets are largely served by depository institutions originating conventional loans. In the white market 71 percent of loans made in the 1993–98 period were made by depository institutions; furthermore this number is higher for white borrowers within the white market, who received 77 percent of their loans from depository institutions. Twenty percent of loans in the white market were FHA loans, and only 9 percent of white borrowers within this market received FHA loans. In the gentrifying market, depository institutions made 83 percent of the loans, and only 6 percent of the loans were FHA-insured.

This is the broad structure of the lending market in Chicago, and it looks like a story of differential branch distribution on the part of depository institutions and differences in the willingness and ability of all lenders to offer products that suit the different markets and people of different races within those markets. But this is not the whole story. For example, there are a large number of bank branches in the Hispanic markets, but mortgage banks seem to be able to compete effectively in those markets. How do they do this? The place to look is in the lending process itself, and, in particular, the network relationship between the real estate broker and the loan officer, which is the key link between a lender and a particular housing market.

Different real estate brokers serve different markets. In my interviews with black brokers, they acknowledged that almost all their clients are black, and that they largely serve the black neighborhoods of Chicago and its increasingly black suburbs to the south of the city. In the same way, real estate brokers with offices located along the North Side lakefront serve the neighborhoods fronting the lake, and also the gentrifying neighborhoods to the west. Though efforts have been made to eliminate racial bias in real estate advertisements by ensuring that photographs of prospective buyers include people of different races, there is no way around the fact that real estate brokers and salespersons of different races serve different markets. For example, in the magazine *Living in Greater Chicago* among the descriptions of different neighborhoods and suburbs there is the occasional photograph of a real estate salesperson. The race or the ethnicity of the salesperson corresponds to the racial composition of the neighborhood or suburb. As was noted in chapter 3, loan officers market their loan products by building relationships with real estate brokers. In a racially segregated and class segregated city, people of different races and classes will meet with and work with different real estate brokers and, therefore, different loan officers.

The Home Mortgage Disclosure Act provides evidence for the widespread existence of these networks. I compared the market shares of all those lenders who took more than 1 percent of the loan applications made by mortgage lenders between 1993 and 1998 in different markets within the city, using a dissimilarity index that has traditionally been used to measure spatial segregation.[13]

In this case, I measured institutional segregation but the idea is the same: it is a measure of the extent to which loan applicants in different markets would have to apply to a different lender for a loan in order for each lender in one market to have the same market share in another market. I particularly focused on mortgage banks, which are the least regulated institutions in the market and also have had a track record of serving a wide variety of markets. The results show that different mortgage banks serve different markets. Different mortgage banks are active in the black markets from those in the Hispanic markets, while the Hispanic markets themselves, the core and the expanding markets, are served in the same way by the same mortgage bankers. Forty-six percent of loan applicants in the working-class black market would have had to have applied for a loan to a different mortgage banker in order for that market to have been served in the same way by the same mortgage bankers that served the core Hispanic market. The same is true for the expanding Hispanic market. In contrast, the core and expanding Hispanic markets are served in almost exactly the same way—the dissimilarity index for the two markets is only 8. Furthermore, the dissimilarity index for depository institutions is far lower when one compares the working-class black and the Hispanic markets. And the dissimilarity index for top mortgage bankers serving the working-class and middle-class black markets is only 17.

When the black markets as a whole are compared with the gentrifying market the results are equally as clear. The dissimilarity index between the black and gentrifying markets is 48, for mortgage bankers with more than 1 percent of the market. In other words, 48 percent of loan applicants in the black markets would have had to have switched lenders in order for those markets to have been served in the same way by the same mortgage bankers as in the gentrifying market. In contrast, the depository institution dissimilarity index for the two markets is 24. When the black markets as a whole are compared with the white market, the results show how lender networks can cross existing neighborhood boundaries. The dissimilarity index between the black markets and the white market, for all applicants regardless of race, is 35 for mortgage banks with more than 1 percent of the market. Just over 2,400 black home buyers applied for loans to mortgage banks with a market share greater than 1 percent in the white market areas between 1993 and 1998. The dissimilarity index between the black markets and the white markets for black applicants is only 18. In other words, the same mortgage bankers are serving blacks in the black markets and blacks in the white market. In contrast, the dissimilarity index between black applicants in the black market and white applicants in the white market is 45, and the index between the latter and black applicants in the white market is 40.

In the same way, Hispanic loan applicants crossing market boundaries are doing so with lenders from the core Hispanic neighborhoods in tow. The dissimilarity index between Hispanics applying for loans in Hispanic neighborhoods and those applying for loans in white ethnic neighborhoods is only 13, for mortgage banks with over 1 percent of market share, while the index between Hispanics and whites applying in the white ethnic market is 28, and the index for Hispanics applying in Hispanic neighborhoods and whites applying in white neighborhoods is 38.

On the face of it, it is surprising that depository institutions with branches predominantly in the white, Hispanic, and gentrifying markets were able during the mid-1990s to have more equal shares of the market in all parts of the city than mortgage bankers. One might assume that the presence of a branch in a particular neighborhood would bias the institution toward a disproportionate market share in that area. Of course the comparisons I made were only for those lenders with the largest market share, greater than 1 percent, and the market share calculations were based on each institution's share of the depository institution market only. Nevertheless, the contrast with the mortgage bankers is striking. In the 1990s depository institutions have been under regulatory pressure to ensure that they serve all parts of the city. This is the result of a combination of two factors: (1) the new Community Reinvestment Act regulations, which are much more results-oriented; and (2) the high level of merger activity, which has given leverage to community groups to demand equal treatment of minority communities because banks have to have a good rating under the Community Reinvestment Act if the regulators are to allow them to merge. As a result, there is a group of large depository institutions that serve the whole city and dominate each individual market to the point that local depository institutions have little impact, overall, on the pattern of lending.

Mortgage banks on the other hand, are largely unregulated and are not required to comply with the CRA. Furthermore, though they often do not have branch locations, mortgage banks are no less beholden to market boundary lines than are depository institutions with branch networks, because they rely on real estate brokers to refer clients to them. Real estate brokers operating within certain market boundaries will refer clients purchasing homes within those boundaries, thus tying the mortgage banker to a particular market area. In a situation where real estate brokers are crossing established market boundaries, as in the case of blacks or Hispanics entering the white ethnic market, mortgage bankers will also cross those boundaries but not necessarily cross over from one racial group of applicants to another. So you can have a situation where applicants of the same race on different sides of a market boundary are served by the same mix of mortgage bankers, but applicants of different races on the same side of a market boundary are served largely by different mortgage bankers.

The network relationships that link lenders with a particular market are not ironclad. The advent of subprime lending in the black markets, documented in Table 5.3, shows that a product that provides an alternative to the strictures of the conventional and FHA loan products can quickly establish a market presence. It is likely that these subprime lenders are entering the markets through mortgage brokers who may already be established in the markets. A review of the 1998/9 Yellow Pages revealed that very few subprime lenders advertise there.[14] So mortgage brokers, who can switch between lenders while maintaining existing market relationships with real estate brokers, can undo the link between a lender and the market. Furthermore, as noted in the previous chapter, loan officers can change lenders while maintaining their relationships with real estate brokers and, as a result, bring a new lender into the market. Nevertheless, the structured nature of the lending market has some important implications for the social construction of risk and an understanding of how racial discrimination can take place.

Table 5.4. Home purchase approval and denial rates by lender type, income, race, and loan type, Chicago, 1993–1998

Institution type	Applicant		Conventional, Prime		FHA	
	Income	Race	Approval rate (%)	Denial rate (%)	Approval rate (%)	Denial rate (%)
Depository	Low–Mod	Black	62	25	71	15
		Hispanic	79	13	81	9
		White ethnic	82	10	78	12
	Low–Mod total		77	14	76	12
	Middle	Black	67	19	76	13
		Hispanic	80	12	85	7
		White ethnic	84	7	83	8
	Middle total		81	10	82	9
	High	Black	68	17	77	11
		Hispanic	78	12	84	9
		White ethnic	84	6	81	7
	High total		82	7	81	9
Mortgage bank	Low–Mod	Black	62	18	72	13
		Hispanic	79	11	86	6
		White ethnic	80	9	78	10
	Low–Mod total		75	12	78	10
	Middle	Black	65	16	78	9
		Hispanic	80	10	89	5
		White ethnic	82	8	86	5
	Middle total		78	10	84	7
	High	Black	65	13	78	11
		Hispanic	71	13	88	4
		White ethnic	82	7	82	6
	High total		79	8	83	7
GRAND TOTAL			80	10	80	10

Source: Federal Financial Institutions Examination Council 1993–1998, author's calculations.

Racial Disparities in Denial Rates in the Context of a Structured Housing Market

In the Chicago housing market, black applicants are far more likely to fail to get a loan than are either white or Hispanic (or Asian) applicants. This is true even if one takes into account the income of the applicant,[15] the type of lending institution making the decision, and the type of loan applied for (Table 5.4).[16] The traditional way to think about this disparity in approval rates is as the result of one of two factors: the failure of more black applicants to meet the loan criteria, and discrimination in the loan application process. Then, traditionally, all the work goes into trying to figure out whether the problem is simply a failure to meet the loan criteria or whether discrimination is at play. Meanwhile, blacks continue to be denied loans.

Another way to think about the disparity is to think of it as the failure of the process to see a black application through to an approval. Within the spatial context of segregated housing markets this does not mean that we can simply blame the loan officer, because a minority applicant is likely to apply through a minority loan officer, and the latter is likely to have an incentive to see the loan get approved. Within the black community, for example, real estate brokers seek out loan officers who, as one broker told me, are able to deal with "blacks and their culture" (reb. 16). Another broker noted: "Most loan officers we deal with are African American . . . they understand what we face . . . therefore an African American can relate better than a white loan officer" (reb. 13). The loan officer has every incentive to make the loan application as good a package as possible so that it can survive the underwriting process, especially if a large portion of his clients are minorities. On the other hand, the underwriter is unlikely to be specifically assigned to minority loan applications and neighborhoods. The applicant's failure to get a loan is a result of the failure of the process in which a good risk profile is generated. The minority applicant's failure to get a loan can be seen, in part, as a failure of a minority loan officer and an underwriter to see the applicant in the same way. Does this mean that the underwriter is solely to blame? Not necessarily, because the loan application process is complicated and the spatial context in which it takes place matters. Let me illustrate this by looking at two phenomena that underlie the racial disparity data: the overwhelming role of credit as a reason why black applicants are denied loans; and the disparity in black approval rates across different housing markets.

Credit and Discrimination

The most important information over which the loan officer has the least control in preparing the loan application for underwriting is the credit report. Not surprisingly, black applicants are disproportionately denied loans by mortgage lenders for reasons of credit: 38 percent of black loan denials were for reasons of credit, while only 27 percent of Hispanic denials and 22 percent of white denials were (Table 5.5). There are two reasons why, of all pieces of information in the loan file, the loan officer has the least control over the credit report. First, he may not have full information about its content at the time of the application, which means that he and the underwriter are looking at different credit profiles. Their disagreement is one over the facts. Second, the credit report requires more

Table 5.5. Reasons for denial by race of applicant, all prime loans, Chicago, 1993–1998

Race of applicant	Reason for denial (%)				Total
	Income	Credit	Collateral	Other	
Black	24	39	6	30	100
Hispanic	32	29	9	31	100
White ethnic	34	23	10	33	100

Source: Federal Financial Institutions Examination Council 1993–1998, author's calculations.

interpretation on the part of the underwriter than do the other credit factors—there is greater room for disagreement. Table 5.5 also includes information on the rate at which applicants are denied for reasons of income, in essence the failure to meet the ratios criteria. These data show that a loan officer cannot fully anticipate what the applicant's final ratios will be once all the information is in the file. In part this is also a problem resulting from the credit report—a full report may show additional debt obligations that increase the back-end ratio (the ratio of housing expense plus other debt obligations) over the threshold set by the underwriting guidelines. It may also be a product of a number of other factors including errors on the part of a loan officer, an applicant who misstated her income, or a difference in interpretation as to what counted as income. In the case of white and Hispanic applicants, 34 percent and 32 percent of applications fail because of problems with the ratios; for black applicants the percentage is less but only because of the inflated number of denials for reasons of credit—if we stipulate that only 23 percent of black denials are for reasons of credit, the black denials resulting from problems with ratios would be 31 percent of the total denials. To the extent that the ratios data show that applicants of all races experience the process in much the same way, it is likely that the special problems that black applicants face with regard to their credit is, at least in part, a result of problems with the interpretation of the information.

One would assume that this problem would manifest itself only when the loan file was manually underwritten; credit scoring or automated underwriting should take care of the problem of interpretation. But the data show that black applicants were disproportionately denied for reasons of credit even after the introduction of credit scores in the mid-1990s. As I described in chapter 3 the underwriter still has the discretion as to whether to work the deal or not in a situation where she uses credit scores in her underwriting of the file, and this may be behind this phenomenon.

But there is also a broader structural problem with credit scores, which   *173*
captures the essence of how lenders' perceptions of risk are a self-supporting social construct.

Credit scores predict the likelihood of default. The higher the score of
an individual the lower the likelihood that he will default on his loan; the
lower the score the higher the likelihood.[17] Setting aside the methodological validity of the model used to construct credit scores, let us examine the
implications of credit scoring in the light of what we know about the correlation of credit scores with the race and income of the individual and the
type of neighborhood in which he lives. In a report to the U.S. Senate regarding automated underwriting, Freddie Mac freely admitted that black
and Hispanic borrowers whose loans they had bought had lower FICO
scores.

> Black borrowers, for example, were about three times as likely to have high-
> risk credit-bureau scores—defined as FICO scores below 620—as were
> white borrowers, based on Freddie Mac's 1994 mortgage purchases. His-
> panic borrowers were about twice as likely as white borrowers to have high-
> risk scores. (1996a, chapter 6)

But what information are credit scores picking up? Avery et al. analyzed
the 1996 credit bureau scores of all individuals and households living in
994 randomly selected zip codes. Their data do not include individual-
level characteristics other than the credit bureau score and zip code location of the individual, but using these data they show that zip codes where
minorities make up more than 25 percent of the households have an average credit score of 706.4, comparing unfavorably to zip codes where less
than 5 percent of households are minority, which have an average score of
779.8. They also found that in zip codes where the median family income
is less than 80 percent of the MSA median income, the average credit bureau score is 722.8, compared to zip codes where the median family income is greater than 120 percent of the MSA median, which have an average credit bureau score of 803.4. They conclude: "Although bureau scores
are often developed without reference to local economic or broader regional information, our results suggest that they may be affected by such
factors" (2000, 544).

In other words credit scores pick up more than just the individual
characteristics of the applicant; they also pick up factors that would normally be considered to be out of the applicant's control. Not surprisingly,
according to Freddie Mac's data, credit scores are predictive of default on
home loans. Their charts in their report to the U.S. Senate show that the

relative foreclosure rate of blacks and Hispanics is almost twice as high as that of whites for those borrowers with scores in the 619 or less and 620 to 660 ranges, and more than twice as high for those in the 661 or greater range (Freddie Mac 1996a, chapter 6, exhibit 11). Freddie Mac did not control for any other credit factors, such as income or downpayment, in the analysis. Given the way that the lending industry understands and uses credit scores—as a separate piece of information in the underwriting process—these charts are insufficient to support Freddie Mac's contention that credit scores are equally predictive across race and income. But the way credit score data pick up causes and effects beyond the control of individuals living in a segregated society also points to a broader problem facing minorities.

Racial and ethnic segregation concentrates the number of low credit score individuals in particular neighborhoods, thus weakening the market for homes in those neighborhoods and increasing the likelihood of foreclosure for two reasons. First, the constraint on credit availability in the market due to the low average credit scores of prospective home buyers decreases the liquidity of the market. A home owner who runs into financial trouble in a strong housing market supported by a large number of mortgage lenders willing to originate loans to prospective buyers in that market can always sell the home to avoid a default.[18] In contrast, a home owner who is in financial trouble and tries to sell a home in a market where many buyers are denied financing is more likely to default on the loan. Thus segregation of people by race serves to exacerbate the problems created by discrimination against individuals in such a way that they affect the group as a whole. Second, the absence of a viable prime mortgage market opens the door for unscrupulous lending practices. The advent of subprime lending, which is often associated with unscrupulous, "predatory" practices, in the black housing markets is a manifestation of a chronic problem that these markets have faced over the years, namely, segregated black markets present themselves as a target for unscrupulous practices. Up until recently these unscrupulous practices have been carried out under the umbrella of the Federal Housing Administration. A study by the National Training and Information Center (1997) of 20 U.S. cities showed a concentration of defaulted FHA loans in a few census tracts, and showed in each city studied that a large number of the defaulted loans were originated by a select few lenders. The study concluded that high default rates in minority neighborhoods were a product of the unscrupulous practices of a particular set of lenders. In Chicago specifically, many of the high default rate census tracts were in the black markets, and the 10 worst lenders were responsible for 64.4 percent of FHA loans that were originated between January 1991 and December 1994 and went into default between January 1992 and December 1995 (ibid., A-18 to A-21).[19] A subsequent study on subprime lenders by the NTIC (2000) shows that they are largely responsible for mortgage loans that go into default within the first two years of the loan's life.

Beyond these factors internal to the housing market, segregation can compound the problems a minority individual faces in the labor market. Of particular significance is the effect of "cognitive maps" on the hiring decisions of employers (Tilly et al. 2000; Bluestone and Stevenson 2000). Based on interviews with representatives of 175 firms in four cities (Atlanta, Los Angeles, Detroit, and Boston) Tilly et al. reached the following conclusion: "Space is a signal to employers: they have well-formed perceptions of certain neighborhoods, and draw inferences about the quality of workers from those neighborhoods. These perceptions, in turn, are strongly colored by the actual or perceived racial (as well as class) composition of neighborhood residents" (2000, 3).

In other words, minorities living in segregated neighborhoods carry the stigma of their neighborhoods when seeking employment. These findings, along with those that show that a spatial mismatch between the location of employers and minority neighborhoods contribute to minority unemployment, highlight the circular self-destructive economic process that minorities must endure because of segregation (Mouw 2000).

The plight of black home buyers operating in a segregated housing market is symptomatic of the way in which the housing market as a whole is structured and sustains itself within that particular structure. Blacks, for both historical and contemporary reasons, have been the target of practices that undermine the viability of their housing market. In the same way, the white housing markets, and especially the gentrifying market, have been the target of practices that support the viability of those markets. There is no doubt that factors external to the housing market have had an impact on the relative viability of different housing markets—labor market conditions and differing educational achievements contribute to differences in the economic strength of different parts of the city. But there is a dynamic internal to the housing market itself that cannot be ignored. This dynamic is constituted by the drawing of spatial boundaries, the perpetuation of both positive and negative network relationships, and a lending process that favors one set of applicants over another on the basis of rules whose content is the product of a particular set of values developed within a particular institutional context. Furthermore, we cannot underestimate the role of segregation in perpetuating inequalities in other

Table 5.6. Black conventional prime loan applications by market area, Chicago, 1993–1998

Market	Applicant's income	Number of applications	Approval rate (%)	Denial rate (%)
Black	Low-Mod	5,505	60	24
	Middle	2,603	65	20
	High	1,601	64	18
	TOTAL	9,709	62	22
White ethnic	Low-Mod	960	71	18
	Middle	796	74	15
	High	680	74	12
	TOTAL	2,436	73	15
Gentrifying	Low-Mod	912	64	23
	Middle	612	67	18
	High	739	68	17
	TOTAL	2,263	66	20

Source: Federal Financial Institutions Examination Council 1993–1998, author's calculations.

parts of society through its impact on spatial maps and the "cognitive maps" employers use in hiring decisions.

Approval Rate Differences across Market Boundaries

The data show that depending on which submarket black applicants are buying in, their experience differs. Table 5.6 shows the approval and denial rates for black applicants in black, white, and gentrifying housing markets when applying for conventional loans to all prime lenders. Black applicants do best in white markets.[20] If, as the data on lender networks suggest, black applicants are being served by the same loan officers in the white markets as in the black markets, then it is not surprising that they do well in the former—they have the advantage of a loan officer working on their behalf. In contrast, black applicants in the gentrifying market do not do as well as in the white market. This is because black applicants in this market are less likely to be dealing with loan officers who normally take applications from such applicants—the gentrifying neighborhoods are both spatially and institutionally separate from the black housing market. Nevertheless, black applicants fare the worst in black markets, and that cannot be due simply to the fact that their applications are being submitted by sympathetic loan officers who are trying to make the deal work, but are being prevented from doing so by underwriters who are unsympathetic. Such loan officers are also operating in the white housing market.

Table 5.7. Average loan amount of black conventional applications by market area, Chicago, 1993–1998

Market	Applicant's income	Average loan amount ($)
Black	Low–Mod	60,610
	Middle	83,264
	High	123,274
	AVERAGE	77,017
White ethnic	Low–Mod	75,769
	Middle	103,546
	High	140,149
	AVERAGE	102,817
Gentrifying	Low–Mod	63,954
	Middle	100,814
	High	188,325
	AVERAGE	114,536
	OVERALL AVERAGE	87,272

Source: Federal Financial Institutions Examination Council 1993–1998, author's calculations.

The income of the applicants does not make a difference to the results. The obvious answer is that it has something to do with the appraisal. Lenders are not reporting appraisals as a problem, but one significant difference between the white and black markets is the average loan amount for which home buyers applied.

Within each income category, the average conventional loan amount applied for in the white market was 25 percent higher than in the black market for low-, moderate- and middle-income applicants and 14 percent higher for higher-income applicants (Table 5.7).[21] The differences were almost the same for FHA loan applications. What is probably going on in the black and white markets is that the same loan officer has a greater monetary incentive to work the deal in the white market than in the black because, being paid on commission, his income from each deal in the former market is greater. Thus the structure of the housing market, in which black and white neighborhoods operate at different price levels, translates into differences in the size of loans applied for and differences in the incentives facing loan officers taking loan applications.[22]

Conclusion

Racial disparities in mortgage lending do not just happen because one group of people is less creditworthy than another group of people. The

178   disparities are a result of a process that takes place within a spatial context. Disparities are a failure of the process, one that is designed for success, to get loans to a particular group of people. And the failure of the process for one application affects the likelihood that future applications will also fail, because of the spatial concentration of those failures. Furthermore, we cannot ignore the fact that blacks have worse credit scores than their white counterparts because they are segregated in neighborhoods that have been neglected by financial institutions for years and carry a stigma that is a barrier to their entry into the labor market. Credit scores may be a reflection of reality, but if they are, it is a reality that says much about the harmful effects of segregation, for which the lending and real estate industries bear a large responsibility.

6

Constructing Risk

W̲e construct risk by trying to quantify uncertainty. In the mortgage lending industry the underwriter's risk decision is based on "what makes sense." In this context, "sense" has a long institutional history grounded in a mix of rules of thumb, accepted norms, theoretical assumptions imposed on reality, and self-fulfilling prophecies. The "what" also has a history, but a shorter one, grounded in the willingness and ability of the loan officer and the underwriter to gather the appropriate information to make a good decision about a loan application. Furthermore, "what makes sense" ends up supporting itself by being part of and promoting a liquid mortgage and housing market.

This account of the construction of risk has both theoretical and practical implications. In this chapter I focus on theory, and in the next I focus on practice. The method I employ to highlight the theoretical implications of my account of the construction of risk in mortgage lending is to look at the extent to which there has been consensus or disagreement within the industry regarding the construct risk. I apply this strategy both to the national-level processes in which institutions and policy-makers construct risk, and to the everyday activities of loan officers, underwriters, and appraisers as they construct the risk profile of a loan applicant. In this way I hope to: integrate the concepts of rules, networks, and the production of space; articulate the role of people and their motivations in constructing risk; and, at the same time, analyze the ways in which people are "locked in" to a consensus or consent to it by convention. I also devote a separate, but related, section to the question of whether we can blame the federal government for any consensus there is—is the lack of what I call the "competition of knowledge" in the industry just another example of government intervention stifling competition?

The Construction of Risk at the National Level

In chapters 1 and 2 I discussed five different components of the process by which lenders construct risk: the appraisal process; the use of debt-to-income ratios; the use of credit reports and credit scores; the use of loan-to-value ratios; and the use of prepayment penalties. Each of these components has a unique institutional history, and each is supported by varying degrees of consensus.

Appraisals

There is widespread consensus in the United States about the definition of value and the methods employed to measure it in the field of residential real estate. The Uniform Residential Appraisal Report is what its title implies, a uniform instrument for formulating and reporting a valuation conclusion. After a scattered beginning, the definition of value and its measurement have largely been brought under the control of the professional associations, with the exception of antidiscrimination efforts made by the Justice Department, Congress, community activists, and, more recently, the FHA, Fannie Mae, and Freddie Mac. Even under FIRREA, Congress delegated the development of uniform standards and state licensing procedures to the Appraisal Foundation.

The road to uniformity was a long one, and highly revealing of the way concepts get constructed. The founders of the appraisal associations wanted to put appraising on a "sound footing"—they wanted to give it some badly needed legitimacy. For the most part this meant basing the practice of appraising on what they saw as good economic theory. But there was also a desire to have consensus for its own sake, for no other reason than that it meant that two appraisers could come to roughly the same conclusion as to the value of a property. To achieve that, association members were willing to compromise on the recommended methodology to be used by appraisers. Hence the three approaches to value and how to reconcile them.

Particular relational networks among a certain set of leaders allowed them to jump-start the process of professionalization through the Home Owners Loan Corporation and the FHA, through which the advocates of professionalization were able to train thousands of real estate appraisers in their methods. Of the four most prominent men in these two government organizations (Philip Kniskern, Arthur Mertzke, Ernest Fisher, and Frederick Babcock), three had affiliations with the Institute for Research in Land Economics and Public Utilities at Northwestern University, located in a suburb immediately neighboring Chicago, and later became active in the National Association of Real Estate Brokers, in Chicago.

Thus, with regard to the definition of value, the initial impetus to develop a unique definition and a consistent approach to its measurement came from a tight-knit network of men motivated by the desire for professional legitimacy. Yet, despite the compromise encompassing the three approaches to value and the jump start from the federal government, it is clear that a large number of lenders did not feel the need to operate within the consensus established by the professional associations. It was only through the increased use of professional appraisers that consensus spread.[1] This in turn was consolidated by the growing power of the secondary market, which required a common definition of value for its operational viability.

In contrast to this painful process of construction, there was always consensus in the appraisal profession about separating people by race and class. Though the savings and loan industry was, initially, not open to the influence of the professional associations in how it defined value, it did follow the profession's lead in how it redlined certain neighborhoods (Jackson 1985, 203). The evidence suggests that the consensus derived from a well-ingrained racism and class-consciousness in the industry, which the professional associations and the federal government institutionalized.

The development of both the appraisal profession and the credit reporting industry was contingent on the production of space in which they took place, and they in turn contributed to that production process. Confronted with the chaos of the metropolis of the 1920s the appraisal profession sought to make sense of it, and then sought to impose its theory of how a metropolis should look onto this chaotic reality. In short, this meant promoting racially and socio-economically homogeneous neighborhoods, in which, for valuation purposes, each housing unit could be treated as a commodity. One could argue that this commodification destroyed space, by making geographic differences irrelevant—a person can move from a suburb of Detroit to a suburb of Phoenix and find the same mix of amenities available at the same price relative to his income. But this ignores the fact that space is continually in production. The boundaries of homogeneous neighborhoods, as Babcock so readily recognized, are not sacrosanct. They have to be preserved, and when they are violated they set in motion a process that draws meaning from the historical fact that there once was a homogeneous neighborhood within the violated boundaries. Thus homogeneity may imply commodification, but it does not necessarily erase meaning. Rather it transforms meaning and makes defense of the neighborhood a priority: keeping out "the barbarians at the gate" comes to define the neighborhood. At the same time, the flow of funds into homogeneous neighborhoods changes the meaning of the experience of those excluded. Their housing conditions are diminished by a lack of funds for upkeep, and their ability to build wealth is impaired, thus depriving their children of the means to leverage new capital to finance their education and investments. This abandonment of neighborhoods is self-fulfilling— the withdrawal of funds takes liquidity out of the market, which increases the risk associated with that market, which in turn leads to a new withdrawal of funds. The appraisal profession helped reconfigure the space of metropolitan America by supporting the flow of funds into conforming neighborhoods and not into others. The process is also eventually self-defeating, because the lack of funds stymies the legitimate demand of millions of people for credit. So they look to the homogeneous neighborhoods for their salvation, thus arriving at the gates of those neighborhoods.

Credit Reports

The story of the development of the appraisal profession is one of a central group of men attempting to evangelize a dispersed group of men with their ideas about how to appraise a home. The story of the credit reporting industry reveals a different dynamic, though it shares a central element: a professional association that was able to quickly recruit a large number of dispersed local credit bureaus into its network of information exchange, so much so that within 20 years of the birth of the association it was prosecuted by the government under federal antitrust laws.

One could argue that the only story here is that the network of credit bureaus was essential to the success of the credit reporting industry because of the increasing geographical mobility of borrowers—if a borrower was able to leave a bad credit report by moving from one place to another then the local credit bureau was an ineffective safeguard against delinquencies and default. But this would be to ignore the circumstances in

which the network emerged. The professional association that promoted
the network was the National Retail Credit Association—an association of
credit *grantors*, not credit reporters. That association was, during its first
20 years, involved in a struggle to justify the expansion of installment
lending. It sought this justification by drawing a close association between
a person's treatment of her credit obligations and her character. The credit
report played an essential role in this association by providing a record of
how a person treated her obligations and, therefore, a record of her character. The NRCA made sure the credit report could play this role by both
setting standards for credit reports and connecting a network of bureaus
through which information could easily be exchanged. It is no accident
that credit reports exchanged through the network up to the 1960s explicitly included character data; it was a product of their social origins. And it
is no accident that the idea that a person's credit report in some way reflects her character survives—derogatory credit that is the result of "extenuating circumstances" is still treated differently from derogatory credit
that is not. The relationship between one's credit history and one's character survives in the reasoning of underwriters and in the rules of the secondary market and the FHA. It has even garnered support from community activists because taking into account "extenuating circumstances" in
underwriting loans to individuals with adverse information on their credit
reports, or low credit scores, is a way to extend credit to those who have
been excluded from the mortgage market in the past. I say more on this in
the next chapter.

The credit reporting industry's need to build a network of credit bureaus across the United States was a direct result of the mobility of people
through space. On the face of it, this network of bureaus destroyed space,
by making the geographic mobility of an individual irrelevant. But such a
conclusion ignores the fact that the network enabled the flow of funds into
areas of the country where there were many new arrivals. So long as they
were internal migrants they carried with them, figuratively speaking, their
credit reports. As a result, they were able to gain access to credit more easily than they might have without a credit report. And, of course, this
process favored those new arrivals who had been able to access credit in
their previous location and those whose behavior conformed to the ideal
embodied in the structure of the credit report. In this way the network of
bureaus contributed to the production of space, a production process that
did not have to rely on closely knit social ties for the extension of credit,
but one that could rely instead on preexisting credit relationships to inform the development of new credit relationships.

Debt-to-Income Ratios

In contrast to the story of value and the story of credit reports, the story of debt-to-income ratios does not involve the development of a professional association or a reporting industry. Nevertheless, it is intriguing in its simplicity. Essentially, it is one of a consensus that emerged out of the everyday business practices of a diverse group of lenders. At least since the first survey of real estate professionals by Herbert Hoover's President's Housing Conference, there has been a consensus not only that the best measure of a borrower's ability to make his mortgage payment is the debt-to-income ratio but also that it should be near 25 percent. The FHA and the VA both followed paths that rejected ratios as inadequate, but both were eventually brought into line by Congress for different reasons—the FHA to promote fairness and the VA to bring its practices closer to those of the private sector.

Though today the ratios that lenders use vary, the idea that they are a valid way to measure a borrower's ability to pay remains. I cannot be certain as to why this is the case, but one possible explanation is that ratios are a good way to sell houses: a broker can quickly match a buyer with a price range by knowing his income. Any other method brings too much uncertainty into the transaction. So the merit of ratios is not necessarily that they are the best predictors of risk, but they are the best given the fact that real estate agents find them easy to use, and lenders depend on these agents for borrower referrals. The spatial implications of this are fairly straightforward. People of the same income and wealth are likely to live in similarly priced houses, and in similar neighborhoods given house price homogeneity, if their capacity to borrow is linked directly to their income by a simple ratio. In this way a simple rule serves to organize people into a particular spatial configuration, and the rule itself is contingent on the need for lenders to maintain their relationships with real estate agents.

Loan-to-Value Ratios

For many years there was a consensus in the industry that the maximum loan-to-value ratio on a residential mortgage loan should be 80 percent, unless mortgage insurance was available. During the New Deal Congress continued the tradition from the states of stipulating the maximum loan-to-value ratio in its legislation establishing the HOLC and the FHA. It failed to impose such a maximum on the savings and loan industry when it established the FHLBB and the FSLIC. Nevertheless, the 80 percent fig-

ure was one with which the savings and loan industry of the 1920s was beginning to experiment, and the FHLBB soon adopted it as its standard
maximum. Though subsequent legislation altered the FHA's maximum
loan-to-value ratio, that figure remains embedded in the congressional
charters of Fannie Mae and Freddie Mac. It is, however, no longer the
norm of the federal regulators of depository institutions—the consensus
has broken down.

Furthermore, the 80 percent rule has lost much of its constraining effect because it has given rise to a large private mortgage insurance industry that has allowed Fannie Mae and Freddie Mac to exceed the 80 percent limit while staying within the limitations established by their charters.
There is no technical reason for the 80 percent limit, as the federal regulators have so clearly indicated by abandoning the imposition of any limitations on the institutions they regulate. But there are good political reasons
why at least Fannie Mae and Freddie Mac are likely to be stuck with the
80 percent limit so long as they have federal charters. Allowing Fannie
Mae and Freddie Mac to exceed these limits would be strongly opposed
by those who believe that the two GSEs already pose an inordinate risk to
the U.S. government, and the private mortgage insurance companies
would be strongly against any such change.

Prepayment Penalties

The rules regarding prepayment penalties were, for a long time, set by
state courts in favor of the lender. There was a judicial consensus based on
legal precedent stretching back to decisions made in English courts. But
in the early 1970s, Fannie Mae and the FHA changed their rules to disal-
low them, and Freddie Mac followed suit in 1979. The way in which this
policy emerged is yet another version of the process of rule-making that
highlights the contingent nature of this process. The opportunity for advocates and the Congress to weigh in on the issue of the prepayment
penalty was a result of the fact that Fannie Mae and Freddie Mac were attempting to develop a uniform set of mortgage instruments. The reason
the prepayment penalty featured in those instruments was that it is part of
the loan contract—it is a way of managing behavioral risk. As a result, advocates were able to make an issue of the penalty and widen the debate
through congressional hearings, resulting in Fannie Mae's policy of disal-
lowing the penalties. Today the GSEs are locked into a position of disal-
lowing prepayment penalties because they are such a politically salient
issue right now, and the private, secondary market conduits do not have

the market power to make loans with prepayment penalties a good investment, because they cannot create a liquid market in which they can be
bought and sold.

Nevertheless, many lenders do make loans with prepayment penalties
because such penalties make sense for lenders, and because there are few
regulatory restrictions on doing so. In the 1990s the penalties became a
matter of dispute within states, and between states and federal regulators
because of their abuse by predatory lenders. The little evidence we have
on the activities of predatory lenders suggests that they target minority
neighborhoods. Given the persistence of racial segregation nationwide
there is a clear spatial dimension to this problem, which may exacerbate
its effects by further weakening already-weakened housing markets. What
we have then is a general lack of consensus on the use of prepayment
penalties stemming from the diverse institutional histories of this risk
management policy, which is now playing out in a debate over predatory
lending and its impact on minority communities.

Constructing Risk through Everyday Practices

The sale of a home constitutes a consensus among all parties involved that
that sale should go forward. The meeting of the minds of the buyer and the
seller is, of course, important. But the consensus required goes far beyond
that exchange nexus. The appraiser has to be able to find comparable sales
that justify the sales price. To do that he must delineate the neighborhood
in which the house is located, or identify an acceptable competing neighborhood. This delineation process is informed by the existing boundaries
of neighborhoods which real estate brokers use to sell homes and which
have themselves received support from previous appraisal and lending decisions. To the extent that these boundaries separate people of different
races, ethnicities, and incomes, they structure a lenders' network of loan
officers in an attempt to engender trust between a loan applicant and the
loan officer. Furthermore, they build on existing trust relationships between real estate brokers and loan officers.

In this context we see the application of rules and the exercise of discretion. Discretion is exercised in two ways, in the choice of information
gathered and in the interpretation of that information. In both cases, discretion is informed by the rules—it seeks to use the rules to achieve a certain end, rather than violate the rules. Letters explaining the extenuating
circumstances that resulted in derogatory credit and compensating factors
that allow a borrower to exceed the ratios are both allowed by the underwriting rules, but it is up to the loan officer or the underwriter to generate

such information because this is not information that has a specific box on the loan application. The interpretation of information also takes place within the rules but is still an exercise of discretion and judgment. An underwriter is looking to make sense of the file and that sense is organized by the underlying logic of the rules. But to make sense of the file the underwriter has to be able to tell the story, which is contingent on her willingness and ability to do so.[2] Automated underwriting changes some of the elements of this story, placing more emphasis on the discretion exercised by the loan officer and the underwriter in the amount of information they gather. But the essence of the decision remains the same: what makes sense?

The dynamic process that produces a consensus that allows a sale to go forward reveals much about how rules, networks, and the production of space interact. As I stated above, networks grounded in trust do not require formal rules; and rules do away with the need for trust because they create standards according to which people can evaluate each other. In this sense, networks and rules are mutually destructive. But the loan officer–real estate broker relationship is premised on the fact that a home buyer has to conform to the underwriting rules if she is to buy a house. The relationship is necessary because there is so much discretion exercised in the application of the rules, whether it be in terms of the information gathered or of the assessment process. In this way rules which require discretion for their implementation, and which are at all complex, require a trust-based relationship to help achieve compliance with them.

The everyday processes of the mortgage loan market also give us some further insight into the relationship between the rules of appraising, lender–broker networks, and the production of space. The interviews with appraisers demonstrated their adherence to the idea of economic segregation. Furthermore, though racial segregation is no longer actively endorsed by the appraisal profession, the logic of the appraisal process dictates that segregation be tacitly acknowledged in the selection of comparable properties—the black, white, and Latino markets are different and not comparable. But the interviews also demonstrated how, in the case of gentrification, appraisers can assist in the creation of new neighborhood boundaries that, on the face of it, violate the idea of economic segregation. In addition, though neighborhood boundaries structure the networks of relationships between lenders and a particular location, these networks cross those boundaries as racial resegregation takes place. This suggests that the thinking of lenders and appraisers is structured by the logic of the rules they use and the preexisting conditions of segregation, but where that logic takes them is contingent on where the everyday decisions of home buyers and real estate brokers take them. Appraisers will support the move into a newly gentrifying area if they can be sure that that new area will become fully gentrified. Hence the need for that newly gentrifying area to be strictly bounded, to harness the power of the self-fulfilling prophecy. And lenders whose strength is in serving their respective minority markets will follow their real estate broker contacts into new white markets to take advantage of the opportunities created by racial re-segregation.

Is It the Government's Fault?

Despite the varied institutional origins of the rules and concepts that underlie the social construction of risk in the mortgage lending industry, the state, in the form of the federal government, has played a critical role in promoting the development of a standardized lending market. Could it be that it has been the interference of the federal government in the mortgage market that has resulted in the particular construction(s) of risk that we have today, rather than the work of nongovernmental actors? There is considerable evidence to support this idea. Some opponents of the creation of the FHA opposed it principally on the basis of their belief that it would promote "uniformity in home ownership." As an insurance scheme it required conformity to accepted standards of underwriting that it developed. The creation of Fannie Mae in 1938 was an act of Congress to create a secondary market purchaser of mortgage loans, a national mortgage association, to promote the free flow of capital from the northeastern region of the country to the west and southwest. It did so in the face of the private sector's failure to create such associations on its own, despite the 1934 National Housing Act provisions for them. In 1970 the Congress created Freddie Mac and rechartered Fannie Mae to jump-start the conventional, conforming loan market. Through Fannie Mae, Freddie Mac, and the FHA the federal government has established powerful institutions that have been able to construct risk for private sector lenders.

Three facts argue against the theory that the federal government was solely responsible for the construction of risk in the U.S. mortgage lending industry. First, the history of the credit reporting industry and debt-to-income ratios shows how private sector institutions have constructed risk, and done so at a national level without government assistance. Furthermore, at the level of everyday practice, appraisers and real estate brokers engage in tacit collusion to define market boundaries—the very idea of a spatially demarcated housing market implies nonmarket coordination.

Second, the federal government has often regulated with a light hand, allowing lenders to construct risk in their own ways. A case in point is the Federal Home Loan Bank System. Though it provided liquidity to its members through its 12 regional banks, it did not, for many years, closely monitor their lending. Instead it limited the amount that any institution could borrow against its assets, monitored their capital structure, and, after passage of the 1934 National Housing Act, required federal deposit insurance through the Federal Savings and Loan Insurance Corporation.

Third, the theory is premised on the idea that there is a clear separation of the private and public sectors in the development of the mortgage lending industry. Such a separation does not stand up to scrutiny. The FHA was the product of business-government cooperation. Not only were major businesses backers of the FHA, but they were involved in drafting the original bill submitted to Congress. The major business opponents of the FHA were the savings and loan associations which had, only two years earlier, received their own federal program in the form of the FHLBS. The creation of Freddie Mac in 1970 was at the request of the FHLBB and the savings and loan industry. The following exchange between the chairman of the Senate Banking and Currency Committee and Preston Martin, chairman of the FHLBB at the time, shows why the industry wanted Congress to set up Freddie Mac:

The Chairman. You say on page 5 of your statement that a good many local associations do not make use of the borrowing right they have with the Home Loan Bank System for reasons of financial conservatism and local mores. You say 2,000 member associations . . . continue to refrain from borrowing. . . . I just don't figure out in my own mind why they do not. Of course you say it is because of the financial conservatism. I think I can understand that. But also because of local mores. What would develop in a community that would discourage getting money were it legitimately available?

Mr. Martin. The institutions themselves tell us, Senator, that it gives them great personal satisfaction and standing in their community to be able to put on their statement of conditions distributed to the public no borrowings. It is a matter of pride and attitude of the local folks, these are smaller communities, mostly, that their financial institutions just do not borrow. On the other hand, the same individuals indicated if there was a secondary market and a great shortage of housing in their community they would be willing providing the price is right to trade in mortgages with our facility. But they have no plans to become borrowers at all. (U.S. Congress, Senate, Committee on Banking, Housing, and Urban Affairs 1970, 61–62)

190   In essence federal intervention has often been good for business, in this case because it was able to bring liquidity to savings and loan institutions without upsetting their balance sheets.

The lesson from the mortgage lending industry and its relationship to the federal government is a simple one, once one realizes how government is good for business. The lending industry often benefits from coordination rather than competition, whether such coordination is brought about through a professional association, a network of credit bureaus, or some other such mechanism.[3] The federal government has proven able and willing to go along with this project of coordination through regulations that promulgate uniform standards and by setting up institutions that assist in market coordination directly. What we have not seen in the mortgage lending industry is any sort of competition of knowledge, where lenders have competed by developing a better way to underwrite a loan or appraise a property. Lenders are far more willing to compete within the rules of the game, because the rules often have broad legitimacy and the standardization that comes with the rules of the game results in increased liquidity and the potential to gain from externality effects of a coordinated lending process.[4]

Conclusion

The framework of rules, networks, and the production of space serves, at the very least, as a list against which we should check any analysis of the construction of risk, and decision-making in general. Unless those making the decisions have complete information, then none of the concepts should be absent from the analysis.[5] Beyond this function as a check-list the framework requires that we look at how people maintain, create, and destroy rules, networks, and space. In each case—maintenance, creation, and destruction—we should look for the ways in which the concepts interact. Out of what networks did certain rules emanate? Around what rules have social networks formed to ensure and maintain compliance? And, how have networks constituted or destroyed social or abstract spaces? On the basis of answers to these questions we can begin to understand the context in which people construct risk out of uncertainty, and the context in which they construct knowledge in general. We can also use the answers to develop public policy solutions to problems created by particular constructions of risk, given the important role that government plays in the construction process.

7

New Policy Approaches to Discrimination and Subprime Lending

I have argued two major points in this book. One is that the context in which people construct risk matters for how they go about doing so. The other is that this context can best be described using the concepts of rules, networks, and the production of space. How are these relevant to the important questions that are currently being debated among those concerned with policies and practices of the mortgage lending industry? The answer lies in the way that the constructivist approach forces us to question those policies and practices in light of evidence that they are not the fruit of some unvarnished search for the most accurate risk assessment, but rather the product of values, rules of thumb, and self-fulfilling prophecies. Furthermore, as I noted at the end of the last chapter, that approach gives us some clear empirical questions to ask within a framework built on the concepts of rules, networks, and the production of space, out of which can evolve some clear policy strategies based on the answers to those questions. In this chapter I discuss the issues of racial and ethnic discrimination, on the one hand, and subprime and predatory lending, on the other hand, within the context of three interrelated strategies for thinking about and dealing with those issues: a rules strategy, a network strategy, and a spatial strategy.

Rules Strategy

A Constructive Antidiscrimination Policy

Despite greater enforcement of fair lending laws and extensive changes in underwriting guidelines in the 1990s, black and Latino applicants for home mortgages continue to be rejected at a far higher rate than whites.[1] From a constructivist perspective these data constitute prima facie evidence for a concerted public policy response that directly addresses their causes and consequences. This is because the data clearly show that the mortgage lending process, a process that is explicitly designed to help a loan applicant succeed in getting a loan, is failing a considerable percentage of minority applicants. There are elements of current public policy that do force lenders, indirectly, to tackle this failure. In the primary market the Community Reinvestment Act's new results-oriented regulations force depository institutions to work out ways to better serve all neighborhoods in which they are located. The evidence from Chicago suggests that this is working. The Home Mortgage Disclosure Act puts a spotlight on the track records of lenders and is a useful tool for community activists and researchers who wish to hold lenders to account. In the secondary market regulations enforcing the 1992 Federal Housing Enterprises Financial Safety and Soundness Act (FHEFSS Act) require that Fannie Mae and Freddie Mac purchase a certain percentage of their loans from targeted tracts, forcing them to develop new loan products and underwriting criteria to enable lenders who sell loans to them to approve applications from minority and low-income applicants. These are indirect methods in that they create incentives for lenders and the secondary market to serve minorities more effectively, but they do not get at the root causes of the failure of the lending process to serve minorities.

Some laws are in place that, ostensibly, result in a more direct method for fixing the process failure, namely the Fair Housing Act and the Equal Credit Opportunity Act. In 1994, 20 years after the latter was put on the books, the Interagency Task Force on Fair Lending issued a statement clarifying what these laws make illegal. As noted in the introductory chapter, they make illegal three types of activity: overt discrimination, disparate treatment, and disparate impact. The statement explains what each of these means:

- "Overt evidence of discrimination," when a lender blatantly discriminates on a prohibited basis;
- Evidence of "disparate treatment," when a lender treats applicants differently based on one of the prohibited factors; and

- Evidence of "disparate impact," when a lender applies a practice uniformly to all applicants but the practice has a discriminatory effect on a prohibited basis and is not justified by business necessity. (Interagency Task Force on Fair Lending 1994, 4)

Since the Task Force's statement, federal regulators have carried out fair lending exams in the banks they supervise. Accounts of how these exams are carried out indicate that for financial institutions with large loan applicant pools the regulators use statistical techniques akin to those used in the Boston Fed study. But these accounts also indicate that federal enforcement policies do take into account the process by which risk is constructed in the loan application process. Thus, for example, the FFIEC's guide to conducting fair lending examinations gives the following advice to examiners comparing marginal loan applications, where it suggests they are most likely to find evidence of discrimination:

> the examiner should simultaneously look for and document . . . any evidence found in marginal files regarding the following:
> - the *extent of any assistance,* including both *affirmative aid and waivers or partial waivers* of credit policy provisions or requirements, that appears to have been provided to *marginal-approved* control group applicants which enabled them to overcome one or more credit deficiencies, such as excessive debt-to-income ratios
> - the extent to which *marginal-denied* target group applicants with similar deficiencies were, or were not, provided similar affirmative aid, waivers or other forms of assistance. (Federal Financial Institutions Examination Council 1999, 18)

Calem and Longhofer (2002) indicate that the examiners are not looking for disparate impacts on minorities because they are evaluating the fate of loan applications based on criteria that the lenders *do* apply, without any assessment of whether they *should* apply them. Without this latter assessment there is no way for an examiner to determine whether a criterion is a business necessity or not. But, as Calem and Longhofer point out, looking at only the criteria that the lender *does* apply solves some considerable methodological problems.

Does the constructivist content of the federal guidelines on conducting fair lending examinations mean that we have in place an effective fair lending policy that is directed at the heart of the problem? No, because the regulators are not constructivists, even though they implicitly endorse the empirical validity of such an approach. As a result, they do not take the constructivist logic to its conclusion. The fair lending exam process should

begin from the premise that a disparity in loan application outcomes
across people of different races and ethnicities should be something that
the lender should fix, whether it is a product of discrimination or not. For
example, in Calem and Longhofer's account the examiners found that 12
of the 14 applications that were denied and were submitted by mortgage
brokers had incomplete/unverifiable information, and 10 of those 12 were
applications from minorities. At the very least the examiners should require the lender to fix this obvious failure in the process, even if they do
not interpret it as discrimination. This simple step makes use of data that
have been laboriously gathered by the examiners to help lenders understand how they might better serve their minority applicants.

A further step that the constructivist logic requires is that fair lending
exams be made public, including information covering the statistical
analysis done by the examiners, a summary of the in-depth file review
they conducted, and a list of the recommendations they made to the lender
about how it might best address some process failures. Such a disclosure
could easily be achieved in connection with the CRA exam disclosure. The
constructivist logic dictates such disclosure because the examiners are
subject to the same influences as any other person attempting to make an
"objective" evaluation. They are operating within a regulatory environment that is very friendly toward the regulated, and most likely with
premises that bias them toward the idea that discrimination is irrational,
and therefore unlikely to be occurring.

Beyond this microlevel approach to fixing the problems minorities
face in negotiating the loan application process, there remains the thorny
question of "business necessity." The historical record of the mortgage
lending industry indicates that very few of the loan underwriting criteria
that have been used in the past could be justified on the basis of a "business necessity," if the test of that condition is a proven link between a criterion and the likelihood of default. Today, many of the past practices that
clearly had no relation to the likelihood of default have been eliminated,
but in a manual underwriting system, the link between many of the underwriting criteria and the likelihood of default remains tenuous. This is why
the focus in a fair lending exam has to be on what the lenders do look at,
not what they should look at. The advent of automated underwriting (AU)
changes this situation in an important way. AU uses a statistical model to
predict the likelihood of default. As a result, it forms the basis for a judgment about whether a lender is using a criterion in its underwriting that
has a business necessity—that is, if the variable is not a statistically significant predictor of default then there is no business necessity for having it
in the model. But even with AU the situation is not completely clear. An

AU model can include a statistically significant variable that is, neverthe- less, an inaccurate predictor of default. This is so for a number of reasons, the most obvious being the following: the data used to generate the model are from the past and, following Keynes, may not be a sound basis for predictions about the future; variables in the model may correlate with each other and with other variables not in the model, making it hard to know exactly which variable is the accurate predictor of default; and, because the data used to create the model are only from the behavior of successful applicants, the model may be biased. Nevertheless, even ignoring the potential inaccuracies of AU, we can not get around the problem that lenders are quite capable of creating the conditions under which a particular criterion is a business necessity — something I discuss in the section on the spatial strategy.

Subprime Lending

Traditionally lenders in the United States have employed a "one-size-fits-all" approach to lending. That is the system I have described in the preceding pages. Fannie Mae and Freddie Mac dominate this one-size-fits-all segment of the market. Though ostensibly stockholder-owned corporations, Fannie Mae and Freddie Mac enjoy the backing of the full faith and credit of the federal government. In exchange for this favored status they have been pressured since the early 1990s to extend the reach of their underwriting policies in order to increase the flexibility of the "one size" to fit more loan applicants, specifically applicants who are minority, lower-income, or buying in urban housing markets (Temkin et al. 1999; Stuart 2000b).[2] Under the FHEFSS Act, HUD has regulatory responsibility for evaluating the safety and soundness of Fannie Mae and Freddie Mac (through the Office of Federal Housing Enterprise Oversight) and their effectiveness in reaching the goals that it sets for them with regard to the reach of their lending.[3] In turn, Fannie Mae and Freddie Mac work with community groups and their own lenders to find ways to serve markets they have traditionally underserved.

What this regulatory structure ensures is some sort of political accountability for the rules that the GSEs promulgate and a results-driven assessment of how well they are keeping up their end of the bargain. The structure is akin to that in place under the Community Reinvestment Act after the development of its new, results-oriented regulations in 1995. The history of that act indicates that this structure places a lot of weight on two variables: the willingness and ability of the regulator to properly oversee the regulated institutions; and the availability of good data. To the extent that, in the case of the GSEs, HUD and its OFHEO are directly accountable to Congress, through its appropriations and oversight, and to the president, through the appointment of their top administrators, the level and type of regulation are consistent with the wishes of these two democratically elected institutions. Furthermore, not only does the public have access to data under the Home Mortgage Disclosure Act to analyze the distribution of mortgage loans in general; it also has access to data that provide information on the types of loans Fannie Mae and Freddie Mac buy or securitize. From this perspective one could argue that we have a structure that allows for a public debate of underwriting guidelines, with some democratic accountability.

What this ignores is Fannie Mae's and Freddie Mac's considerable political power, which undermines the democratic nature of the current regulatory structure.[4] Furthermore, the increasing use of automated underwriting by Fannie Mae and Freddie Mac has severely affected the public's ability to understand and debate their underwriting criteria. Both entities have disclosed limited information on the way their AU systems work, but nothing that could not be gleaned from their manual underwriting guidelines.[5] Finally, to the extent that the GSEs create the markets in which they operate, they can continue to justify their lack of purchases from many minority, low-income, and urban markets because of the risks those markets and their residents represent—risks created by the inactivity of the GSEs themselves.

The FHEFSS Act also mandated a study of the viability of revoking the congressional charters of Fannie Mae and Freddie Mac. One premise behind this study was that these two institutions stifle market competition and that, left to its own devices, the mortgage lending industry would provide credit in a more efficient and effective manner.[6] Apart from allowing new institutional forms of risk-sharing, competition holds out the promise of creating a dynamic in which underwriting systems, most likely automated, become increasingly accurate in their ability to assess risk—the assumption being that greater accuracy results in greater profits. But this is premised on the idea that there can be a real competition of knowledge. It is possible to imagine every lender having its own AU system reflecting its risk perspective, but this raises two further questions. Do lenders have a real interest in seeing such a situation come about? If so, how would such a situation come about?

As I have argued, uniformity is good for business. So long as lenders need to access the capital markets to sell or borrow against their mortgage loans, they will have to use an underwriting system that is generally accepted in the capital markets. General acceptance is necessary if investors are going to be able to buy and sell loans, or mortgage-backed securities, as and when they like—if they are going to be able to benefit from a liquid market in these loans. So there seems little incentive for lenders to compete on the basis of knowledge. But if they did want to do so, there is a solution of sorts, which entails the lender retaining some of the risk exposure when it sells a loan. For example, FHLBS's Mortgage Partnership Finance Program has the lender share the risk of the loan even after it sells it. Under this program the lender underwrites the loan according to its own guidelines, but the amount of risk it must take on to be able to sell the loan under the program is determined by the FHLBS (www.fhlbc.com/mpf.htm, Pollock 1999, 5).[7] In other words, the FHLBS system splits the risk in two—the risk that the FHLBS deems acceptable, and the risk it does not deem acceptable but the lender does.[8]

Competition in such a situation is highly contingent. It is contingent on the extent to which different system developers have an incentive to develop unique systems, as against systems that ensure that their clients are not deviating from the norm established by the FHLBS or any other secondary market actor operating in the same way. The history of the lending industry indicates that lenders place a premium on legitimacy. Systems developers, as professionals, also value legitimacy, and their legitimacy will be questioned if the system they develop for a lender continuously "disagrees" with that of the secondary market. This is especially likely given the fact that the "test" to see which system is right will not occur for a number of years—the time it takes for bad loans to reveal themselves through delinquencies and default. Finally, competition is contingent on the ability of prospective borrowers to be able to compare systems, something I discuss further in my examination of network strategies.

We seem to be at an impasse: the current regulatory system, though ostensibly one in which there is some democratic control over the construction of risk, is weak because of the political power of the regulated; and the probability that there might be a competition of knowledge in the absence of Fannie Mae and Freddie Mac is low. But a development outside of the mainstream sector promises a way round this impasse. We are moving beyond the world of one-size-fits-all risk assessment into a world of risk-based pricing, using automated underwriting. The promise of this new world is that lenders can offer borrowers a continuum of loan prices contingent on their particular risk profile.

Subprime lending is a step in this direction, in that borrowers are offered varying interest rates contingent on what risk category they fall into—A-, B, C, or D. To people on both sides of the debate about how the mortgage lending industry should conduct itself, subprime lending constitutes a solution to the problem facing those excluded from securing loans from prime lenders. In particular, the evidence from HMDA data shows that subprime lenders have a greater share of the minority market than they do of the white market.

Yet despite the fact that the subprime market has thrived in the least regulated sector of the mortgage lending industry it is unclear that it really constitutes much of an innovation. First, its scope of operations is defined by the prime market — wherever the prime lenders are absent the subprime market flourishes. Thus, it is unclear that it has developed any new underwriting tools that make it any better at assessing risk. It is simply willing to take on more of the risk, as perceived by the prime market, in exchange for a higher interest rate. In fact, there are indications that the subprime market's main niche is refinance loans to high-equity home owners who somehow fail to fit the prime market's underwriting criteria. Second, in recent years subprime lenders have suffered considerable losses, in large part due to the liquidity crisis they faced in 1998 as a result of the capital market's "flight to quality" in the wake of the Russian debt crisis. In other words, during the 12 years since the SEC changed its regulations to put it on the same disclosure footing as the GSEs, the private secondary market has been unable to find a way to provide consistent liquidity to this market. Finally, subprime lending has provided the context for overcharging borrowers and for predatory lending. There is a continuum of abuses that lenders can mete out to unwitting borrowers in the mortgage market. In the prime market lenders can charge borrowers "overage," which is a rate over and above the rate that the lender is willing to charge prime borrowers. There is a limit to how much overage a prime lender can charge in the prime market if the borrower has any idea of what current rates are. In the subprime market the situation is the same — a loan officer can quote a rate to the applicant that is higher than the one the lender is willing to grant such an applicant with that risk profile. Unlike in the prime market, even if the borrower has some idea of what the current rates are she is still at a considerable disadvantage, because a higher rate can always be justified on the basis of the fact that the borrower falls into a higher risk category. In other words, a borrower with general market knowledge has no way of detecting when she is being charged overage. Beyond this problem facing borrowers is the willingness of some lenders, mostly in the refinance market, to use the loan contract to extract as much money out of the borrower as possible, through predatory practices.[9]

There are good reasons for trying to mainstream subprime lending by promoting an expansion of Fannie Mae, Freddie Mac, and FHA activities in this market. From a business perspective this will provide liquidity to the market. From a constructivist perspective it will bring the market under the auspices of institutions over which the public has some ostensibly democratic control. This will give those interested in regulating the practices of subprime lenders another means by which to curb abusive practices. But Fannie Mae, Freddie Mac, and the FHA should not simply enter the market as it is now constituted. This would simply be providing liquidity to a market open to abuse. Rather, they should enter the market through an automated, risk-based pricing system with a mutual insurance feature. In such a system borrowers are offered a rate that is commensurate with their risk profile. There is a basic rate and then there is a premium reflecting the greater risk that a borrower represents according to the assessment of the automated underwriting system. The lender places the borrowers in pools with other borrowers representing the same risk. So long as all the borrowers in the pool pay off the loan, they will pay the basic rate and will be reimbursed the full amount of the premium they have paid minus their prorated share of any payouts from the insurance fund to cover losses on loans in the pool.

The FHA is in the best position to adopt such a scheme because it is already an insurer of mortgage loans, and this structure is the same as the original FHA structure first adopted in 1934.[10] Fannie Mae and Freddie Mac are also in a position to adopt such an insurance scheme, though they would have to take in-house the insurance functions that are currently the bailiwick of the private mortgage insurers. Essentially, purchasers of mortgage-backed securities issued by the GSEs would be purchasing the equivalent of basic-rate loans regardless of the rating or premium the GSEs would charge the borrower. The GSEs would simply use those premiums to enhance the quality of the lesser quality loans. If the FHA, Fannie Mae, and Freddie Mac were all able to offer loans on this basis, they could generate a basic rate which covers a pool of buyers whose risk profile is the same, and which is large enough to cover the costs of systemic risk that affects all home owners—such as an economic downturn. Beyond the basic rate, borrowers will pay a premium, and should be pooled with others who have the same profile. The purpose here is to allow borrowers who have the same rating to test whether the underwriting system has evaluated them correctly. If the system has been too conservative, there should be a premium surplus that can be returned to the borrowers as they pay off their loan.

This is not just a technical solution to the problem of how to best implement a risk-based pricing system. It raises a number of political issues, which are part of its attraction. First and foremost, the idea of pooling people by risk, and having each pool member's final interest payment be contingent on the payment performance of all the other members casts the lending decision in a new light. Up until now the discussion has been in terms of a borrower-lender relationship, where the lender assesses whether it wants to take the risk the borrower represents. This dyadic presentation of the situation is a product of the way the mortgage lending has traditionally operated, that is, on a one-size-fits-all basis. Implicit in the criteria of the one-size-fits-all model is the idea that an applicant belongs only if his likelihood of default fits within the range that allows the lender to charge all borrowers a particular rate. Borrowers' behavior could affect the costs facing other borrowers, but only in future pools. Risk-based pricing allows lenders to place borrowers with different profiles into different pools, and, again, the borrower-borrower relationship is significant only between current and future borrowers. The mutual insurance feature changes this—the behavior of current borrowers in the pool affects the loan costs of other borrowers. This makes the question of who belongs in what pool a matter of concern not just for the lender but also for the other borrowers in the pool.

A public debate on the criteria by which people should be pooled would raise some fundamental issues about how people in this country relate to one another. For example, a group of people may share exactly the same risk profile, except that some are more vulnerable to a systemic risk, such as the effects of a general economic downturn, than others. Should this risk be shared? Or should those who are most susceptible pay more? Our cultural tradition is mixed on this. On the one hand, the credit assessment allows for the consideration of "extenuating circumstances" in relation to derogatory credit. This acknowledges that people should not be held responsible for events outside their control. Following this logic, borrowers who are more susceptible to systemic risk should be in the same pool as those who are not, but share other, *individual* risk characteristics with them. On the other hand, public policy and private practices endorse the idea of racial and class segregation, and, as a result, the segregation of people with differing vulnerabilities to systemic risk. Such de facto segregation may result in the segregation of people into different risk pools based on their race or income.[11]

On top of raising questions about how to segregate borrower pools, the mutual insurance feature would allow for an accurate monitoring of what we might call the "black tax" that is a product of underwriting errors. The "black tax" refers to what minorities pay who receive inferior goods and services for inflated prices. Today subprime and predatory lending are likely to be allowing lenders to collect a new form of black tax—that is, interest payments that are higher for blacks than they are for whites with the same risk profile. Allowing the FHA, Fannie Mae, and

Freddie Mac to engage in risk-based pricing with a mutual insurance feature would create a direct measure of the cost to borrowers of errors generated by their respective underwriting systems—the greater the surplus for any given pool of borrowers the greater the error. If it becomes clear that the errors systematically disadvantage a group of people, for example blacks, then the owner of the underwriting system responsible should pay a fine. Otherwise, the only punishment the owner of an error-prone system should face is the burden of managing the surplus funds it generates and has to redistribute, and charges of incompetence by the interested public.

There is one step further that this system would allow us to take, because of the way in which it creates a clear measure of who bears what financial risk in the current U.S. housing market. If the data also show that minorities are paying more for their loans, and that this seems to be justified based on their default rates, then we also have a direct measure of what it costs to be a minority in the current market. Given the history of discrimination in housing and lending, and the persistence of segregation, should we not then ask: are not these higher rates a measure of past and present systemic injustices that demand a response?

Many lenders who currently originate subprime loans are subsidiaries of lenders that sell A paper loans to the secondary market, and also originate FHA loans. Why should they shift their subprime business to the GSEs and the FHA? The most compelling positive reason is the liquidity these institutions offer. More telling is why they might not do so. By the logic of market competition, the profit on a subprime loan should be no different from the profit from an A paper loan, because the extra interest charged on the subprime loan should be just sufficient to cover the additional losses the lender will incur.[12] So there should be no difference between selling a subprime loan on the secondary market under the mutual insurance system and selling it through a private secondary market conduit. But, as we know, the market does not work like this. Incomplete information on the lender's side makes the pricing process hit or miss, and incomplete information on the borrower's side, within a market structured by networks of relations, makes price gouging highly likely. The reason why a lender would decline the opportunity to sell its subprime loans into the risk-based, mutual insurance system I have described is because it is earning profits through gouging—it is charging A paper borrowers A- or B rates and pocketing the premium. In other words, only lenders with good intentions will opt into the system. Those opting out of the system should be subjected to greater scrutiny, in particular regarding their pricing practices across people of different races and ethnicities.[13]

Network Strategy

What is needed to accompany the risk-based pricing mutual insurance system is an aggressive advertising campaign and lender endorsement process, which raise public awareness of the distinction between lenders opting into the system and those choosing a different route.[14] Real estate brokers and other network ties into the subprime market could be recruited into the outreach effort through an incentive system—borrowers receiving reimbursement checks from the mutual insurance fund would do so through the broker. This incentive system might violate the anti-kickback provisions of the Real Estate Settlement Procedures Act (RESPA). But this simply reveals the flaw of RESPA—the intent was to destroy network ties in the market by outlawing kickbacks from lenders to real estate brokers, without understanding that those ties would persist. A better approach is to work out ways to make network ties work positively for the consumer.

More generally, the problem of price gouging could become irrelevant if taking loan applications over the Internet becomes more widespread. Today, home buyers with access to the Internet, and the financial knowledge to correctly enter data into an online form, have the option of applying for a loan this way. The promise of the Internet is a decrease in "shoe leather" costs: technically a borrower can submit applications to a number of different lenders, maybe by filling out only one application sent to a central clearing system, at very little cost. As a result, even if the borrower has a B paper risk profile he can shop around for the best rate because all lenders will be quoting rates on the basis of that applicant's unique profile. In an ideal world, lenders would offer feedback with their rate quote that offers the borrower ways in which he could lower his interest rate by providing additional, contextual data. In this way the applicant is not dependent on the loan officer's willingness and ability to present the best loan profile.

We are still a long way from universal access to the Internet and the level of financial sophistication required to complete mortgage application forms. Nevertheless there is a way to provide loan applicants with greater access to this loan application network. A burgeoning industry of nonprofit credit counselors exists, whose purpose is to educate prospective home buyers about the costs and benefits of home ownership and prepare them to be home owners. In the process the counselors also prepare them for the loan application process to increase their chances of being approved for a loan. The quality of the counseling services is highly variable, from extended seminars on all aspects of home ownership, to short videos, to pro forma worksheets filled out in an hour.

The challenge these counselors face is the wish of prospective home buyers to realize their desire for home ownership, their "dream," immediately. Under the old, one-size-fits-all system, borrowers faced a barrier, the rules, that prevented them from realizing their dream immediately and gave the counseling agencies a strategic role. In the new world of subprime lending and risk-based pricing, that barrier has been removed, at a price to the borrower in higher interest rates. To regain the strategic advantage they had, counseling agencies need to be able to provide a service to prospective home owners that they want. The most beneficial service is access to the secondary market's automated underwriting systems, which will allow counseling agencies to show prospective borrowers the added costs of an immediate home-buying decision over a delayed one, where the borrowers use the delay to improve their risk profile. When they are ready to buy a home and apply for a mortgage, the borrowers who have been through counseling can run their profile through the system one last time to determine their risk rating and the interest rate they should expect to pay. Counselors currently do not have full access to the automated system, because Fannie Mae and Freddie Mac have been reluctant to grant such access. There is no reason why the FHA should not grant access to its system, as a way to gain a competitive advantage over Fannie Mae and Freddie Mac.

The difficulty a counseling agency faces in delivering such a service is that it is contrary to the interests of the real estate broker, who is the first point of contact people have with the housing market. So long as brokers can also provide borrowers with access to the automated underwriting system through their relationships with loan officers, they will be able to effectively shut counselors out of the loan origination process. Integrating the counselor into the process will likely require a mandate that all borrowers who receive a risk rating that is higher than the minimum must be referred to a counseling agency. This can be easily implemented if loan applicants go through the systems controlled by the FHA, Fannie Mae, and Freddie Mac, but it is unclear whether there is the political will to force all lenders to comply with such a requirement.

The network strategy is a complement to the rules strategy. Both are based on a clear understanding of the way risk is constructed in the mortgage lending industry. Thus the network strategy is designed to help people comply with the rules, regardless of whether they are correct or not, while the rules strategy is designed to compensate borrowers as best as possible for the inevitable errors in the risk assessment process.

Spatial Strategy

Clearly there has to be a spatial strategy to address the failings of the mortgage lending industry. This is true in regard to formulating a constructive response both to discrimination and to subprime lending. Discrimination and subprime lending can both be justified on the basis of the fact that a particular market is too risky for prime lending, or any lending at all, setting up a self-fulfilling prophecy.

A lender may argue that more conservative underwriting criteria or a higher interest rate are justified as a business necessity when lending in a minority neighborhood, because it has a weak housing market. This ignores the fact that the lender itself contributes to the relative strength or weakness of that market in the way that it lends there. This effect is compounded by the fact that the most likely source for information about market strength or weakness, at the neighborhood level, comes from appraisers who are still required to rate a neighborhood on the URAR by noting whether housing prices are declining, stable, or rising there. To the extent that appraisers are also serving other lenders, their appraisals can give rise to an unintentionally coordinated influx or withdrawal of capital. The effect is further compounded if lenders are making decisions based on secondary market criteria, and thus are reacting in the same way. This is not necessarily a problem if the lenders are building a strong market, but it is a problem if they are weakening it. In particular, homes in neighborhoods where house prices are declining cannot receive maximum financing under GSE guidelines, a situation that directly contributes to the decline of the market.[15] It may be necessary for lenders and GSEs to continue to gather information on neighborhood price trends for their own risk management purposes, but instead of taking a passive approach to the information by denying maximum financing to neighborhoods with declining values or, in a risk-based pricing world, charging a higher rate they should act on the information in a positive fashion. They should first verify that the information is correct, identify the causes of the problem, and work with and fund the efforts of community development organizations and local government departments to ameliorate the situation. They should not do this on an ad hoc basis in response to community cries for help; they should integrate a proactive response into their everyday corporate practices.

A lender may also deny a loan from a minority applicant because she has a low credit score, and the use of the score is justified as a business necessity because of its predictive qualities. There is evidence that part of what underlies the credit score is the socio-economic and racial status of the neighborhood. To the extent that lenders contribute to the production of segregated neighborhoods, they are in part responsible for the credit scores of the individuals whose loans they deny.

At the heart of these problems is the persistence of racial, ethnic, and income segregation. Given the fact that we understand how segregation is produced and reproduced, both through the actions of the lending industry and through the actions of others, there are some simple, but politically difficult, policy changes that should be made. I see no reason why the Department of Housing and Urban Development cannot force the FHA, Fannie Mae, and Freddie Mac to expunge any reference to the connection between homogeneity and house price stability from their underwriting guidelines. There is no business necessity for such a language in the guidelines. This change is important for two reasons. First, it has real symbolic value—arguments against the development of lower-income housing in well-to-do neighborhoods should not be based on its lowering values. If home owners in a neighborhood have a class prejudice against lower-income people they should say so, and not hide behind the veneer of economics. Second, if ever there were to be neighborhoods that experienced a transformation from homogeneity to heterogeneity, they should not be penalized for undergoing such a transition by the withdrawal of capital driven by appraisals based on the homogeneity assumption.

Beyond changes in the way GSEs treat information on the URAR and define stable neighborhoods, we need to attack the underlying structure that continues to reproduce segregation. Within cities the processes of gentrification and resegregation are contingent on the boundary-drawing strategies of real estate brokers and appraisers. An obvious strategy for those concerned with undoing the inevitability of this process is to try to disrupt the boundary-drawing process. Municipal governments are in the strongest position to do this because they have resources they can use to physically change neighborhoods and boundaries. Often they exacerbate the process, rather than mitigate it, by helping to draw boundaries around areas marked for redevelopment. They do so because they have an interest in attracting and retaining middle-class residents who, through increased property values, contribute to the city's tax base. But this comes at a cost, both material and moral. The concentration of poverty created by economic and racial segregation fueled by boundary-drawing creates a demand for city services that could be mitigated through the promotion of integration. Furthermore, once one admits that gentrification and resegregation are not inevitable, it is immoral to stand by and watch them hap-

206   pen. The most important strategy in the face of the dynamics of gentrification and resegregation is to find ways to expand the areas in which they are happening in such a way as to cool the processes.

In the suburbs, which saw a huge growth in the minority population in the 1990s, the dynamic of segregation is also contingent on boundary-drawing, but here the boundaries have been drawn by government—specifically by municipal authorities and school districts. Furthermore, the dynamics are exacerbated by exclusionary zoning, which takes advantage of the lower wealth and income of minorities to exclude them from neighborhoods and whole towns. So long as exclusionary zoning funnels minorities into particular lower-income suburbs, resegregation will seem inevitable. If minorities and lower-income whites are given the opportunity to live in higher-income suburbs, the likelihood of integration will increase dramatically. All that lies between the current sorry state of affairs and a new suburban housing market in which people are free to move where they will is a Supreme Court decision, *Euclid v. Ambler*, made in 1926.

Conclusion

The constructivist approach to policy-making is purposefully disruptive of established policies, practices, and lines of debate. The intent is not simply to act as a "bomb-thrower," but to find alternative ways to construct a viable policy that gives access to resources in a just manner. This requires understanding the values and interests behind current policy positions and the institutional structures that support and perpetuate them. So the intent here has been twofold: first, to recommend certain strategies for amending current institutional arrangements so that a genuine debate about values and interests can take place; and, second, to make value statements that position this author in such a debate. The institutional structure I favor is one that allows public, informed debate about "who gets what" in terms of access to capital; the value I most cherish in the context of this discussion is the ability of people of all races, ethnicities, and incomes to live in any neighborhood, subdivision, or suburb they choose.

Appendix

Following pages: Freddie Mac Form 70, Uniform Residential Appraisal Report, dated 6/93. Reprinted with permission from Freddie Mac, McLean, Va.

UNIFORM RESIDENTIAL APPRAISAL REPORT   File No.

S U B J E C T

Property Address		City		State	Zip Code

Legal Description			County		

Assessor's Parcel No.		Tax Year	R.E. Taxes $	Special Assessments $

Borrower		Current Owner		Occupant	Owner	Tenant	Vacant

Property rights appraised	Fee Simple	Leasehold	Project Type	PUD	Condominium (HUD/VA only)	HOA$	/Mo.

Neighborhood or Project Name	Map Reference	Census Tract

Sales Price $	Date of Sale	Description and $ amount of loan charges/concessions to be paid by seller

Lender/Client	Address	

Appraiser	Address	

N E I G H B O R H O O D

Location	Urban	Suburban	Rural	Predominant occupancy	Single family housing		Present land use %	Land use change	
					PRICE $ (000)	AGE (yrs)			
Built up	Over 75%	25-75%	Under 25%				One family	Not likely	Likely
Growth rate	Rapid	Stable	Slow	Owner	Low		2-4 family	In process	
Property values	Increasing	Stable	Declining	Tenant	High		Multi-family	To: ___	
Demand/supply	Shortage	In balance	Over supply	Vacant (0-5%)	Predominant		Commercial		
Marketing time	Under 3 mos.	3-6 mos.	Over 6 mos.	Vacant (over 5%)			( )		

Note: Race and the racial composition of the neighborhood are not appraisal factors.

Neighborhood boundaries and characteristics: _____

Factors that affect the marketability of the properties in the neighborhood (proximity to employment and amenities, employment stability, appeal to market, etc.):

Market conditions in the subject neighborhood (including support for the above conclusions related to the trend of property values, demand/supply, and marketing time - - such as data on competitive properties for sale in the neighborhood, description of the prevalence of sales and financing concessions, etc.):

P U D

Project Information for PUDs (If applicable) - - Is the developer/builder in control of the Home Owners' Association (HOA)?   Yes   No

Approximate total number of units in the subject project _____ . Approximate total number of units for sale in the subject project _____ .

Describe common elements and recreational facilities:

S I T E

Dimensions _____	Topography
Site area _____ Corner Lot Yes No	Size
Specific zoning classification and description _____	Shape
Zoning compliance Legal Legal nonconforming (Grandfathered use) Illegal No zoning	Drainage
Highest & best use as improved Present use Other use (explain)	View

Utilities	Public	Other	Off-site Improvements	Type	Public	Private		
Electricity			Street				Landscaping	
Gas			Curb/gutter				Driveway Surface	
Water			Sidewalk				Apparent easements	
Sanitary sewer			Street lights				FEMA Special Flood Hazard Area Yes No	
Storm sewer			Alley				FEMA Zone ___ Map Date ___	
							FEMA Map No.	

Comments (apparent adverse easements, encroachments, special assessments, slide areas, illegal or legal nonconforming zoning use, etc.): _____

D E S C R I P T I O N   O F   I M P R O V E M E N T S

GENERAL DESCRIPTION	EXTERIOR DESCRIPTION	FOUNDATION	BASEMENT	INSULATION
No. of Units	Foundation	Slab	Area Sq. Ft.	Roof
No. of Stories	Exterior Walls	Crawl Space	% Finished	Ceiling
Type (Det./Att.)	Roof Surface	Basement	Ceiling	Walls
Design (Style)	Gutters & Dwnspts.	Sump Pump	Walls	Floor
Existing/Proposed	Window Type	Dampness	Floor	None
Age (Yrs.)	Storm/Screens	Settlement	Outside Entry	Unknown
Effective Age (Yrs.)	Manufactured House	Infestation		

ROOMS	Foyer	Living	Dining	Kitchen	Den	Family Rm.	Rec. Rm.	Bedrooms	# Baths	Laundry	Other	Area Sq. Ft.
Basement												
Level 1												
Level 2												

Finished area above grade contains: Rooms;   Bedroom(s);   Bath(s);   Square Feet of Gross Living Area

INTERIOR	Materials/Condition	HEATING	KITCHEN EQUIP.	ATTIC	AMENITIES	CAR STORAGE:
Floors		Type	Refrigerator	None	Fireplace(s) #	None
Walls		Fuel	Range/Oven	Stairs	Patio	Garage # of cars
Trim/Finish		Condition	Disposal	Drop Stair	Deck	Attached
Bath Floor		COOLING	Dishwasher	Scuttle	Porch	Detached
Bath Wainscot		Central	Fan/Hood	Floor	Fence	Built-In
Doors		Other	Microwave	Heated	Pool	Carport
		Condition	Washer/Dryer	Finished		Driveway

C O M M E N T S

Additional features (special energy efficient items, etc.): _____

Condition of the improvements, depreciation (physical, functional, and external), repairs needed, quality of construction, remodeling/additions, etc.: _____

Adverse environmental conditions (such as, but not limited to, hazardous wastes, toxic substances, etc.) present in the improvements, on the site, or in the immediate vicinity of the subject property: _____

COST APPROACH			Comments on Cost Approach (such as, source of cost estimate, site value, square foot calculation and, for HUD, VA and FmHA, the estimated remaining economic life of the property): _____
ESTIMATED SITE VALUE. = $ _____			
ESTIMATED REPRODUCTION COST-NEW OF IMPROVEMENTS:			
Dwelling _____ Sq. Ft @ $ _____ = $ _____			
_____ Sq. Ft @ $ _____ = _____			
= _____			
Garage/Carport _____ Sq. Ft @ $ _____ = _____			
Total Estimated Cost-New . . . . = $ _____			
Less Physical	Functional	External			
Depreciation _____ = $ _____			
Depreciated Value of Improvements . . . . = $ _____			
"As-is" Value of Site Improvements . . . . = $ _____			
INDICATED VALUE BY COST APPROACH . . . . = $			

ITEM	SUBJECT	COMPARABLE NO. 1		COMPARABLE NO. 2		COMPARABLE NO. 3	
Address							
Proximity to Subject							
Sales Price	$		$		$		$
Price/Gross Liv. Area	$ ☑	$ ☑		$ ☑		$ ☑	
Data and/or							
Verification Sources							
VALUE ADJUSTMENTS	DESCRIPTION	DESCRIPTION	+ (-) $ Adjustment	DESCRIPTION	+ (-) $ Adjustment	DESCRIPTION	+ (-) $ Adjustment
Sales or Financing Concessions							
Date of Sale/Time							
Location							
Leasehold/Fee Simple							
Site							
View							
Design and Appeal							
Quality of Construction							
Age							
Condition							
Above Grade	Total Bdrms Baths	Total Bdrms Baths		Total Bdrms Baths		Total Bdrms Baths	
Room Count							
Gross Living Area	Sq. Ft.	Sq. Ft.		Sq. Ft.		Sq. Ft.	
Basement & Finished							
Rooms Below Grade							
Functional Utility							
Heating/Cooling							
Energy Efficient Items							
Garage/Carport							
Porch, Patio, Deck, Fireplace(s), etc.							
Fence, Pool, etc.							
Net Adj. (total)		+ ☐ – ☐ $		+ ☐ – ☐ $		+ ☐ – ☐ $	
Adjusted Sales Price of Comparable		$		$		$	

(Left margin vertical label: SALES COMPARISON ANALYSIS)

Comments on Sales Comparison (including the subject property's compatibility to the neighborhood, etc.): _____

ITEM	SUBJECT	COMPARABLE NO. 1	COMPARABLE NO. 2	COMPARABLE NO. 3
Date, Price and Data Source for prior sales within year of appraisal				

Analysis of any current agreement of sale, option, or listing of the subject property and analysis of any prior sales of subject and comparables within one year of the date of appraisal:

INDICATED VALUE BY SALES COMPARISON APPROACH . . . . = $ _____

INDICATED VALUE BY INCOME APPROACH (If Applicable) Estimated Market Rent $ _____ /Mo. x Gross Rent Multiplier _____ = $ _____

This appraisal is made ☐ "as is" ☐ subject to the repairs, alterations, inspections, or conditions listed below ☐ subject to completion per plans and specifications.

Conditions of Appraisal: _____

(Left margin vertical label: RECONCILIATION)

Final Reconciliation: _____

The purpose of this appraisal is to estimate the market value of the real property that is the subject of this report, based on the above conditions and the certification, contingent and limiting conditions, and market value definition that are stated in the attached Freddie Mac Form 439/Fannie Mae Form 1004B (Revised _____).

I (WE) ESTIMATE THE MARKET VALUE, AS DEFINED, OF THE REAL PROPERTY THAT IS THE SUBJECT OF THIS REPORT, AS OF _____

(WHICH IS THE DATE OF INSPECTION AND THE EFFECTIVE DATE OF THIS REPORT) TO BE $ _____

APPRAISER:	SUPERVISORY APPRAISER (ONLY IF REQUIRED):		
		☐ Did	☐ Did Not
Signature _____	Signature _____	Inspect Property	
Name _____	Name _____		
Date Report Signed _____	Date Report Signed _____		
State Certification # _____ State	State Certification # _____		State
Or State License # _____ State	Or State License # _____		State

Freddie Mac Form 70   6–93   10 CH.   PAGE 2 OF 2   Fannie Mae Form 1004   6–93

Abbreviations

ACB of A	Associated Credit Bureaus of America
AIREA	American Institute of Real Estate Appraisers
AU	automated underwriting
CHBP	Community Home Buyer Program
CHHB	Chicago House Hunt Book
CRA	Community Reinvestment Act
DU	Desktop Underwriter
ECOA	Equal Credit Opportunity Act
FDIC	Federal Deposit Insurance Corporation
FFIEC	Federal Financial Institution Examination Council
FHA	Federal Housing Administration
FHEFSS Act	Federal Housing Enterprises Financial Safety and Soundness Act
FHFB	Federal Housing Finance Board
FHLBB	Federal Home Loan Bank Board
FHLBS	Federal Home Loan Bank System
FHLMC	Federal Home Loan Mortgage Corporation
FICO	Fair, Issac and Company
FIRREA	Financial Institutions, Reform, Recovery and Enforcement Act
FNMA	Federal National Mortgage Association
FRB	Federal Reserve Board
FSLIC	Federal Savings and Loan Insurance Corporation
FTC	Federal Trade Commission
GNMA	Government National Mortgage Association
GSE	Government Sponsored Enterprise
HMDA	Home Mortgage Disclosure Act
HOAP	Home Ownership Assistance Program
HOLC	Home Owners Loan Corporation
HUD	Department of Housing and Urban Development

212	IRLEPU	Institute for Research in Land Economics and Public Utilities
	LP	Loan Prospector
	LTV	loan-to-value
	MAF	minimum assessment feedback
	MBS	mortgage-backed security
	MIP	mortgage insurance premium
	MSA	Metropolitan Statistical Area
	NAMA	National Association of Mercantile Agencies
	NAREB	National Association of Real Estate Brokers
	NCCRC	National Consumer Credit Reporting Corporation
	NRCA	National Retail Credit Association
	NRCMA	National Retail Credit Men's Association
	NTIC	National Training Information Center
	OCC	Office of the Comptroller of the Currency
	OFHEO	Office of Federal Housing Enterprise Oversight
	OTS	Office of Thrift Supervision
	PMI	private mortgage insurance
	RESPA	Real Estate Settlement Procedures Act
	SEC	Securities and Exchange Commission
	SREA	Society of Real Estate Appraisers
	TILA	Truth In Lending Act
	URAR	Uniform Residential Appraisal Report
	VA	Veterans Administration

Notes

Introduction

1. The data on the number and volume of originations in 2000 are from Mortgage Bankers Association of America (2000a and b), while the data on the volume of outstanding loans are from the Congressional Budget Office (2001).

2. Investors who buy loans on the secondary mortgage market invest a lot of energy in trying to anticipate future changes in interest rates and the behavior of borrowers. In this way, they try to pass on the cost of prepayment to the original lender, who, in turn, passes it on to the borrower in the form of higher interest rates. There is more on this in chapter 2.

3. Both Knight (1921) and Keynes ([1921] 1979) are credited with formulating the distinction between risk and uncertainty in the economics literature, though the latter's formulation was not explicit (Lawson 1985, 913). Knight explicitly makes the distinction I have drawn above between risk and uncertainty:

"The practical difference between the two categories, risk and uncertainty, is that in the former the distribution of the outcome in a group of instances is known (either through calculation *a priori* or from statistics of past experience), while in the case of uncertainty this is not true, the reason being in general that it is impossible to form a group of instances, because the situation dealt with is in a high degree unique" ([1921] 1979, 233).

Keynes's treatment of the distinction between risk and uncertainty stems from his work on probability. He defines probability as the relationship between a proposition and a set of relevant evidence: the probability of proposition *a* given evidence *h*. For example, the proposition "there is a one in three probability that a borrower will default on his mortgage loan if his credit score falls below 540" defines a probability-relation. For Keynes this relationship between proposition and evidence is a logical one, not subject to "human caprice" ([1921] 1979, 4). Thus a probability-relation is a relation we know with certainty, and, because Keynes defines risk in terms of probability, a risk decision is a decision made with certainty. But measuring or even comparing probability-relations is full of difficulties, and these difficulties result in uncertainty. Specifically, uncertainty exists either where someone is incapable of reasoning from the evidence to the conclusion or where the probability-relation itself is not measurable or comparable with other probability-relations.

4. Thus in the final paragraph of the *Treatise on Probability* Keynes argues: "the practical usefulness of inference, here termed Universal and Statistical Induction, on the validity of which the boasted knowledge of modern science depends, can only exist—and I do not now pause to inquire again whether such an argument *must* be circular—if the universe of phenomena does in fact present those peculiar characteristics of atomism and limited variety" ([1921] 1979, 427).

5. This incentive is in addition to the fact that the lender's exposure to loss is far less because the initial loan is below the value of the home, the gap being made up by the borrower's downpayment. The quality of this coverage is contingent on the lender's being able

to perform an adequate assessment of the value of the home—translating uncertainty into risk.

6. This formulation is a simplification because it is very common in the mortgage lending industry for the servicing of the loan to be divorced from the loan itself. An investor may buy the loan but contract with the original lender or another organization to service the loan. The contractual relationship does, of course, mean that the borrower has an indirect relationship with the "lender."

7. Myrdal elaborates a negative version of a similar process, which he calls cumulative causation, with regard to the "Negro problem":

> White prejudice and discrimination keep the Negro low in standards of living, health, education, manners and morals. This, in its turn, gives support to white prejudice. White prejudice and Negro standards thus mutually "cause" each other. . . . If either of the factors changes, this will cause a change in the other factor, too, and start a process of interaction where change in one factor will continuously be supported by the reaction of the other factor. The whole system will be moving in the direction of the primary change, but much further. This is what we mean by cumulative causation. (1996, 75–76)

In the instance Myrdal describes, white prejudice is a self-fulfilling prophecy because of the effect it has on the status of African Americans.

8. This consensus does not mean that lenders do not compete. They may compete in terms of marketing or price by finding innovative ways to more effectively reach potential borrowers and to keep operating costs down. The argument here is that they do not compete in how they construct risk—how they assess it, manage it, and where they lend.

9. How wide the coverage must be depends on the extent of the market the lender serves, and the extent to which people enter and leave it. As I argue later, the geographical mobility of Americans forced lenders early on to support a national network of credit bureaus.

10. Both ideas can be found in the work of Granovetter. His embeddedness concept (1985) is consistent with the first idea, while his more general thesis regarding the "social construction of economic institutions" (1992) is consistent with the second idea.

11. This is consistent with the argument Stone makes: "Portraying a problem as a decision is a way of controlling boundaries: what counts as problematic and what does not, how the phenomenon will be seen by others, and how others will respond to it. Each step in the rational model can be seen as part of a strategy to *control* a decision rather than merely to get through the agony of deciding" (1988, 194–95). See also Jasanoff 1998.

12. Commissioner Philip Brownstein made this announcement in a letter to the directors of the FHA's field offices (see U.S. Congress, House, Committee on Banking, Finance, and Urban Affairs 1972, 270–71). Before this announcement Congress had already moved to provide mortgage insurance, through the FHA, to areas designated for urban renewal under the 1961 Housing Act, Sections 220(h), 203(k) and 221(d)(3).

13. The CRA's regulations were changed in 1995 to make them much more results oriented. The new regulations took effect on January 1, 1996, though many lenders were able to elect to be examined under the old rules for a year after that.

14. For an extensive review of the literature see Turner and Skidmore 1999.

15. I cite the 1992 working paper rather than the 1996 journal article in the *American Economic Review* because the latter omits this statement; see Munnell et al. 1996.

16. For example, Martin argues:

> Money is not just an economic entity, a store of value, a means of exchange or even a 'commodity' traded and speculated in for its own sake; it is also a *social relation*. Financial markets are themselves structured networks of social relations, interactions and dependencies—they are

communities of actors and agents with shared interests, values and rules of behaviour, trust, co-operation and competition. Face-to-face contact, personal recommendation and informal word-of-mouth have always been central to the conduct of financial business and transactions, and remain so even in an age of advanced telecommunications—geography matters. These social relations are an important part of the embedded micro-regulation (accepted mores, norms, customs and rules) of business practice and behaviour in financial institutions and markets. Those practices in turn incorporate and reproduce specific structures of power, exploitation and domination." (1999, 11)

17. This has been found to be an effective tool in the field of microfinance in developing countries, where lenders use peer lending groups and other social structures to enhance their ability to get borrowers to repay. Though I do not cover it in this book, the lending industry has improved its ability to manage behavioral risk through monitoring the behavior of borrowers through their payment record and their general credit record. This is further bolstered, in situations where the loan is on the point of default, by aggressive loss mitigation procedures by which the lender helps the borrower restructure the loan in such a way that he is in a position to repay it.

18. See Gottdiener 1985 and 1993 for more on Lefebvre's trichotomous treatment of the production of space.

19. The Justice Department enforces fair lending laws, but the bank regulators conduct fair lending tests as part of their overall regulatory examination.

20. "Conventional" has a specific meaning in the mortgage lending industry. It means a loan that is not government-insured. A "conforming" loan is one that falls below the maximum loan limit that Congress has set for Fannie Mae and Freddie Mac purchases. In 1999 this limit was $252,700 for a single-family home ($379,050 in Alaska, Guam, Hawaii, and the Virgin Islands, where housing costs are higher).

21. In 1999 the system had 7,383 members, of which 5,329 are commercial banks, 1,610 are thrifts, and 440 are other types of institution such as credit unions (Federal Housing Finance Board 1999, 3).

22. There is some room for variation within this system in that borrowers with high loan-to-value ratios have access to private mortgage insurance, and the FHA offers borrowers who cannot get a conventional loan an alternative. In both cases, borrowers do not pay different interest rates but they do pay a mortgage insurance premium, which is essentially the same thing.

23. Most likely a warehouser, an organization that pools mortgages from a number of different sources in amounts sufficient to qualify for sale to Fannie Mae or Freddie Mac.

24. Up to 80 percent loan-to-value ratio and a 20-year loan term.

25. Until 1988 only thrifts were allowed to own Freddie Mac stock. Now the stocks are publicly traded.

Chapter 1. The Meaning of Value

1. McMichael refers to the summation (cost) method as "the common premise on which valuations have been based in past years" (1931, 2). Bodfish, in his survey of Ohio thrifts, sent out a sample appraisal problem which he structured in such a way as to be amenable to the cost theory (1927, 23). Furthermore in his discussion of how appraisal practices could be improved, all the suggestions for improvement were made within the context of the cost theory, and a discussion of different methods was limited to a discussion of methods of estimating building costs (ibid., 28–35). Finally, Register notes: "In the past there were many theories and methods in the valuation of property, one of the most common method used being the *summation method*, by which the total value of a property was derived by adding together incompatible values of fractional parts of the property" (1931, 83–84).

2. Bonright goes further and argues that this was "a concept of market value which, in-

216   stead of being borrowed from the economic textbooks or from the language of the street, seems to have been created by the law" (1937, 59). See also Commons (1934, 61–63) for the judicial origins of this concept. Note also Marx's comment: "In bourgeois society the economic *fictitio juris* prevails, that everyone, as a buyer, possesses an encyclopaedic knowledge of commodities" (1977, 44 n. 2).

3. Babcock (1924) devoted a whole chapter to the subject. Functional obsolescence results from changes in taste and technology that render an existing function of a building out of date. Economic obsolescence results from changes in the economy of the city, district, and neighborhood that render the building currently standing on the lot to be inappropriate to the lot — the building is no longer the highest and best use of the lot.

4. Abrams's focus, like that of many writers who follow him, is on the racist attitudes of the real estate industry at the time. Some of his quotes also include the idea that people of the same "social standing" prefer to live near each other, but he makes little of these. Abrams's quote from Fisher (1923) ends "people of similar social standing live near together" (Abrams 1955, 155). But he leaves out the very next few sentences, quoted above, which highlight the explicitly class nature of this sentiment.

5. Mertzke disagreed with the inevitability of value decline in the face of the incursion of apartment buildings. He noted that the more intensive use of land that such buildings generated raised land values to such an extent that single-family home owners would be willing to vote in favor of rezoning their block to allow the building of such apartments. They could then take advantage of the raised land values by selling their homes to "apartment builders" (1927, 4–5).

6. It should be noted that Hurd's book contains little reference to race, and none that could be considered significant to land valuation.

7. This list was generated both from existing bibliographies in other publications and from a search of Online Computer Library Center, Inc.'s "Worldcat" database, which includes all materials cataloged by member libraries, covering over 41 million records.

8. The organization was initially associated with the University of Wisconsin at Madison, but in 1925 it moved to Evanston, Illinois, and began its association with Northwestern University.

9. This statement was drafted by the Committee on Standards of Practice, Appraisal Division of NAREB, composed of Henry A. Babcock, John P. Hooker (a Chicagoan), and Arthur J. Mertzke.

10. Cutmore was a tax assessor for Cook County, Illinois, which encompasses Chicago.

11. Fisher and Babcock continued their institutional association after working together at the IRLEPU; both had appointments at the University of Michigan Business School before receiving their federal appointments.

12. I make this assertion based on a review of a small sample of the HOLC's maps held at the National Archives. For example, the Chicago map was not completed until April 1940, and the map of Kenosha, Wisconsin, was not completed until December 1937.

13. In addition to its commitment of loan monies the HOLC implemented a comprehensive property management program that ensured that properties that came into its possession as a result of foreclosure did not further deteriorate before they were sold.

14. This is an estimate provided by Frances Perkins, secretary of labor, to the House Committee on Banking and Currency during hearings regarding the act (U.S. Congress, House, Committee on Banking and Currency 1934, 66).

15. Babcock made the same point in the discussion printed in the first edition of the *Appraisal Journal*:

> There is a difference between something which we can call market value or market price . . . and the thing which we can call a warranted or justified price. A great deal of our law is apparently

predicated on the idea of price or value being what a property will command in the market, and very frequently we talk carelessly and say that the test of our valuation is found when the property is sold. I submit that that is not entirely correct. The figure we arrive at when we appraise real estate is not market price and is not market value. That is not what we are after. What we are really after is the amount of money which some one is warranted in paying for a piece of property. There is a distinction between what people actually do pay for property and what they should pay for property, and I think it is the latter figure that constitutes the security for the loan and the compensation to people where their property is taken away from them, and practically all the purposes for which we require valuations. (American Institute of Real Estate Appraisers 1932, 23)

16. In the subsequent discussion of the "Use of Data in Dwelling Valuation," the Manual clearly states that sales price data should not be relied upon as the sole measure of value (FHA 1936, pt. I, para. 307 (1)–(3)). Furthermore, the Manual also provided a justification for the practical usefulness of the income capitalization method, based on the ready availability of rental data, especially at the time, because the Depression had resulted in a large number of single-family homes being rented out (pt. I, para. 312(2) and 313(1)). This was in contrast to Babcock's advocacy of the sales comparison method in his 1924 and 1932 books. The Manual also noted that the particular skills and data needed to carry out an accurate income capitalization appraisal were not prevalent in the profession at that time (pt. I, para. 334(4)).

17. In contrast, the University of Chicago's Social Science Research Committee identified 75 community areas in the 1920s, Hunter (1974) identified 206 neighborhoods based on a survey conducted in 1968, and a map of Chicago neighborhoods printed in 1992 showed 183 neighborhoods.

18. The concept of risk rating seems to have emanated from the work of the Twentieth Century Fund which, in a draft housing bill presented by John Fahey, a trustee of the Fund and chairman of the board of the FHLBB, introduced the idea that the FHA's insurance fund should work on a "mutual" basis. Each borrower would be pooled with borrowers of a similar risk profile, and they would equally contribute to the insurance fund for their pool. Any proceeds remaining in the insurance fund for the pool at the end of its life would be reimbursed to the borrowers equally. Such a plan would prevent cross-subsidization of poor risks by good risks. But to implement this idea required an extensive risk rating system, which Babcock and his cohorts provided.

19. The appraiser can translate the uncertainty involved in the valuation process into a risk statement by stating that there is $y\%$ chance that the value of the home is x, or lies between x_1 and x_2, where the dollar value(s) given is/are the most probable of all.

20. The mark of Homer Hoyt is very apparent in the location rating section of the Manual. He joined the FHA as chief economist in the fall of 1934 and developed his economic background and sector theories of the city in 1935, when the Manual was being written (Hoyt 1970, 774). My emphasis on the principle of uniformity and its relationship to the warranted value theory is not designed to deemphasize Hoyt's influence. But it should be noted that Hoyt's theory of city structure and growth is almost identical to that of Hurd (1903), who developed it based on a specific definition of value. The broader point here is that the theories of urban dynamics underlying the FHA Manual are grounded in, though not necessarily logically following from, a particular theory of value.

21. The "Livability and Functional Plan" rating required that "the inspector determine the degree of practical usefulness for residential purposes to the typical family likely to occupy the subject property" (FHA 1936, pt. II, para. 131). But the rest of the rating was against an absolute benchmark. For example, the rating also required that the inspector "must determine whether or not the layout of the structure is economical, practical, and efficient. An economical layout is one which presents the greatest proportion of usable floor

218   area in relation to the gross floor area" (ibid.). The other such mixed benchmarks were "Mechanical and Convenience Equipment" and "Architectural Attractiveness."

22. The one exception was the "Topography and Special Hazards" rating.

23. I say "almost" because it is possible to have an area of uniform land values in which a variety of functions, each yielding the same rate of return, are performed, the variety being sufficient to satisfy the needs of all those living and working in the area.

24. Evidence that the Manual was correctly characterizing the policies of private sector organizations can be seen in the issue on "Real Estate Problems" in the *Annals of the American Academy* (1930) in an article by H. H. Richardson, vice-president of the Security Land Insurance Company, which insured the owners of land against the loss in its value. In the article he cited three factors which would exclude an area from his company's insurance activities: first, if it was a "non-progressive" city with a stagnant population; second, if it was a city dependent on one industry only; and third, cities "without a constructive plan or well-enforced zoning ordinance" because "the absence of such plans causes many 'blighted districts' in cities, resulting in lowered valuations and loss of confidence by the investing public" (Richardson 1930, 84).

25. In addition minorities and lower-income people were excluded as a result of the minimum property standards, which made many areas of central cities ineligible for mortgage insurance (Jackson 1980, 436). It was in the central cities that minorities and lower-income people were often confined by residential segregation.

26. It is unclear whether black properties were considered competitive with each other, and therefore could be rated in that way—there is no evidence this was considered possible.

27. Though the Manual emphasized homogeneity in its definition of a neighborhood, it noted that considerable variance in properties' final risk rating within a neighborhood was likely (pt. II, para. 208).

28. When an appraiser went to rate a property in a particular neighborhood he took the appropriate card with him and compared the information on the card to the benchmark property itself, which it described, to give him a sense of the relationship between the characteristics of the property and its rating. He then used this information when he went on to look at the subject property: he could easily come to a rating based on a comparison of that property with the benchmark and the information on the card.

29. See Harvey 1989, 177–78, for a discussion of the inherent tension resulting from the ability to freely buy and sell real property. The Manual sought to solve this tension by giving home owners of different classes the means to separate themselves from others—this is an example of the "powers of domination" to which Harvey refers. Ironically, the Manual achieved this, in part, by deepening the commodification of real property rather than denying its ability to be bought and sold.

30. For an amusing "philosophical" discussion of the meaning of value by members of Congress and VA bureaucrats, see the hearings before the House Committee on World War Veterans Legislation on the Amendments to the Servicemen's Readjustment Act in 1945.

31. For more on this see chapter 2.

32. Herman Walther was credited as a research assistant in Dorau and Hinman 1928, viii, working at the Institute for Research in Land Economics and Public Utilities at Northwestern University. He went on to become a lecturer in real estate at the university's School of Commerce.

33. The AIREA's *Appraisal Terminology and Handbook* 1950 edition defined value purely in terms of market value.

34. As Ekdahl (1964) notes, the Board was closely allied with the savings and loan industry until the 1960s, when McMurray was appointed its chair. His appointment was an accident of politics: he was initially slated to head the Housing and Home Finance Adminis-

tration, but that position went to Robert Weaver, whom the Kennedy administration had picked to be the first black cabinet member.

35. Citations in this format are to references in the Federal Register.

36. The Standards define value as the following:

The most probable price which a property should bring in a competitive and open market under all conditions requisite to a fair sale, the buyer and seller each acting prudently and knowledgeably, and assuming the price is not affected by undue stimulus. Implicit in this definition is the consummation of a sale as of a specified date and the passing of title from seller to buyer under conditions whereby:

1. The buyer and seller are typically motivated.
2. Both parties are well informed or well advised, and each is acting in what they consider their best interest.
3. A reasonable time is allowed for exposure in the open market.
4. Payment is made in terms of cash in United States Dollars or in terms of a financial arrangement comparable thereto. The price represents the normal consideration for the property sold unaffected by special or creative financing or sales concessions. (Quoted in U.S. Department of Housing and Urban Development 1999, Ch. 4–2)

37. Fannie Mae and Freddie Mac through automation are at the same time decreasing the amount of information the appraiser gathers, depending on the type of loan and its risk profile. Freddie Mac's Minimum Assessment Feedback (MAF) program tells loan processors the detail required in the appraisal and the correct form to use. The MAF program is based on Freddie Mac's own "Home Value" statistical model, which uses data from transactions to check the sales price and evaluate if it is supported by the model and the data (Freddie Mac 2002a, 44.1, and Freddie Mac 2002b, Sec. 7). Fannie Mae allows streamlined appraisals depending on the assessment of the mortgage risk made by its automated underwriting program, Desktop Underwriter (Fannie Mae 1996).

38. All references to Freddie Mac 2002a and b and Fannie Mae 1999, 2000, and 2002 are from the on-line subscription service www.allregs.com. Each reference to or quotation of material from this source was verified in August 2002. Hard copies of all referenced and quoted material are available from the author.

Chapter 2. Rules for Assessing the Borrower and Managing Behavioral Risk

1. Initially the FHLBB issued regulations to charter institutions called Charter E, which specified a 75% limit, but in 1937 it introduced Charter K, which, though it had a limit of 75%, also allowed it to be exceeded subject to the authorization of the institution's members and FHLBB regulations, which set the limit at 80% (1938 CFR 202.9 and 203.10(b)).

2. McAvoy was a real estate builder and appraiser who had, 20 years earlier, built a house for Senator Robert F. Wagner, who sat on the Banking and Currency Committee (see U.S. Congress, Senate, Committee on Banking and Currency 1934, 328).

3. The differential would have directed FHA-insured lending away from the market for existing homes, thus ensuring that savings and loan associations would not face competition in a market in which they had a well-established presence.

4. Basing the loan-to-value calculations on an acquisition cost that included the MIP raised the total amount that could be financed with an FHA-insured mortgage, while basing the downpayment on the cost of acquisition exclusive of the MIP lowered the downpayment amount because it was calculated as the percentage of a lower amount. The FHA justified its liberal policy by citing data showing that, though default rates rose as the loan-to-value ratio went from 95 to 97 percent, increases in the loan-to-value ratio beyond 97 percent were not correlated with higher default rates. The "acquisition cost" definition would have its greatest impact in raising loan-to-value ratios that were already above 97 percent (48 FR 28794).

The FHA did not address the fact that its policy would increase the number of loans with a ratio greater than 97 percent as a proportion of the FHA's overall portfolio, thus increasing its overall risk exposure.

5. The Price Waterhouse study remained at the center of the political debate about the fate of the FHA during the early 1990s. In 1992 a follow-up study showed that the original study had severely underestimated the losses facing the FHA. This was used as an excuse by community advocates and housing industry representatives to pour scorn on the Price Waterhouse risk model and to rescind the risk-based premium policy.

6. This citation refers to the United States Code of Federal Regulations.

7. Section 203(b)(1) of the 1934 National Housing Act has not been amended since it was first written and simply states:

"(b) To be eligible for insurance under this section a mortgage shall—(1) Have, or be held by, a mortgagee approved by the Administrator as responsible and able to service the mortgage properly" (12 USCS 1709). The Federal Home Loan Bank Board's regulations and Fannie Mae's and Freddie Mac's charters are silent on the issue.

8. When a loan carries a 6 percent interest rate over a 15-year term, fully amortizing, the two ratios are equivalent to the nearest percent.

9. The secondary market's guidelines also included what is called a "back-end ratio," which is the ratio of monthly housing expenses plus all other recurring monthly debts to monthly income. This ratio is 36% today.

10. In 1972 and 1982 the FHA's back-end ratio was 50 percent, and today it is 41 percent. The change in the type of income that formed the basis for the calculation of the ratios, from net effective income to gross income, occurred in 1989.

11. Furthermore, in the late 1980s and 1990s, Fannie Mae and Freddie Mac increased the debt-to-income ratio cut-offs for certain loan products targeted at lower-income home buyers.

12. I can state only what the NRCA's standard report was because I have no copies of the wide variety of reports produced by the hundreds of different credit bureaus around the country. A study of the costs and timeliness of reports conducted by the Research Division of the NRCA in 1935 cited a Dayton, Ohio, bureau manager who noted that there was a wide discrepancy in the amount and depth of information in a report, depending on which bureau produced it (National Retail Credit Association 1935, 9–10). Nevertheless, as I discuss below, the NRCA's standard report was the only one that could be used in the exchange of reports between its member credit bureaus.

13. The NCCRC began life in 1906 as the National Association of Mercantile Agencies (NAMA), which was set up by a group of local agencies meeting in New York. The purpose of this organization seems to have been to facilitate the exchange of information among local credit bureaus, so they could provide information on applicants for credit from out of town to local stores. In 1912 the National Retail Credit Men's Association was formed at the annual convention of the NAMA in Spokane, Washington. (NRCMA–"credit men" made the decisions as to whether to grant applicants credit; women were confined to the work of collecting and supplying information in the offices of credit bureaus.) The purpose of this association was to serve as a national forum for credit grantors. In 1921 the two associations merged under the auspices of the NRCMA, with the NAMA becoming the "Credit Service Exchange Division" of the NRCMA. In 1927 the NRCMA became the National Retail Credit Association (NRCA) and at the August 1932 convention in Washington, D.C., the NCCRC was created; in 1934, it replaced the "service division" (*Credit World* 1926–1932, passim; Truesdale 1927, 13–17; and Blake 1987, 24–33).

14. The first savings and loan associations held a lottery to determine who got a loan—everyone eventually got a loan but the lottery determined the order in which loans were made.

15. Dun and Bradstreet did not, and does not, make reports on individuals, which were the types of reports that the FHA mostly required. The Retail Credit Company is now known as Equifax, Inc., having changed its name in 1979 (Rourke 1988, 24). Though Equifax is now heavily involved in credit reporting, and is one of the "big three" agencies, its prominence in this field is largely a post-computerization phenomenon (since 1970). In 1968 its president, W. Lee Burge, stated that only 6 percent of its volume was credit reporting and by far the largest part of its volume was in providing information services to the insurance industry. Insofar as the Retail Credit Company was involved in credit reporting, it seems to have done this through the local credit bureaus it had bought. Its post-1970 expansion into credit reporting was a direct result of such buying activity (ibid.). The local bureaus it bought were likely to be members of the National Retail Credit Association and affiliated to the NCCRC (which, in 1937, became the Associated Credit Bureaus of America).

16. Copies of credit reports can be found in U.S. Congress, House, Committee on the Judiciary 1968, 143, 151, and 160. Credit Bureau Reports, Inc. was, at that time, operating as a national sales organization. It bought reports from local credit bureaus, most of which were members of ACB of A.

17. Investigative reports were reports based on more in-depth investigations into the life of an individual, which included information-gathering techniques such as interviews with neighbors.

18. Feins and Lane (1981, 113) note that by the 1970s direct assessment of a person's character was no longer carried out by lenders, but that it was also not clear how lenders treated the more "objective" information presented by the credit history.

19. Computerization has dramatically decreased the costs of organizing and transmitting credit data. As a result, it has destroyed the network externalities that allowed the ACB of A to dominate the industry up to the 1960s. Essentially the organizations providing merged credit reports act as a bridge between the three networks linked to the three reporting agencies, though many credit grantors report to more than one reporting service. The current structure of the industry does raise a question about the extent to which network externalities are really such strong structural constraints, rather than simply the product of a monopoly strategy by one organization that already has an extensive network. Could there have been, before computerization, a set of disparate agencies, served by their own set of local bureaus, which supplied information to organizations that merged their data into one report?

20. Fannie Mae's latest automated underwriting system, Desktop Underwriter 5.0, does not use FICO scores. I discuss this development further in chapter 4.

21. They also use the score in a third way, as a key indicator in their selection of files for post-closing quality control review. Those files with low credit scores are more likely to be reviewed by Fannie Mae and Freddie Mac underwriters (Fannie Mae 1995b; Freddie Mac 1996b, 1997).

22. Fannie Mae has a similar policy for all derogatory credit when underwriting the credit history manually and makes the same exception for Chapter 13 bankruptcies as Freddie Mac does: "We generally require four years to elapse before we will consider the borrower to have a reestablished credit history. We will, however, consider two years as an acceptable interval for reestablishing a credit history when the derogatory information in the borrower's credit record resulted from documented extenuating circumstances or when the derogatory information relates to a Chapter 13 bankruptcy (regardless of the reasons that contributed to the bankruptcy)" (Fannie Mae 2002, X, 803.02). A Chapter 13 bankruptcy is one in which the debtor agrees to pay off all his creditors according to a monthly installment plan agreed to by the courts. It provides relief from creditors only insofar as it establishes this agreed-upon schedule; no debts are written off. In a Chapter 7 bankruptcy all the debts are written off.

23. According to Alexander (1987) the decisions made in the early nineteenth century, on which most subsequent decisions have been based, were not well founded, and before that time the courts had in some cases allowed prepayment of a loan without penalty.

24. Both the FHA and FHLBB had regulations in place regarding these penalties. The FHA's regulations required that the mortgagee pay the FHA a penalty of 1 percent of the original mortgage amount upon full payment of the mortgage loan (3 FR 364), but was silent on the size of the penalty that a mortgagee could charge a mortgagor. In 1969 this rule was changed to apply to only the first ten years of the loan (34 FR 197951). Alexander (1987, 326–27) documents the FHLBB's regulations over the years.

25. Among the opponents of the prepayment penalty were Senator William Proxmire, who was the second most senior Democrat on the Senate Committee on Banking at the time, and Ralph Nader's Public Interest Research Group. Prepayment was not the only issue that was controversial in the uniform instruments; others included payment of interest on escrow accounts, a 30-day acceleration clause, and a requirement that all borrowers pay their taxes and insurance payments into an escrow account managed by the lender (U.S. Congress, Senate, Committee on Banking, Housing, and Urban Affairs 1971).

26. The purpose of this legislation was to ensure that nonfederally chartered housing creditors were not put at a competitive disadvantage in the supply of nonstandard mortgage products because of state regulations, to which federally chartered financial institutions were not subject.

27. For a discussion of OTS's statutory authority to preempt state laws see General Accounting Office 2000. In April 2000 the OTS issued an "Advanced notice of proposed rule-making" in which it proposed to amend its regulations regarding preemption because of evidence that lenders were using the Parity Act to avoid state laws designed to curb abusive practices, commonly known as predatory lending (65 FR 17811). At the time of writing the OTS has not changed its rule.

28. It was only in 1985 that the FHLBB issued regulations prohibiting regulated institutions from charging such prepayment penalties (50 FR 46744).

Chapter 5. The Loan Application Process

1. I conducted two sets of interviews to understand the lending process. In 1992 and 1993 I interviewed 65 people involved in the home purchase and lending process: 19 real estate brokers, 18 loan officers, 15 underwriters, one loan processor, 4 Community Reinvestment officers, and 8 other senior officers of lending institutions. The employees of lending institutions were drawn from: 6 mortgage banks, 5 thrifts (4 savings and loans and one federal savings bank), 4 banks, 2 mortgage brokers, and one warehouser (bundles the individual loans of a number of lenders for sale on the secondary market). I found people to interview in multiple ways: cold telephone calling from industry directories, letters, contacts through other interviewees, and direct solicitation (walking in off the street and asking for an interview). I make no pretense that this sample of people was generated using formal techniques of randomization, and there was some obvious self-selection going on in the case of many lenders who were willing to talk to me because they were undergoing changes in their policies to enable them to serve low-income borrowers more effectively. The only population that was probably overlooked in my interviews was that of the very small depository institutions, but they do a very small proportion of the lending in Chicago. I feel I have a representative sample of lenders doing most of the business in Chicago, given the constraints imposed by trying to interview people whose time is money.

In 2000 I interviewed another 10 underwriters to update my information, paying particular attention to the impact of credit scoring and automated underwriting on the process. I also surveyed 29 real estate brokers working in a black neighborhood in Chicago, and another 18 working in a white and Hispanic neighborhood in the same city. The focus of the survey was on the extent to which brokers maintain relationships with loan officers.

I cite quotes from interviewees by code in order to protect their identities. I identify real estate brokers by the code "reb. #"; the # refers to a particular broker by number. I identify loan officers, underwriters, and other institution officers by the code "len. #"; the # refers to a particular institution. The # may be followed by a letter if more than one member of the institution is cited in the text. It will be clear from the text what position the individual holds within the institution. In the following chapter I identify real estate appraisers by the code "ap. #"; the # refers to a particular appraiser by number.

2. Another study reports evidence that the influence of real estate brokers is exaggerated and cites the recommendation of friends and past experience with a lender as the two most important reasons for contacting a lender (Duncan 1999). Nevertheless, though there may be a number of ways that a buyer comes to choose a lender, the predominant channel is one based on some sort of personal referral, most likely from a real estate broker. To the extent that referral networks are neighborhood-based, the buyer's choice of a lender is structured by the existing housing market structure, something that I address in the next chapter.

3. There are exceptions to this rule, but these are rare. Only one underwriter I interviewed met with the applicant as a part of her standard operating procedures.

4. Throughout this chapter and the next I sometimes paraphrase the account of a situation described to me by an interviewee, or I describe a situation I observed. These appear in the format used here. Direct quotes from interviews (except for sentence fragments in the text) appear as block quotations.

5. In some cases lenders will not make such loans. These tighter guidelines for investment properties are a result of the belief that such properties constitute a greater risk. The reasoning here is that a mortgagor who lives in a property is far less likely to be able to or want to walk away from it if he runs into financial trouble, than one who does not. This reasoning is akin to that which goes into the interpretation of an application file by an underwriter.

6. Despite the emphasis on patterns of credit mishandling, signs of individual cases of mishandling in the past two years can sink a loan.

7. There have now been three updates to DU version 5 since the release of 5.0 in July 2000. Though they are different from each other I refer to them generically as version 5, unless specified.

8. Fannie Mae's press release regarding version 5.0 and subsequent news stories make no mention of this feature, though the lenders who first tested version 5.0 in late 2000, two of whose underwriters I talked to, described the system to me. The new *Selling Guide*, released in 2002, provides details on expanded approval, though it is available only to approved lenders. Expanded approval works in combination with a product Fannie Mae launched in 1999 called "Timely Repayments" that extends loans to applicants with poor credit. The borrowers pay a half to two percentage points more in interest, which is then reduced by one percentage point if they stay current on their loan for two years (Strickland 1999).

Chapter 4. Constructing Housing Markets

1. It is worth noting that Schelling says nothing about where a collective definition of a neighborhood comes from. This undermines his contention that he is using "micromotives" to explain "macrobehavior" because in the bounded neighborhood model he is assuming a collectively defined neighborhood, a "macrobehavior" in which "micromotives" play out.

2. Put yourself in the shoes of a real estate broker showing properties to a white home buyer. By law he cannot ask the buyer her racial preferences and so he has to discern them in some way. Or he can choose the default option of assuming that they are racist and show her only properties in white neighborhoods.

3. I generated home buyer data from the Home Mortgage Disclosure Act by looking at the distribution of loans for home purchases where the borrower indicated that she would be occupying the home.

4. Low- and moderate-income applicants are those with incomes at or below 80 percent of the median income of a family of four in the Metropolitan Statistical Area, as calculated annually by the U.S. Department of Housing and Urban Development. Middle-income applicants are those with incomes greater than 80 percent of the median and less than or equal to 120 percent. High-income applicants are those with incomes greater that 120 percent of the median. In 1998 the median income in the Chicago Metropolitan Area was $59,500.

5. Pulaski Avenue as a boundary has an interesting status. According to the most recent edition of the *Chicago Sun-Times' Living in Greater Chicago*, this street serves as the western boundary of Gage Park, whereas the *Chicago Tribune*'s description of the community follows the Burgess community area boundaries. The predecessor to *Living in Greater Chicago*, the *House Hunt Book*, also followed the Burgess community area boundaries on its map of Gage Park.

6. For the purposes of this analysis "upper-income" is defined as 120 percent or more of the metropolitan area's median income for each year in the time series.

7. The example of the boulevards of Logan Square speaks to an alternative process of white settlement, which does not necessarily result in the problems of gentrification, even if we assume that white home owners want to be around other white home owners. Why could we not observe a process by which small clusters of white home buyers congregate around a set of dispersed nodes throughout the West Town, Logan Square, and Humboldt Park community areas, where the nodes are centered on such favored places as parks, subway stations, and stretches of boulevards? The result would be a large, spatially integrated area.

8. As Sharon Zukin so aptly put it: "The basic problem . . . is not . . . that capitalism eventually transmutes all ideas into commodity fetishes. Rather, the danger is that the realization of ideas in urban space re-creates an unequal distribution of the benefits these ideas represent" (quoted in Caulfield 1994, 228).

9. The mantra of the real estate industry is "location, location, location," but it is not a particular point in space that matters, but rather what surrounds that point in space, what the neighborhood is like.

Chapter 5. Lending Discrimination

1. The historical data show that this legitimacy is a socially constructed one, rather than stemming from "objective" economic analysis. Nevertheless, the studies accepted the legitimacy of many of the factors that they were criticized for omitting, and so these criticisms were legitimate in the eyes of all parties to the debate.

2. The period covered by these data is 1993–98. Beginning in 1993, new regulations came into effect which increased the number of mortgage banks covered by HMDA. Mortgage banks have traditionally been more likely to serve minorities, so comparing post-1992 data with pre-1993 data can lead to biased conclusions.

It is important to isolate prime lenders from subprime lenders in these calculations because the latter have very high denial rates, reflecting a different approach to the loan application process—they are more likely to take an application that they will subsequently deny. The Department of Housing and Urban Development has developed a list of subprime lenders and lenders specializing in lending to purchasers of manufactured homes. For details on this see Scheessele 1999.

3. Author's calculations from HMDA data released by the Federal Financial Institutions Examination Council, 1993–1998. See chapter 4 n. 4 for income category definitions.

4. More generally, it is unclear that there is a good link between default rates and profit

maximization: what the studies should really look at is whether, after taking into account all 225 costs and fees, lenders make more or less profit on loans to minorities than they do on loans to whites.

5. Note that the cultural affinity hypothesis shares a premise with the standard articulations of statistical discrimination: lenders make decisions about loan applications on the basis of imperfect information. As originally articulated by Phelps, statistical discrimination encompasses the mechanisms inherent in the idea of cultural affinity. Though his emphasis is on the role of background information in the decision (in his case) of the employer, in terms of both its negative content and its reliability (1972, 660), Phelps also introduces a "further case" in which the reliability of test scores varies across racial groups (661). This "further case" is the mechanism by which cultural affinity has its effect.

6. An easy way to understand how this might work is to think of the pool of minority applicants as divided into three groups with different true credit scores: 54 with scores of 650, 30 with scores of 660, and 18 with scores of 670. Assume the lender measures their true score with the following degree of accuracy: 1/3 of the time they get the score exactly right, 1/3 of the time they are 15 points too high, and 1/3 of the time they are 15 points too low. Also assume the lender uses a cut-off score of 659. If the lender could measure minority applicants with complete accuracy, as we assume it does for whites, then it would approve 48 loans. But owing to its errors it approves 1/3 of the 650 applicants, 2/3 of the 660 applicants, and 2/3 of the 670 applicants, thus approving a total of 50 applicants (18 + 20 + 12). Thus, *as a group*, minorities gain greater access to credit, but still there are a number of *individual* minority applicants who are denied loans because of the lender's error.

7. For example, Calomiris, Kahn, and Longhofer conceptualize the dynamics of cultural affinity along the following lines: "Loan officers must expend time and effort in evaluating the prospects of a loan. This evaluation includes not only consideration of objective financial factors but also the loan officer's opinion as to whether or not the applicant is likely to repay. This opinion is the result of a complex array of subtle signals: firmness of handshake, dress, local characteristics, posture, nervous habits can play a part in a banker's appraisal of an applicant's character" (1994, 650).

This captures some of the complexities of the interaction between an applicant and a loan officer, but it mistakenly puts the loan decision in the hands of the loan officer, whereas it is most likely to be in the hands of an underwriter who has never met the applicant. On the other hand, Ferguson and Peters (1997) are able to develop a model of disparate treatment of minorities without the decision-maker having knowledge of the minority status of the applicant, because minorities look different in light of the information gathered about them. To understand whether such a situation is likely requires us to understand more clearly how minorities might look different in the first place—in other words, how the information gathered in the loan application process results in minorities looking different.

Cornell and Welch, though not writing explicitly about lending discrimination, have a more detailed exposition of the sources of affinity. They discuss people of a "similar cultural type" which is "interpreted broadly to include groups defined by language, religious belief, ethnic background, race, sex, sexual preference, neighborhood upbringing, schooling, or membership in social organizations" (1996, 543).

8. There is evidence that looking within the process can produce promising results for our understanding of racial disparities in denial rates. Squires and Kim (1995) show that lenders who employ a greater percentage of minorities on their staff are more likely to be successful in serving the minority community. They do not specify the positions, beyond being managerial and professional, that the minority employees hold, so the findings do not allow us to specify the causal mechanisms by which this relationship comes about. Turner and Skidmore (1999) provide a case study that demonstrates the extent to which employees of one lender were ignorant of the consequences of their loan application process for minori-

ties. What this case study demonstrates is that the lending industry itself may not understand what it is doing in its treatment of minorities.

9. The data from Olcott's *Blue Book* are also the product of the views of real estate professionals. As they state in their explanatory introduction on land values:

> The valuation herein given is arrived at by making a careful survey each year of the whole City and Suburbs, interviewing local dealers for data on sales, asking prices, and rentals in their neighborhood. Occupancy and collections are also inquired into. In the office of the publication, files are compiled of transfers and advertised prices, and all other information obtainable as to the trend of the market. The valuations may be said to be quotations of land values, rather than estimates of them. (1990, A5)

10. Land values are given in dollars per front foot, of a standard 125 foot–deep Chicago lot. These values are used in order to control for the type of building on the land. Thus these values do not compare single-family homes with 3–flats. They also control for the level of deterioration of buildings on the land. The problem with using land values is that they do not easily translate into house prices, which is what lenders are interested in. But all in all they do reflect the level of confidence that the industry has in a location.

11. This is not to say that this lack of homogeneity is a stable condition. In the two established gentrified communities of Lake View and Lincoln Park the percentage of the population which is white increased between 1980 and 1990—two of only three community areas in the city to experience such an increase, the other being the Near North Side.

12. This recognition by the mainstream real estate industry was supported by a black loan officer I interviewed. She took me on a tour to demonstrate the soundness of the market she served, which covered the Southeast Side middle-class neighborhoods.

13. I used a 1 percent cut-off to limit the lenders included in the comparison to those which had a more than passing relationship with the market. For the most part there were 20 to 30 lenders in this group, and they usually took more than 65 percent of the loans in the market.

14. I compared the list of subprime lenders created by the Department of Housing and Urban Development for 1998 who were active in the Chicago lending market with the list of lenders advertising in the 1998–99 Chicago Yellow Pages in the "Mortgage Loans" category.

15. Given my characterization of the lending process, the income of the applicant should make little difference in whether she gets a loan or not, because real estate brokers and loan officers take the applicant's income into account when constructing her risk profile. This is borne out in the case of white loan applicants, whose success rate in getting a loan was 82 percent in the case of low- and moderate-income applicants and 84 percent in the case of all other applicants with known incomes (FFIEC 1993–1998, author's calculations).

16. These do not add up to 100 percent because some applications may be approved and not accepted by the applicant, others may be withdrawn by the applicant before the application process is complete, and still others may have their files closed out because the applicant failed to provide sufficient information for a decision to be made. The approval rate is the most important measure of the extent to which the process is working because it shows the extent to which loan officers and underwriters are achieving their mission—generating loans from applications.

17. Fair, Isaac and Company's Website lists the five important factors that go into determining an individual's credit score: payment history, the amount owed, the length of the credit history, whether new credit has been taken out recently, and the mix of accounts (www.fairisaac.com).

18. See Dymski 1995 for a model of the self-fulfilling dynamic of the loan market operating in a segregated housing market.

19. The NTIC defined worst lenders as those lenders who had the highest number of defaults in high default census tracts.

20. The FHA loan denial rates are lower across the board, but the differences across market areas are the same.

21. In the highest income category the average loan amounts for which black home buyers applied in devastated and middle-class housing markets were almost the same as the average in the white market. Nevertheless, black applicants fared better in the white market than in these markets, contradicting the argument presented here. In the devastated market it is likely that the high-income applicants were applying for loans to purchase and rehabilitate long-neglected historic mansions—deals that many lenders find complicated to finance and that are therefore likely to fall through. In the case of the middle-class market the high loan amount applications mostly came from The Gap neighborhood, where the average amount was $168,000 and where, again, many of the high-income deals would likely have involved a more complex purchase and rehabilitation process, compared to $126,000 in the rest of the middle-class market.

22. This last explanation is not completely satisfactory because high-income black applicants in black neighborhoods have a higher average loan amount than low-income applicants in the white markets, yet the latter are approved at a higher rate. Two other possible explanations are that people of the same income and race applying for loans in a different market have different risk profiles, or that appraisals are causing a problem of some sort and lenders are simply not reporting these as the reason for denying the loan. The only way to adjudicate between these explanations is through a close examination of the particular processes that produced the data, something I touch on in chapter 7.

Chapter 6. Constructing Risk

1. The viability of a market approach to valuation, which was, by the 1960s, the consensus in the appraisal profession, was given additional support by the development of local associations in which appraisers could exchange appraisal information. The Society of Residential Appraisers further promoted the development of such information exchange within the profession with its Market Data Centers.

2. This interaction between rules and judgment is the essence of being a professional, as those first involved in the efforts to professionalize appraising were only too aware. On the one hand, a profession involves the promulgation of accepted rules; on the other hand, it is the exercise of judgment that is the mark of a professional because one is a professional not only because of one's training but also because of one's intelligence and character. Bureaucrats and hacks implement rules, professionals exercise judgment.

3. Adam Smith warned against this very problem when he argued: "though the law cannot hinder people of the same trade from sometimes assembling together, it ought to do nothing to facilitate such assemblies; much less to render them necessary. . . . The pretence that corporations are necessary for the better government of the trade, is without any foundation. The real and effectual discipline which is exercised over a workman, is not that of his corporation, but that of his customers" (Smith 1976, 144). If you substitute the word *profession* for the word *trade* you get an idea of what Smith might have thought about professional associations. Of course, professionals will argue that their knowledge-based activities cannot be compared to those of a workman in a trade because a lay person has no ability to judge the quality of a professional's work.

4. Despite its advantages this consensus does not cover the whole mortgage market. The consensus excludes a large number of potential borrowers. It is here that the subprime lenders operate. The defining characteristic of these lenders is that they are willing to work outside the consensus, at a price. One might hope that they would be the source of innovative ideas about how to underwrite mortgage loans, but it is unclear that they are in any but

228   one respect: they are willing to vary the interest rate they charge depending on the risk the
borrower represents. I take this up in the next chapter.

5. Of course, it is hard to see how one can say that people acting with complete information (including information about their own desires) are making decisions. They are simply automata following preordained routes.

Chapter 7. New Policy Approaches to Discrimination and Subprime Lending

1. In 1998 only 46 percent of black applicants for conventional, prime home purchase
loans nationwide were approved, while 59 percent of Latinos and 73 percent of whites were
approved (author's calculations based on data in Scheessele 1999).

2. For example, beyond the instances cited in previous chapters, underwriting guidelines regarding employment stability have changed from requiring that applicants have been
in the same job for two years to requiring that they have been employed for two years; and
considerable efforts have been made to make it easier for immigrants to get loans.

3. On October 31, 2000, HUD issued its final rule for its new targets for Fannie Mae
and Freddie Mac. These targets stipulate that for 2001 through 2003: 50 percent of the loans
they buy must be loans to families earning below the area median family income; 31 percent
must be in targeted geographical areas, identified as low-income census tracts and high minority census tracts; 20 percent must be special affordable housing loans; and the equivalent
of 1 percent of the average amount of their purchases from 1997 through 1999 must be devoted to affordable multifamily loan purchases.

4. HUD testimony before the Senate Subcommittee on Consumer and Regulatory Affairs in 1991 revealed that though in 1978 HUD was given the task of reviewing Fannie
Mae's lending in cities, it received data that it could use to do so only from 1978 to 1980. In
1982 an agreement between HUD and Fannie Mae expunged information on the census
tract, age, and price of the property and the income of the borrower from the data Fannie
Mae submitted to HUD (U.S. Congress, Senate, Committee on Banking, Housing, and
Urban Affairs 1991). Stanton (1996, 17 fn. 36) quotes a 1991 report from the secretary of
the Treasury which stated: "The principal GSEs are few in number; they have highly qualified staffs; they have strong support for their programs from special interest groups; and
they have significant resources with which to influence political outcomes." There is no indication that this political power has decreased since then, though in recent years the two entities have needed to flex their political muscle more forcefully in the face of criticisms not
only from community activists but also from organizations advocating revocation of their
federal charters. Part of this flexing has been an increase in political donations. According to
the Center for Responsive Politics (www.opensecrets.org), Fannie Mae soft money contributions increased from $500,000 in 1997/8 to $1.2m in 1999/2000; Freddie Mac soft money
contributions increased from $876,000 to $2.15m in the same period.

5. The argument against a full disclosure of the models underlying the AU systems is
that they are "proprietary." Making them public would allow their replication by other financial institutions. Fair, Isaac and Company uses this argument against making the model
underlying the credit scoring system public, and in addition argues that public knowledge of
the model would undermine its ability to predict credit behavior because the public would
act on its knowledge of the model to circumvent it.

6. HUD's Office of Policy Development and Research finally issued a report in May
1996. Though there remain some vocal critics of Fannie Mae and Freddie Mac, including
Rep. Richard Baker (R-La.), there is very little likelihood that they will lose their charters
for the reasons discussed in the previous note.

7. For this pattern of lending to become generalized, Fannie Mae and Freddie Mac
would have to adopt it. Their charters do allow them to share risk with primary lenders in
the event that a loan exceeds the 80 percent loan-to-value ratio, and the only other constraint

they face is that their charters require that whatever loans they buy must "be of such quality, type, and class as to meet generally the purchase standards imposed by private institutional mortgage investors" (Emergency Home Finance Act 1970, Sec. 305(a)(1) for Freddie Mac).

8. Such a split also seems to occur in the private secondary market where the lender retains exposure to a certain percentage of the losses on a pool of loans.

9. The three most common practices are: up-front fees charged for credit and other types of insurance; loan "flipping" whereby a borrower is induced to repeatedly refinance her loan and is charged high up-front fees each time; and large prepayment penalties that lock borrowers into high interest rate loans. All three practices have one thing in common: a large lump-sum payment to the lender that is financed by the subsequent loan. The reason predatory lending is largely confined to the refinance market is because in this market there are borrowers with a large, illiquid asset—their home—which can act as security for loans that finance these lump-sum payments. So not only does the lender extract money from the borrower, but also it has a well-secured loan.

10. Today the FHA has a watered-down version of this structure still in place—everyone is in the same pool, but they are eligible for an insurance reimbursement. With the advent of a huge FHA surplus, HUD is considering reimbursing some of the premiums to its borrowers.

11. There is also likely to be a debate about the allocation of penalty fees for late payments. These can be a considerable sources of income for those servicing a loan, even taking into account the losses that result when a borrower defaults. Do these penalties actually belong to the pool, not to the servicer of the loan? If so, how should the servicer be compensated for the extra work it put into those loans that are delinquent, and what incentive can it be given to do its utmost to ensure the borrower does not default?

12. This assumes that lenders are risk-neutral. Someone who is risk-neutral is someone who does not care if the distribution of losses and gains from a decision is wide or narrow, so long as the expected value of the pay-off is the same.

13. The Federal Reserve Board is in the process of promulgating new HMDA disclosure rules that would require lenders to include interest rate information in their reports.

14. The mutual insurance system does not have to be limited to Fannie Mae, Freddie Mac, or the FHA. Any lender could set up such a system, with the approval and supervision of regulators.

15. Freddie Mac's rules state:

> 23.5: Maximum Financing (05/05/00)
> Financing to the maximum LTV ratio, as set forth in Section 23.4 and other sections that limit the LTV ratio for certain products or Mortgage types, is acceptable when property values are stable or increasing. The lender may not offer financing to the maximum LTV ratio in any instance in which property values are declining. In such cases, the LTV ratio must not exceed an amount that is 5 percentage points less than the maximum LTV ratio allowed for the specific type of Mortgage or product. (Freddie Mac 2002b, 23.5)

Fannie Mae's rules state:

> The appraiser must indicate whether property values in the subject neighborhood are "increasing," "stable," or "declining." Maximum financing is acceptable when property values are stable or increasing. The lender generally must not offer maximum financing in any instance in which property values are declining. However, we do make some exceptions to this policy. For example, we permit maximum financing . . . for "no cash-out" rate/term refinance transactions that involve Fannie Mae-owned or-securitized mortgages even if the property is located in a declining market. (Fannie Mae 2002, XI, 403.03)

The rules recognize a role for Fannie Mae in addressing the problems of a declining market, but it is up to the lender to request Fannie Mae's assistance:

230   We will consider granting a waiver of our prohibition against maximum financing in declining markets if the lender can demonstrate that it is (or will be) participating in a focused local redevelopment effort that is designed to infuse capital and provide lending programs as a means of revitalizing or stabilizing a neighborhood in which values are declining. "Focused local redevelopment efforts" must concentrate on a specific neighborhood or community that has been targeted for substantial and coordinated investment activity that is intended to help arrest or reverse declining property values by doing such things as improving the public or private infrastructure, providing increased levels of public services, building new schools or modernizing existing ones, establishing local enterprise zones to encourage business development, offering special housing finance programs, etc. While special housing finance programs (such as those offered by Fannie Mae and others) are an important component of the overall community development, they must not be the only component; the redevelopment effort should also consist of specific nonhousing components. The "infusion of capital and lending programs" can come from local, state, or federal government programs that are targeted to specific neighborhoods or communities or from programs that are funded by either the nonprofit sector or public-private partnerships that were created to revitalize a particular neighborhood or community.

To request a waiver of our prohibition against maximum financing in declining markets, a lender must submit its written request to its lead Fannie Mae regional office. (ibid.)

In a 1971 letter to Fannie Mae, Senator William Proxmire objected to this very same practice of conservative lending in "declining" markets:

If FNMA will not purchase a loan in a so-called declining neighborhood, it is doubtful any private lender will supply credit even if he has been making such loans in the past. Your procedures could actually reduce the amount of credit now going into "declining neighborhoods," thus converting the anticipated decline into a self-fulfilling prophecy. (U.S. Senate, Committee on Banking 1971, 36)

References

Abrams, C. 1955. *Forbidden Neighbors: A Study of Prejudice in Housing.* New York, Harper Bros.

Alexander, F. 1987. "Mortgage Prepayment: The Trial of Common Sense." *Cornell Law Review* 72: 288–343.

American Institute of Real Estate Appraisers. 1932. "Value." *Appraisal Journal* 1 (1): 17–26.

Anderson, E. 1990. *Streetwise.* Chicago, University of Chicago Press.

Appraisal Institute. 1996. *The Appraisal of Real Estate.* Chicago, Appraisal Institute.

Avery, R., et al. 2000. "Credit Scoring: Statistical Issues and Evidence from Credit-Bureau Files." *Real Estate Economics* 28 (3): 523–47.

Babcock, F. 1924. *The Appraisal of Real Estate.* New York, Macmillan.

Babcock, F. 1931. "The Errors Valuators Make." In H. Babcock, *Real Estate Appraisals.*

Babcock, F. 1932. *The Valuation of Real Estate.* New York, McGraw-Hill.

Babcock, F. 1935. "The Determination of Mortgage Risk." *Appraisal Journal* 3 (4): 316–23.

Babcock, F., J. Maurice, and R. Massey. 1938. "Techniques of Residential Location Rating." *Appraisal Journal* 6 (2): 133–40.

Babcock, H., ed. 1931. *Real Estate Appraisals: Discussions and Examples of Current Technique.* Chicago, National Association of Real Estate Boards.

Barnes, J. 1933. "Character Is an Asset: Today as Always." *Credit World* 21 (8): 22–23.

Bartholomew, H. 1925. "The Prevention of Economic Waste by City Planning." *Journal of Land and Public Utility Economics* 1 (1): 83–88.

Becker, G. S. 1993. "Nobel Lecture: The Economic Way of Looking at Behavior." *Journal of Political Economy* 101 (3): 385–409.

Beckman, T. 1930. *Credits and Collections in Theory and Practice.* New York, McGraw-Hill.

Blake, H. 1987. "History of the International Credit Association." *Credit World* 75 (Jan./Feb.): 24–33.

Bluestone, B., and M. H. Stevenson. 2000. *The Boston Renaissance: Race, Space, and Economic Change in an American Metropolis.* New York, Russell Sage Foundation.

Bodfish, M. H. 1927. *Money Lending Practices of Building and Loan Associations in Ohio.* Columbus, Ohio State University Press.

Bonright, J. 1937. *The Valuation of Property.* New York, McGraw-Hill.

252   Bradford, C. 1979. "Financing Home Ownership: The Federal Role in Neighborhood Decline." *Urban Affairs Quarterly* 14 (3): 313–35.

Bush, V. 1997. "The Ground Floor: Big Lenders Offer Home Loans with Penalties for Early Repayment, but Investors Are Unimpressed." *Barron's* 77 (16): 41.

Calder, L. 1999. *Financing the American Dream: A Cultural History of Consumer Credit.* Princeton, Princeton University Press.

Calem, P., and S. Longhofer. 2002. "Anatomy of a Fair Lending Exam: The Uses and Limitations of Statistics." *Journal of Real Estate Finance and Economics* 24 (3): 207–37.

Calomiris, C. W., C. M. Kahn, and S. D. Longhofer. 1994. "Housing-Finance Intervention and Private Incentives: Helping Minorities and the Poor." *Journal of Money, Credit, and Banking* 26 (3, part 2): 635–74.

Carruthers, B. 1996. *City of Capital: Politics and Markets in the English Financial Revolution.* Princeton, Princeton University Press.

Carruthers, B., and A. Stinchcombe. 1999. "The Social Structure of Liquidity: Flexibility, Markets, and States." *Theory and Society* 28 (3): 353–82.

Caulfield, J. 1994. *City Form and Everyday Life: Toronto's Gentrification and Critical Social Practice.* Toronto, University of Toronto Press.

Chicago Fact Book Consortium, ed. 1984. *Local Community Fact Book: Chicago Metropolitan Area: Based on the 1970 and 1980 Censuses.* Chicago, Chicago Review Press.

Chicago Fact Book Consortium, ed. 1995. *Local Community Fact Book, Chicago Metropolitan Area: Based on the 1990 Census.* Chicago, University of Illinois at Chicago.

Chicago Rehab Network. 1990 and 1993. *The Chicago Affordable Housing Fact Book: Visions for Change.* Chicago, Chicago Rehab Network.

Chicago Sun-Times. 1990. *Pocket Guide to the Chicago Market.* Chicago, Chicago Sun-Times.

Commons, J. 1934. *Institutional Economics: Its Place in Political Economy.* New York, Macmillan.

Congressional Budget Office. 2001. *Federal Subsidies and the Housing GSEs.* Washington, D.C., Congressional Budget Office.

Cornell, B., and I. Welch. 1996. "Culture, Information, and Screening Discrimination." *Journal of Political Economy* 104(3): 542–71.

Cutmore, H., and F. Taylor. 1932. "Value." *Appraisal Journal* 1 (1): 17–27.

Dexter, S. 1894. *A Treatise on Cooperative Savings and Loan Associations.* New York, D. Appleton.

DiMaggio, P. 1990. "Cultural Aspects of Economic Action and Organization." In *Beyond the Marketplace: Rethinking Economy and Society,* edited by R. Friedland and A. F. Robertson. New York, Aldine de Gruyter.

Dorau, H., and A. Hinman. 1928. *Urban Land Economics.* New York, Macmillan.

Douglas, M. 1985. *Risk Acceptability according to the Social Sciences.* New York, Russell Sage Foundation.

Douglas, M. 1986. *How Institutions Think.* Syracuse, N.Y., Syracuse University Press.

Douglas, M., and A. Wildavsky. 1982. *Risk and Culture.* Berkeley, University of California Press.

Dow, S. 1999. "The Stages of Banking Development and the Spatial Evolution of

Financial Systems." In *Money and the Space Economy,* edited by R. Martin. Chichester, U.K., John Wiley and Sons.

Duncan, D. 1999. "How Do Borrowers Shop?" *Mortgage Banking* (December): 38–48.

Dunham, C. 1991. *The Unknown Lenders: The Role of Mortgage Banks in the Chicago Metropolitan Area.* Chicago, Woodstock Institute.

Dymski, G. A. 1995. "Theory of Bank Redlining and Discrimination: An Exploration." *Review of Black Political Economy* 23 (3): 37–74.

Easley, B. J. 1935. "The F.H.A. Plan of Mortgage Insurance." *Credit World* 23 (6).

Ekdahl, J. N. 1964. "The Federal Home Loan Bank Board: A Political Entity and Its Implications for Group Theory." Cambridge, Harvard University.

Ely, R., and E. Morehouse. 1924. *Elements of Land Economics.* New York, Macmillan.

Fannie Mae. 1993a. *Originating Residential Mortgages.* Washington, D.C., Fannie Mae.

Fannie Mae. 1993b. *Underwriting the Borrower: Basics of Sound Underwriting.* Washington, D.C., Fannie Mae.

Fannie Mae. 1995a. *Single-Family Annoucements and Letters, LL02-95.* Washington, D.C., Fannie Mae.

Fannie Mae. 1995b. *Single-Family Annoucements and Letters, LL09-95.* Washington, D.C., Fannie Mae.

Fannie Mae. 1996. *Single-Family Annoucements and Letters, LL07-96.* Washington, D.C., Fannie Mae.

Fannie Mae. 1998. *Welcome to Fannie Mae.* Washington, D.C., Fannie Mae.

Fannie Mae. 1999. *Guide to Underwriting with Desktop Underwriter.* Washington, D.C., Fannie Mae.

Fannie Mae. 2000. "Desktop Underwriter, Version 5.0 Release Notes." Washington, D.C., Fannie Mae.

Fannie Mae. 2001. "A Statistical Summary of Housing and Mortgage Finance Activities." Washington D.C., Fannie Mae.

Fannie Mae. 2002. *Selling Guide.* Washington, D.C., Fannie Mae.

Federal Deposit Insurance Corporation. 2000. Bank and savings and loan branch locations data file. Available from author.

Federal Financial Institutions Examination Council. 1993–1998. *Home Mortgage Disclosure Act Data.* CD-ROM. Washington, D.C., Federal Financial Institutions Examination Council.

Federal Financial Institutions Examination Council. 1999. Interagency Fair Lending Examination Procedures. Washington, D.C., Federal Financial Institutions Examination Council.

Federal Home Loan Bank Board. Office of Examinations and Supervision. 1968. Memorandum T-15. Washington, D.C., Federal Home Loan Bank Board.

Federal Home Loan Bank of Chicago. 2000. *Mortgage Partnership Finance Program, 2000.* Chicago, Federal Home Loan Bank of Chicago.

Federal Housing Administration. 1934–1940. "Letters to the Chief Underwriters." U.S. National Archives, Records of the Federal Housing Administration, record group 31, 1930–1970, box 85.

Federal Housing Administration. 1936. *Underwriting Manual: Underwriting and Valuation Procedure under Title II of the National Housing Act.* Washington, D.C., GPO.

234   Federal Housing Administration. 1947. *Underwriting Manual: Underwriting and Valuation Procedure under Title II of the National Housing Act.* Washington, D.C., GPO.

Federal Housing Administration. 1959. *The FHA Story in Summary.* Washington, D.C., Federal Housing Administration.

Federal Housing Finance Board. Federal Home Loan Bank Office of Finance. 1999. *Federal Home Loan Bank System: Facts and Myths.* Washington, D.C.

Feins, J. 1977. "Urban Housing Disinvestment and Neighborhood Decline." Ph.D. diss., University of Chicago.

Feins, J., and T. S. Lane. 1981. *How Much for Housing? New Perspectives on Affordability and Risk.* Cambridge, Mass., ABT Books.

Ferguson, M. F., and S. R. Peters. 1995. "What Constitutes Evidence of Discrimination in Lending?" *Journal of Finance* 50 (2): 739–48.

Ferguson, M. F., and S. R. Peters. 1997. "Cultural Affinity and Lending Discrimination: The Impact of Underwriting Errors and Credit Risk Distribution on Applicant Denial Rates." *Journal of Financial Services Research* 11 (1, 2): 153–68.

"FHA's Insurance Fund Shored Up." 1990. *Congressional Quarterly,* 657–61.

Fisher, E. M. 1923. *Principles of Real Estate Practice.* New York, Macmillan.

Fisher, E. M. 1930. *Advanced Principles of Real Estate Practice.* New York, Macmillan.

Freddie Mac. 1996a. "Automated Underwriting: Making Mortgage Lending Simpler and Fairer for America's Families." Washington, D.C., Freddie Mac.

Freddie Mac. 1996b. *Single-Family Bulletins and Letters, 96-6.* Washington, D.C., Freddie Mac.

Freddie Mac. 1997. *Single-Family Bulletins and Letters, 97-9.* Washington, D.C., Freddie Mac.

Freddie Mac. 1999. *Single-Family Bulletins and Letters, 99-1.* Washington, D.C., Freddie Mac.

Freddie Mac. 2002a. *Loan Prospector Training and User Guide.* Washington, D.C., Freddie Mac.

Freddie Mac. 2002b. *Single-Family Seller/Servicer Guide.* Washington, D.C., Freddie Mac.

Garfinkel, H. 1984. *Studies in Ethnomethodology.* Oxford, Polity.

General Accounting Office. 1990. *Government-Sponsored Enterprises: The Government's Exposure to Risks.* Washington, D.C., GPO.

General Accounting Office. 2000. *Role of the Office of Thrift Supervision and Office of the Comptroller of the Currency in the Preemption of State Law.* Washington, D.C., GPO.

Gottdiener, M. 1985. *The Social Production of Space.* Austin, University of Texas Press.

Gottdiener, M. 1993. "A Marx for Our Time: Henri Lefebvre and the Production of Space." *Sociological Theory* 11 (1): 129–34.

"The Government Seeks Injunction against the National Retail Credit Association." 1933. *Credit World* 21 (11): 16–18.

Granovetter, M. 1985. "Economic Action and Social Structure: The Problem of Embeddedness." *American Journal of Sociology* 91 (3): 481–510.

Granovetter, M. 1992. "Economic Institutions as Social Constructions: A Framework for Analysis." *Acta Sociologica* 35: 3–11.

Gries, J. 1925. "Housing in the United States." *Journal of Land and Public Utility Economics* 1 (1): 23–35.

Haar, C. M. 1960. *Federal Credit and Private Housing: The Mass Financing Dilemma*. New York, McGraw-Hill.

Haig, R. 1926. "Toward an Understanding of the Metropolis: The Assignment of Activities to Areas in Urban Regions." *Quarterly Journal of Economics* 40 (2): 179–208; (3): 402–34.

Hanson, P. 1933. "The Meaning of Value." *Appraisal Journal* 1 (1): 289–97.

Harvey, D. 1989. *The Urban Experience*. Oxford, Basil Blackwell.

Hays, R. A. 1985. *Federal Government and Urban Housing*. Albany, State University of New York Press.

Heimer, C. 1981. "Reactive Risk and Rational Action: Managing Behavioral Risk in Insurance." Ph.D. diss., University of Chicago.

Henriques, D. 2000. "Hidden Charges: A Special Report." *New York Times*, October 27, 1.

Hoyt, H. 1933. *One Hundred Years of Land Values in Chicago*. Chicago, University of Chicago Press.

Hoyt, H. 1939. *The Structure and Growth of Residential Neighborhoods in American Cities*. Washington, D.C., Federal Housing Administration.

Hoyt, H. 1970. *According to Hoyt: 55 Years of Homer Hoyt, 1916 to 1969*. Washington, D.C., n.p.

Hunter, A. 1974. *Symbolic Communities: The Persistence and Change of Chicago's Local Communities*. Chicago, University of Chicago Press.

Hunter, W. C., and M. B. Walker. 1996. "Cultural Affinity Hypothesis and Mortgage Lending Decisions." *Journal of Real Estate Finance and Economics* 13: 57–70.

Hurd, R. 1903. *Principles of City Land Values*. New York, Record and Guide Company.

Interagency Task Force on Fair Lending. 1994. *Policy Statement on Discrimination in Lending*. Washington, D.C. www.fdic.gov/regulations/laws/rules/5000-3860.html #5000policyso3.

Jackson, K. 1980. "Race, Ethnicity, and Real Estate Appraisal: The Home Owners Loan Corporation and the Federal Housing Administration." *Journal of Urban History* 6 (4): 419–52.

Jackson, K. 1985. *Crabgrass Frontier: The Suburbanization of the United States*. New York, Oxford University Press.

Jasanoff, S. 1998. "The Political Science of Risk Perception." *Reliability Engineering and System Safety* 59: 91–99.

Jensen, R. 1972. "Mortgage Standardization: History of Interaction of Economics, Consumerism, and Governmental Pressure." *Real Property Probate and Trust Journal* 7: 397–434.

Kelly, A. 1995. "Racial and Ethnic Disparities in Mortgage Prepayment." *Journal of Housing Economics* 4 (4): 350–72.

Keynes, J. M. [1921] 1979. *Treatise on Probability*. New York, AMS Press.

Keynes, J. M. 1937. "The General Theory of Employment." *Quarterly Journal of Economics* 51 (2): 209–23.

Knight, F. 1921. *Risk, Uncertainty, and Profit*. New York, Houghton Mifflin.

Knox, C. 1924. *Principles of Real Estate Appraising*. Youngstown, Ohio, Robert C. Knox.

256 Kollock, P. 1994. "The Emergence of Exchange Structures: An Experimental Study of Uncertainty, Commitment, and Trust." *American Journal of Sociology* 100 (2): 313—45.

Kulkosky, E. 1996. "Norwest Sampling Shows Value of Realtor Referrals." *American Banker,* November 21, 14.

Lauerman, C. 1992. "There Goes the Neighborhood: Will Wicker Park and Buck Town Survive Gentrification?" *Chicago Tribune Magazine,* October 18.

Lawson, T. 1985. "Uncertainty and Economic Analysis." *Economic Journal* 95 (380): 909—27.

Lefebvre, H. 1991. *The Production of Space.* Oxford, Basil Blackwell.

Linn, A. 1992. "Underwriting Criteria Are Focal Point of New Scrutiny." *Chicago Tribune,* August 31, sec. 1, p. 6.

Longhofer, S. D. 1996. "Cultural Affinity and Mortgage Discrimination." *Economic Review: Federal Reserve Bank of Cleveland* 32 (3): 12–25.

Longhofer, S. D., and S. R. Peters. 1999. "Self-Selection and Discrimination in Credit Markets." Working Paper 9809, Federal Reserve Bank of Cleveland.

Lynch, J. 1925. Quoted in "Urges Less Buying of Non-essentials." *New York Times,* August 9, sec. 2, p. 7.

MacEwan, E. 1931. "Your Credit and the Credit Bureau." *Credit World* 20 (4): 15–16, 30–32.

Martin, R. 1994. "The End of Geography?" In *Money, Power and Space,* edited by S. Corbridge, R. Martin, and N. Thrift. Oxford, Blackwell.

Martin, R. 1999. "The New Economic Geography of Money." In *Money and the Space Economy,* edited by R. Martin. Chichester, U.K., John Wiley and Sons.

Marx, K. 1977. *Capital.* London, Lawrence and Wishart.

Massey, D., and N. Denton. 1993. *American Apartheid: Segregation and the Making of the Underclass.* Cambridge, Harvard University Press.

McMichael, S. L. 1931. *McMichael's Appraising Manual: A Real Estate Appraising Handbook for Field Work and Advanced Study Courses.* New York, Prentice-Hall.

McMichael, S. L., and R. F. Bingham. 1923. *City Growth and Values.* Cleveland, Stanley McMichael.

McMichael, S. L., and R. F. Bingham. 1928. *City Growth Essentials.* Cleveland, Stanley McMichael.

Mertzke, A. 1927. *Real Estate Appraisal.* Chicago, National Association of Real Estate Boards.

Meyers, G. 1999–2000. *Living in Greater Chicago.* Chicago, Meyers Communications Group.

Meyers, G., and D. DeBat, eds. 1990. *Chicago House Hunt Book.* Chicago, House Hunt.

Mortgage Bankers Association of America. 2000a. "Number and Dollar Volume of Retail Originations by Loan Type and Purpose—Nation (2000)." Data-on-Demand Service Report 3050-036.

Mortgage Bankers Association of America. 2000b. "Number and Dollar Volume of Wholesale Originations by Loan Type and Purpose—Nation (2000)." Data-on-Demand Service Report 3050-037.

Mouw, T. 2000. "Job Relocation and the Racial Gap in Unemployment in Detroit and Chicago, 1980 to 1990." *American Sociological Review* 65 (Oct.): 730–53.

Munnell, A., et al. 1992. "Mortgage Lending in Boston: Interpreting HMDA Data." Working Paper 92-7, Federal Reserve Bank of Boston.

Munnell, A., et al. 1996. "Mortgage Lending in Boston: Interpreting HMDA Data." *American Economic Review* 86 (1): 25–53.

Myrdal, G. 1957. *Economic Theory and Under-developed Regions.* London, Gerald Duckworth.

Myrdal, G. 1996. *American Dilemma.* 2 vols. New Brunswick, N.J., Transaction Books.

National Association of Real Estate Boards. 1925–1934. *Annals of Real Estate Practice.* Chicago, National Association of Real Estate Boards.

National Association of Real Estate Boards. 1929. "Standards of Appraisal Practice for Realtor Appraisers and Appraisal Committees of Member Boards." *Annals of Real Estate Practice*: 885–97.

National Retail Credit Association. Legislative Committee. 1934. "What Our Legislative Committee Has Done for You." *Credit World* 22 (12): 26–27.

National Retail Credit Association. Research Division. 1935. *Credit Reports: An Analysis of the Costs of Credit Reports and Time Required to Complete Them in Credit Bureaus Located in Cities of Approximately 250,000 Population.* St. Louis, National Retail Credit Association.

National Training and Information Center. 1997. *The Devil's in the Details: An Analysis of Federal Housing Administration Default Concentration and Lender Performance in 20 U.S. Cities.* Chicago, National Training and Information Center.

National Training and Information Center. 1999. *Preying on Neighborhoods: Subprime Mortgage Lending and Chicagoland Foreclosures.* Chicago, National Training and Information Center.

Nichols, J. 1929. "A Developer's View of Deed Restrictions." *Journal of Land and Public Utility Economics* 5 (2): 132–42.

Office of Federal Housing Enterprise Oversight. 1999. *1999 Report to Congress.* Washington, D.C.

Office of Thrift Supervision. 1996. *Re: Effect of Parity Act on Wisconsin Prepayment Penalty Statute.* Washington, D.C.

Olcott, G. C., and Co. 1990. *Land Values Blue Book of Chicago and Suburbs.* Park Ridge, Ill., G. C. Olcott.

Phelps, E. S. 1972. "The Statistical Theory of Racism and Sexism." *American Economic Review* 62 (4): 659–61.

Piquet, H. S. 1931. *Building and Loan Associations in New Jersey.* Princeton, Princeton University Press.

Pollock, A. 1999. "A New Housing Finance Option in the USA: MPF vs. MBS." *Housing Finance International* 13 (3): 3–9.

President's Conference on Home Building and Home Ownership. 1932. *Home Finance and Taxation.* Washington, D.C., National Capital Press.

Price Waterhouse. 1990. "MMI Fund Analysis." Washington, D.C., Price Waterhouse.

Raban, J. 1992. *Hunting Mister Heartbreak.* New York, HarperCollins.

Register, J. A. 1931. "Fallacies of the Summation Method." In H. Babcock, *Real Estate Appraisals.*

258   Richardson, H. 1930. "Land Value Insurance." *Annals of the American Academy* 148 (237): 81–87.

Roberts, K. 1993. "Prepayment Penalties in Texas: The Triumph of Logic and the Need for Legislative Reform." *Baylor Law Review* (Summer): 585–631.

Rourke, E. 1988. "Equifax, Inc." In *International Directory of Company Histories*, edited by P. Kepos. Detroit, St. James Press.

Rule, J. 1974. *Private Lives and Public Surveillance: Social Control in the Computer Age.* New York, Schocken Books.

Rule, J., et al. 1976. "The Dossier in Consumer Credit." In *On Record: Files and Dossiers in Americnan Lives*, edited by S. Wheeler. New Brunswick, N.J., Transaction Books.

Russell, H. 1956. *Savings and Loan Associations*. Albany, N.Y., Matthew Bender.

Scheessele, R. 1999. *1998 HMDA Highlights*. House Finance Working Paper Series HF-009. Washington, D.C., U.S. Department of Housing and Urban Development.

Schelling, T. 1978. *Micromotives and Macrobehavior.* New York, Norton.

Simon, H. 1983. *Reason in Human Affairs*. Stanford, Stanford University Press.

Smith, A. 1976. *An Inquiry into the Nature and Causes of the Wealth of Nations*. Chicago, University of Chicago Press.

Society of Residential Appraisers. 1941. "Current Survey on Appraisal Practices and Policies." *Review of the Society of Residential Appraisers* 7 (9): 6–11.

Squires, G., and S. Kim. 1995. "Does Anybody Who Works Here Look like Me? Mortgage Lending, Race, and Lender Employment." *Social Science Quarterly* 76 (4): 823–38.

Stanton, T. 1991. *A State of Risk: Will Government-Sponsored Enterprises Be the Next Financial Crisis?* New York, HarperCollins.

Stanton, T. 1996. "Restructuring Fannie Mae and Freddie Mac: Framework and Policy Options." In *Studies on Privatizing Fannie Mae and Freddie Mac*. Office of Policy Development and Research. Washington, D.C., U.S. Department of Housing and Urban Development.

Stone, D. 1988. *Policy Paradox and Political Reason*. Glenview, Ill., Scott, Foresman.

Street, H. N. 1927. "Installment Credit." *Credit World* 15 (8): 6–8, 30.

Strickland, D. 1999. "Fannie Mae Moves to Loosen Home Loan Credit Rules." *Los Angeles Times*, October 1, C1.

Stuart, G. 2000a. "The Production and Management of Information in the Home Mortgage Loan Application Process." *Chicago Policy Review* 4 (1): 23–38.

Stuart, G. 2000b. "Mortgage Lending to Minority and Low-Income Home Buyers in the 1990s: Underwriting Changes, Automated Underwriting and Subprime Lending." Washington, D.C., Local Initiative Support Corporation.

Suttles, G. 1972. *Social Construction of Communities*. Chicago, University of Chicago Press.

Temkin, K., et al. 1999. "A Study of the GSEs' Single Family Underwriting Guidelines." Washington, D.C., Urban Institute.

Thorson, I. 1933. "Relation of Value to the Purpose of the Appraisal." *Appraisal Journal* 1 (2): 105–22.

Thrift, N. 1994. "On the Social and Cultural Determinants of International Financial Centres: The Case of the City of London." In *Money, Power, and Space*, edited by S. Corbridge, R. Martin, and N. Thrift. Oxford, Blackwell.

Tilly, C., et al. 2000. "Space as a Signal: How Employers Perceive Neighborhoods in Four Metropolitan Labor Markets." In *Urban Inequality: Evidence from Four Cities*, edited by A. O'Connor, C. Tilly, and L. Bobo. New York, Russell Sage Foundation.

Tootell, G. M. B. 1993. "Defaults, Denials, and Discrimination in Mortgage Lending." *New England Economic Review* (Sept./Oct.): 45–51.

Truesdale, J. 1927. *Credit Bureau Management*. New York, Prentice-Hall.

Tucker, D. 1991. *The Decline of Thrift in America: Our Cultural Shift from Saving to Spending*. New York, Praeger.

Turner, M. A., and F. Skidmore, eds. 1999. *Mortgage Lending Discrimination: A Review of Existing Evidence*. Washington, D.C., Urban Institute.

United States v. Associated Credit Bureaus, Inc. 1972. No. 71 C 716(A), United States District Court for the Eastern District of Missouri, Eastern Division, 345 F. Supp. 940; 1972 U.S. Dist. LEXIS 12744; 1972 Trade Cas. (CCH) P74,107, July 14, 1972, Filed.

United States v. National Retail Credit Assn. 1933. In Equity No. 10420, United States District Court for the Eastern District of Missouri, Eastern Division, 1933 U.S. Dist. LEXIS 957; 1953 Trade Cas. (CCH) P67,608, October 6, 1933, and October 19, 1953.

U.S. Building and Loan League. 1937. "Committee on the FHA, Report." *Building and Loan Annals*: 557–67.

U.S. Congress. House. Committee on Banking and Currency. 1934. *National Housing Act*. 73d Cong., 2d sess. May 18, 25, 26, 28–31, June 1, 2, 4.

U.S. Congress. House. Committee on Banking and Currency. 1937. *Amendments to National Housing Act*. 75th Cong., 2d sess. November 30, December 1–3, 7–10, 1937.

U.S. Congress. House. Committee on Banking and Financial Services. 2000. *Predatory Lending Practices*. 106th Cong., 2d sess. May 24.

U.S. Congress. House. Committee on Banking, Finance, and Urban Affairs. Subcommittee on Housing. 1972. *Real Estate Settlement Costs, FHA Mortgage Foreclosures, Housing Abandonment and Site Selection Policies: Hearings on H.R. 1337*, parts 1 and 2. 92d Cong., 2d sess. February 22 and 24, March.

U.S. Congress. House. Committee on Government Operations. 1986. *Impact of Appraisal Problems on Real Estate Lending, Mortgage Insurance, and Investment in the Secondary Market*. 99th Cong., 2d sess. H. Rept. 99-891. September 25.

U.S. Congress. House. Committee on Government Operations. Special Subcommittee on Invasion of Privacy. 1968. *Commercial Credit Bureaus*. 90th Cong., 2d sess. March 12–14.

U.S Congress. House. Committee on the Judiciary. Subcommittee on Antitrust and Monopoly. 1968. *The Credit Industry: Credit Bureaus and Reporting*. 90th Cong., 2d sess. December 10–11.

U.S. Congress. House. Committee on Veterans Affairs. 1986. *VA Home Loan Guaranty Program, Fiscal Year Budget Proposals and S. 1887*. 99th Cong., 2d sess. March 5.

U.S. Congress. Senate. Committee on Banking and Currency. 1934. *National Housing Act*. 73d Cong., 2d sess. May 16–19, 21–24.

240   U.S. Congress. Senate. Committee on Banking, Housing, and Urban Affairs. 1970. *Secondary Mortgage Market and Mortgage Credit.* 91st Cong., 2d sess. March 2–6.

U.S. Congress. Senate. Committee on Banking, Housing, and Urban Affairs. 1971. *Conventional Mortgage Forms: Federal National Mortgage Association Public Meeting.* 92d Cong., 1st sess. S. Doc. 92-21. April 5–6.

U.S. Congress. Senate. Committee on Banking, Housing, and Urban Affairs. Subcommittee on Consumer and Regulatory Affairs. 1989. *Discrimination in Home Mortgage Lending.* 101st Cong., 1st sess. October 24.

U.S. Congress. Senate. Committee on Banking, Housing, and Urban Affairs. Subcommittee on Consumer and Regulatory Affairs. 1991. *Secondary Mortgage Markets and Redlining.* 102d Cong., 1st sess. February 28.

U.S. Department of Housing and Urban Development. 1976. *Housing in the Seventies: Working Papers.* Washington, D.C.

U.S. Department of Housing and Urban Development. 1982. *Handbook 4000.2 Rev-1: Mortgagees' Handbook: Application through Insurance (Single Family).* Washington, D.C.

U.S. Department of Housing and Urban Development. 1995. *4155.1 REV-4, CHG-1: Mortgage Credit Analysis for Mortgage Insurance on One- to Four-Family Properties.* Washington, D.C.

U.S. Department of Housing and Urban Development. 1996. *Studies on Privatizing Fannie Mae and Freddie Mac.* Rockville, Md., Department of Housing and Urban Development.

U.S. Department of Housing and Urban Development. 1999. *Handbook 4150.2, CHG-1: Valuation Analysis for Single-Family One- to Four-Unit Dwellings.* Washington, D.C.

U.S. Department of the Treasury. 1991. *Report of the Secretary of the Treasury on Government-Sponsored Enterprises.* Washington, D.C.

U.S. Savings and Loan League. 1938–1973. *Savings and Loan Annals.* Cincinnati, Ohio, U.S. Savings and Loan League.

Wagner, P. 1936. "Appraisal Procedures of Federal Agencies." *Appraisal Journal* 5 (3): 240–47.

Wendt, P. F. 1974. *Real Estate Appraisal.* Athens, University of Georgia Press.

Wilken, A. 1956. "The Effect of the GI Guaranty Loan Program." *Appraisal Journal* 22 (July): 400–408.

Williams, F. B. 1922. *The Law of City Planning and Zoning.* New York, Macmillan.

Woodlock, D. 1926. "Good Credit and the New Year." *Credit World* 15 (4): 3.

Woodstock Institute. 1986–1993. *Community Lending Fact Book.* Chicago, Woodstock Institute.

Yezer, A. M. J., et al. 1994. "Bias in Estimates of Discrimination and Default in Mortgage Lending: The Effects of Simultaneity and Self-Selection." *Journal of Real Estate Finance and Economics* 9 (3): 196–215.

Zangerle, J. A. 1924. *Principles of Real Estate Appraising.* Cleveland, Stanley McMichael.

Zekas, J. 1992. "Chicago's Hottest Neighborhoods? Buena Park, Sheridan Park, and Margate Park Reach Critical Mass." *Apartments and Homes, Supplement.*

Zukin, S. 1995. *The Cultures of Cities.* Cambridge, Mass. Blackwell.

Index

Abrams, C., 34, 216 n. 4

African Americans. *See* Blacks

American Institute of Real Estate Appraisers (AIREA), 10, 39, 44–46, 62–67

Appraisal and appraisers: and automated underwriting, 125; and benchmark properties, 55, 218 n. 28; books published on, 38, 40–43; and class segregation, 26, 33, 67, 68, 181, 187; and ethnic succession, 146; and gentrification, 148–49, 154, 187–88; and housing markets, 188, 204; and loan-to-value ratios, 75, 78; and neighborhoods, 8, 14, 17, 27, 134, 138–40, 153–54, 186, 205; professionalization of, 45, 181, 227 n. 2; and property value definition, 26, 29, 30, 31, 39, 44–45, 64, 67–68, 181; racist policies of, 10, 26, 30, 34, 66–67, 68, 142, 181, 216 n. 4; and risk construction, 179–82; rules for, 47–56, 59, 187, 227 n. 2; and savings and loan industry, 61–64, 65, 68; and underwriters, 111, 119; and uniformity principle, 35–36, 58, 59–67, 141–42, 181–82; and Veterans Administration, 60, 66

Appraisal Foundation, 65, 180

Appraisal Institute, 65, 138–39

Associated Credit Bureaus of America, 92, 94, 221 n. 19

Babcock, Frederick: and adverse influence protection, 57; and economic background rating, 54–55; and economic obsolescence, 216 n. 3; and Federal Housing Administration, 38, 45, 47; on market value, 216–17 n. 15; and National Association

of Real Estate Brokers, 38–39, 67, 181; and neighborhood decline, 37, 38, 50, 56; and risk rating procedure, 50–52, 53; and Society of Real Estate Appraisers, 62; and uniformity principle, 35–37, 48–49, 182; and urban structure, 136; and warranted value theory, 32–33, 44, 48

Bingham, R. F., 34, 215

Blacks: approval rates of, 176–77; and black tax, 200–201; and credit scoring, 173, 174, 178; and loan application assessment, 156–57; and loan denials, 11–12, 170, 171, 192; neighborhoods of, 54–56, 106–7, 136, 159–68, 174–75, 177, 187, 218 n. 26; and voluntary prepayment, 103

Bodfish, Morton, 73, 75, 91

Borrowers: ability to make payments, 4, 6, 70, 71, 79–83, 110, 184; and behavioral risk, 6–7, 14, 26–27, 185; and character, 70, 71, 83–92, 95–96, 98, 183; and counseling agencies, 202–3; and credit reporting industry, 83, 90–98, 182, 183; and loan-to-value ratios, 75–77; and marital status, 11; and networks, 13, 131, 215 n. 17; pre-screening of, 107–8; willingness to make payments, 4, 6, 70, 71, 83–99, 110, 128

Burgess, Ernest, 134, 135, 151

Chicago: denial rates of, 170; and gentrification, 147–49, 151; and loan defaults, 174–75; and neighborhoods, 134–35, 143–46, 149–54, 159–62; and Residential Security Maps, 49; and risk assessment, 27

Civil rights advocates, 102–3